Lecture Notes in Artificial Intelligence   12998

Subseries of Lecture Notes in Computer Science

More information about this subseries at http://www.springer.com/series/1244

Andrey Ronzhin · Gerhard Rigoll ·
Roman Meshcheryakov (Eds.)

Interactive Collaborative Robotics

6th International Conference, ICR 2021
St. Petersburg, Russia, September 27–30, 2021
Proceedings

 Springer

Editors
Andrey Ronzhin 🆔
St. Petersburg Federal Research Center
of the Russian Academy of Sciences
St. Petersburg, Russia

Gerhard Rigoll 🆔
Technical University of Munich
Munich, Germany

Roman Meshcheryakov 🆔
V. A. Trapeznikov Institute
of Control Sciences
Moscow, Russia

ISSN 0302-9743   ISSN 1611-3349   (electronic)
Lecture Notes in Artificial Intelligence
ISBN 978-3-030-87724-8   ISBN 978-3-030-87725-5   (eBook)
https://doi.org/10.1007/978-3-030-87725-5

LNCS Sublibrary: SL7 – Artificial Intelligence

This Springer imprint is published by the registered company Springer Nature Switzerland AG
The registered company address is: Gewerbestrasse 11, 6330 Cham, Switzerland

Preface

The 6th International Conference on Interactive Collaborative Robotics (ICR 2021) was organized as a satellite event of the 23rd International Conference on Speech and Computer (SPECOM 2021) by the St. Petersburg Federal Research Center of the Russian Academy of Sciences (SPC RAS, St. Petersburg, Russia) in cooperation with the Technical University of Munich (TUM, Munich, Germany).

ICR 2021 was held during September 27–30, 2021, and focused on challenges of human–robot interaction, robot control and behavior in social robotics and collaborative robotics, as well as applied robotic and cyber–physical systems.

During the conference an invited talk "Enabling Robots to Cooperate and Compete: Distributed Optimization and Game Theoretic Methods for Multiple Interacting Robots" was given by Mac Schwager (Stanford University, Stanford, USA).

Due to the ongoing COVID-19 pandemic, for the second time, SPECOM 2021 including ICR was organized as a fully virtual conference. The virtual conference, in the online format via Zoom, had a number of advantages including an increased number of participants because listeners could take part without any fees, essentially reduced registration fees for authors of the presented papers, no costs for travel and accommodation, a paperless green conference with only electronic proceedings, free access to video presentations in YouTube after the conference, comfortable home conditions for presenters, etc.

This volume contains a collection of 19 papers presented at ICR 2021, which were thoroughly reviewed by members of the Program Committee consisting of more than 20 top specialists in the conference topic areas. Theoretical and more general contributions were presented in oral sessions. Problem oriented sessions as well as discussions then brought together specialists in niche problem areas with the aim of exchanging knowledge and skills resulting from research projects of all kinds.

Last but not least, we would like to express our gratitude to the authors for providing their papers on time, to the members of the conference reviewing team and Program Committee for their careful reviews and paper selection, and to the editors and correctors for their hard work preparing this volume. Special thanks are due to the members of the Organizing Committee for their tireless effort and enthusiasm during the conference organization. We hope that you benefitted from both the SPECOM and ICR 2021 events.

September 2021

Andrey Ronzhin
Gerhard Rigoll
Roman Meshcheryakov

Organization

ICR 2021 was organized by the St. Petersburg Federal Research Center of the Russian Academy of Sciences (SPC RAS, St. Petersburg, Russia) in cooperation with the Technical University of Munich (TUM, Munich, Germany). The conference website is located at: http://www.specom.nw.ru/icr2021/.

Program Committee

Roman Meshcheryakov
  (co-chair), Russia
Gerhard Rigoll (co-chair), Germany
Andrey Ronzhin (co-chair), Russia
Christos Antonopoulos, Greece
Branislav Borovac, Serbia
Sara Chaychian, UK
Ivan Ermolov, Russia
Oliver Jokisch, Germany
Dimitrios Kalles, Greece
Igor Kalyaev, Russia
Alexey Kashevnik, Russia
Dongheui Lee, Germany

Viktor Glazunov, Russia
Mehmet Guzey, Turkey
Evgeni Magid, Russia
Iosif Mporas, UK
Viacheslav Pshikhopov, Russia
Mirko Rakovic, Serbia
Yulia Sandamirskaya, Switzerland
Jesus Savage, Mexico
Hooman Samani, UK
Evgeny Shandarov, Russia
Lev Stankevich, Russia
Tilo Strutz, Germany
Sergey Yatsun, Russia

Organizing Committee

Anton Saveliev (chair)
Irina Podnozova
Dmitry Ryumin
Natalia Kashina
Irina Vatamaniuk

Dmitriy Levonevskiy
Anastasiya Molotilova
Irina Novikova
Natalia Dormidontova
Polina Chernousova

Contents

Prioritized SIPP for Multi-agent Path Finding with Kinematic Constraints

Zain Alabedeen Ali[1](✉) and Konstantin Yakovlev[1,2]

[1] Moscow Institute of Physics and Technology, Moscow Oblast, Russia
ali.za@phystech.edu
[2] Federal Research Center "Computer Science and Control" RAS, Moscow, Russia
yakovlev@isa.ru

Abstract. Multi-Agent Path Finding (MAPF) is a long-standing problem in Robotics and Artificial Intelligence in which one needs to find a set of collision-free paths for a group of mobile agents (robots) operating in the shared workspace. Due to its importance, the problem is well-studied and multiple optimal and approximate algorithms are known. However, many of them abstract away from the kinematic constraints and assume that the agents can accelerate/decelerate instantaneously (Fig. 1). This complicates the application of the algorithms on the real robots. In this paper, we present a method that mitigates this issue to a certain extent. The suggested solver is essentially, a prioritized planner based on the well-known Safe Interval Path Planning (SIPP) algorithm. Within SIPP we explicitly reason about the speed and the acceleration thus the constructed plans directly take kinematic constraints of agents into account. We suggest a range of heuristic functions for that setting and conduct a thorough empirical evaluation of the suggested algorithm.

Keywords: Multi-agent path finding · Robotics · Artificial intelligence · Heuristic search · Safe interval path planning

1 Introduction

Recently, robots became highly engaged in e-commerce warehouses to accelerate the process of collecting the orders especially in peak times [18]. Furthermore, groups of robots are used to tow the parked planes in airports to decrease the cost and pollution. In these two practical examples and many others, groups of robots are moving to do specific tasks, and in order to complete them, the robots need to organize their movements to avoid the collisions and minimize the trip costs. This problem is known as the Multi-Agent Path Finding (MAPF). Many variants of MAPF exist [15]. They differ in the assumptions on how the agents can move, how the conflicts are defined etc. The most studied version of MAPF is the so-called *classical* MAPF. In this setting the time is discretized and both move and wait actions have the uniform duration of one time step. Numerous algorithms can solve classical MAPF. Some of them are tailored to find optimal solutions

© Springer Nature Switzerland AG 2021
A. Ronzhin et al. (Eds.): ICR 2021, LNAI 12998, pp. 1–13, 2021.
https://doi.org/10.1007/978-3-030-87725-5_1

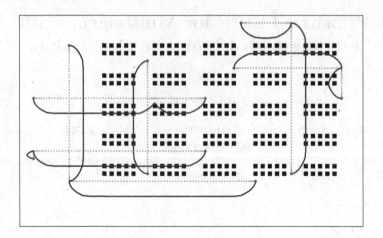

Fig. 1. A scenario of MAPF with kinematic constraints in a warehouse environment. There are six robots that must reach their goals. The path of each robot is highlighted in yellow. The blue lines depict the velocity profiles and one can note the gradual increase and decrease of the speed while the robot is moving. (Color figure online)

(see [11,12,14]), which might be time-consuming in practice (as it is known that solving MAPF optimally is NP-hard [22]). Others target approximate solutions ([13,17]) that can be obtained much faster. In any case, applying the acquired solutions to the real-world robotic settings is problematic as kinematic constraints of the robots are not taken into account in classical MAPF. One way to mitigate this issue is to post-process the agents plans so the constraints associated with the movements of the robots (e.g. speed and acceleration limits) are met [7]. Another way is to modify the problem statement to include these constraints and to develop more advanced algorithms that are capable of solving such modified MAPF problem statements [1,2,8,16,21]. In this work we follow the second approach. Moreover, unlike many other works we reason not only about the speed of the robots but about the acceleration limits as well, i.e. we do not assume that robots accelerate/decelerate instantaneously (see Fig. 1). We build our solver from the well-known in the community building blocks: prioritized planning [3] and SIPP algorithm [10,20]. We elaborate on how we develop the variant of SIPP that takes the considered constraints into account. Moreover, we suggest a range of admissible heuristic functions that are specially designed for planning with speed and acceleration. We evaluate the suggested MAPF solver empirically showing that it is capable of solving large MAPF problems from the logistics domain (i.e. the automated warehouse setting) in reasonable time.

2   Multi Agent Path Finding with Kinematic Constraints (MAPFKC)

MAPF problem is commonly defined by a graph $G = (\mathcal{V}, \mathcal{E})$ and a set of start and goal configurations for k agents that are confined to this graph. The configuration is defined by the graph node and, possibly, some other parameters (e.g. orientation, speed, etc.) depending on the variant of the problem. Anyway, each agent has to reach its goal configuration from the start one by moving from one vertex to the other and waiting at the vertices. A solution of the problem is a set of conflict-free paths for all agents. What makes the paths conflict-free, again, depends on the variant of MAPF. Next we overview the most common MAPF variant called classical MAPF and then define the MAPF problem we are interested in.

2.1   Classical MAPF

In classical MAPF no assumption about the underlying graph is explicitly stated, however other assumptions (discretized timeline, uniform duration of move actions etc.) make the 4-connected grid a natural choice for this problem setting. Therefore, the node u in $\mathcal{V}$ can be represented by the coordinates of the center of the corresponding cell: $u = (x, y)$. Each cell can be either free or an obstacle. In case the cell is an obstacle, no agent can get to this cell at any time. The speed of agents is fixed and it is equal to one cell per time step. There are two kinds of collisions, node-collision and edge-collision. Node collision occurs when two agents get to the same node at the same time step. Edge-collision occurs when two agents cross the same edge in opposite directions at the same time. A solution of this version is a set of trajectories of all agents $\Pi = \{\pi_{ag} : ag \in A\}$ where π_{ag} is the trajectory of the agent ag and it consists of time-increasing array of states $[ag.s_{t_1}, ag.s_{t_2}, ...] : t_1 = 0$ and $t_{i+1} = t_i + 1$ and $ag.s_t = [ag.cfg, t]$. State consists of the time t and the configuration (which is equal to the position $cfg = p = (x, y)$) which the agent ag must have at the time t. The transition between two consecutive states in the trajectory $s_{t_i}, s_{t_{i+1}}$ must be achievable (e.g. by controller) in the corresponding system (whether it is e.g. virtual system (video game) or real life system) with respect to all system constraints. In classical MAPF the transition can be either discrete wait action or discrete move action (i.e. $s_i = [(x, y), t] \rightarrow s_{i+1} \in \{[(x, y), t+1], [(x+1, y), t+1], [(x-1, y), t+1], [(x, y+1), t+1], [(x, y-1), t+1]\}$). We define the cost of a state s as the time to get to this state (i.e. $s.t$) and the cost of a trajectory by the first time to get and stay at the goal state. We define the cost of a solution by the *sum-of-costs* of trajectories of all agents. Intuitively, the optimal solution is the solution with minimal cost i.e. with minimal sum of costs of its trajectories.

2.2   MAPFKC

We define MAPFKC by adding the following ingredients to classical MAPF: agents' shapes, headings, acceleration limits. Reasoning about agents' shapes requires more involved techniques to detect inter-agents collisions. In this work we assume that given an agent's plan one can identify all the grid cells that are swept by the agent and for each cell a sweeping interval can be computed. Overlapping sweeping intervals now define a collision between the agents. In other words, no agent is allowed to enter any cell at time t if at this time the cell is being swept by another agent. The described approach allows planning for agents of different shapes and sizes. In our experiments we consider the agents to be disk-shaped.

Besides the geometry we wish to take into account the kinematics of the agents as well. We assume that each agent may move with a speed from the interval $[0, v_{max}]$, where v_{max} is the given maximum speed. Moreover, the speed can not be changed instantaneously but rather acceleration/deceleration is needed. The latter is limited by the given thresholds: a_{max}^+ (maximum acceleration) and a_{max}^- (maximum deceleration).

Additionally, in this work we assume that the placement of agents in G is *well-formed* [4] i.e. for every agent there is a path in G which connects its initial position with its goal position without passing from any other initial positions or goal positions.

3 Prioritized SIPP for MAPF

In prioritized planning [5], all agents are assigned unique priorities and paths are planned one by one in accordance with the imposed ordering using some (preferably complete) algorithm. When planning for the agent with the priority i the trajectories for the higher-priority agents $1, ..., i-1$ are assumed to be fixed and the current agent has to avoid collisions with them. Moreover, when planning in well-formed infrastructures the individual planner is suggested to avoid start and goal locations of all robots at all times to guarantee completeness [4].

In this work we suggest using SIPP [10] as the individual planner. SIPP is the heuristic search algorithm, which is a variant of the renowned A* [6] algorithm. In the considered setting A* should operate with the search nodes that are defined by the tuples *(configuration, time step)* to take the time dimension into account (as the same configuration might be blocked/available at different time steps due to the dynamic obstacles). SIPP algorithm can be thought as the pruning technique that reduces the number of the considered A* search nodes. To prune the nodes SIPP introduces the notion of the *safe interval*. The latter is a time range for a configuration, during which it is safe to occupy it (i.e. no collision with the dynamic obstacles happen). Safe intervals are considered to be maximal in a sense that extending the interval is impossible as it will lead to a collision. Overall, SIPP prohibits to generate multiple search nodes of the form (cfg, t), for which t belongs to the same safe interval. In other words, per each safe interval only one node is generated and maintained (the one with the lowest time step). Please note, that in original SIPP notation [10], the search node is identified by the safe interval and the configuration of the agent. However, in our work, we will keep the terminology of spatial-time A* (i.e. $s = [cfg, t]$) and implicitly use the *safe intervals* when checking for states duplicates.

SIPP heuristically searches the state-space using A* strategy, e.g. it iterates through the set of candidates states (called OPEN) choosing the one with the minimal f-value, and expanding it (i.e. generating the successors and adding them to the search tree if needed). f-value of the state s is calculated as the

Algorithm 1. SIPP-MAPFKC

Function Plan($grid$, $agents$)
$rsrvTable \leftarrow \phi$
preComputeSpeedTransitions() *
for every ag in A **do**
    $P = $ SIPP($grid$, $rsrvTable$, $ag.cfg_{init}$, $ag.cfg_{goal}$)
    Update $rsrvTable$ with P
end for

Function preComputeSpeedTransitions() *
for every vel_i in V **do** *
    for every vel_j in V **do** *
        if vel_j is achievable from vel_i w.r.t a_{max} passing distance equal to d **then** *
            $acheivableSpeeds[vel_i].insert(vel_j)$ *
            $moveCost[vel_i][vel_j] = $ minimal time to make the transition from vel_i to
vel_j using fixed acceleration $-a_{max}^- \leq a \leq a_{max}^+$ *
        end if *
    end for *
end for *

Function SIPP($grid$, $rsrvTable$, cfg_{init}, cfg_{goal})
OPEN $= \phi$, CLOSED $= \phi$
insert $[cfg_{init}, 0] \rightarrow$ OPEN
while OPEN $\neq \phi$ **do**
    $s \leftarrow$ state from OPEN with minimal f-value,
    remove s from OPEN, insert $s \rightarrow$ CLOSED
    if $s.cfg = cfg_{goal}$ **then**
        return p the path from cfg_{init} to cfg_{goal}
    end if
    for every x in getSuccessors(s, $grid$, $rsrvTable$) **do**
        if $x \notin$ CLOSED **then**
            if $x \in$ OPEN **then**
                if $cost(x)$ from OPEN $> x.t$ **then**
                    update x in OPEN by $x.t$
                end if
            else
                insert $x \rightarrow$ OPEN
            end if
        end if
    end for
end while
return ϕ

Function getSuccessors(s, $grid$, $rsrvTable$)
if $s.speed = 0$ **then** *
    return states in all neighboring cells <u>with all V</u> in all safe intervals with corresponding costs.
end if *
$res \leftarrow \phi$ *
$nxtCell$ is the next cell w.r.t $s.\theta$ *
for every v in V **do** *
    $t = s.t + moveCost[s.v][v]$ *
    if $\{t, nxtCell\}$ is in a safe interval in $rsrvTable$ **then** *
        Add $[nxtCell, s.\theta, v, t] \rightarrow res$ *
    end if *
end for *
return res *

---

sum of the cost of the state, $g(s) = t$, plus the heuristic value, $h(s)$, which is the optimistic estimate of the cost of the path from $s.cfg$ to goal configuration cfg_{goal}. At the beginning, we initialize OPEN by adding the state $[cfg_{init}, 0]$. Every time a state is chosen from OPEN to be expanded, we check if its configuration matches the goal configuration. If it matches, then we terminate the search and return the path from the initial state to the this state. Otherwise we expand it by trying adding its successors to OPEN. Successors' generation involves iterating through the configurations reachable from the current one, calculating their safe intervals and estimating the earliest arrival time for each interval. The latter is used to update the time in the state. In case time does not fit inside the safe interval the successor is pruned. A successor state x is added to OPEN iff x was not expanded before, and either it does not exist in OPEN or its newly discovered cost is lower than the previously known one. In the latter case, the old node is replaced by the new one. Search continues until the goal state is chosen to be expanded or the set of the candidate nodes becomes empty which is the case when we fail to get a solution (path).

The pseudo-code of the algorithm is presented in Algorithm 1 with the additions for MAPFKC are marked with * sign for whole-lines additions and are underlined for partial additions. We first review the general pseudocode of the original planner and then describe the modifications.

Function Plan(*grid*, *agents*). Function plan is the main function of the algorithm. It starts with initializing the reservation table $rsrvTable$ by reserving the positions of start and goal locations of all agents for all times. $rsrvTable$ is a data structure that stores for each position in the environment the intervals of times when this position is not available (i.e. reserved for some other agent). The function continues as follows. Sequentially (according to the defined priority) for each agent a single-agent planner function SIPP is called that returns a path P. After that, $rsrvTable$ is updated, i.e. for each cell that is in collision with P in the predefined time range the corresponding record is added to $rsrvTable$. Thus, next agents must avoid these reservations and, therefore, collision with the higher priority agents.

Function SIPP(*grid*, $rsrvTable$, cfg_{init}, cfg_{goal}). SIPP finds the path for a specific agent avoiding both static and dynamic obstacles. As mentioned before, SIPP algorithm follows A* algorithm with the difference on how to account for the time dimension. Specifically, whenever we check for a state $s = [cfg, t]$ if it is in CLOSED or not, in A* we check if a state with the same configuration cfg and the same t in CLOSED, but in SIPP we check for a state with the same configuration cfg and the *safe interval* $[t_1, t_2]$ where t is contained, instead of t. The same thing is applied when we check for the cost $cost(x)$ of a state x i.e. we search for the cost of a state with the same configuration and the same *safe interval*. Therefore, SIPP prunes many states from A* search space which makes it much faster. SIPP preserves the optimality and completeness properties of A* when the time is discretized and no kinematic constraints are applied [10], and when time is not discretized and the agents move with maximum real speed (but unlimited acceleration) [19].

Function getSuccessors(s, $grid$, $rsrvTable$**).** This function returns all available states which can be achieved from state s. In classical MAPF where the agent has fixed speed and infinite acceleration, getSuccessors returns the states with the following parameters: its position p is one of the 4-neighbor cells of the position in s, and its time t is the minimum time which can be achieved (if possible) in each *safe interval* of the *safe intervals* of p. Details on this function for MAPFKC will be discussed further on.

4   Prioritized SIPP for MAPFKC

To account for limited maximum acceleration, we add the speed (in discrete way) of the robot to the robot state. In this way, we change the transitions between the states not only according to the position of the robot, but also its speed w.r.t the maximal acceleration and the orientation of the robot. Intuitively, storing the real speed of the robot in the search state in SIPP would produce infinite states because from one speed (e.g. starting from the beginning with zero speed) the robot can arrive at the next cell with an infinite number of different real speeds. Therefore, we choose to discretize the maximum speed into a set V of finite number of speeds by fixing a speed-step discretization stp. In this case we will have $V = \{0, stp, 2 * stp, ..., \lfloor \frac{v_{max}}{stp} \rfloor * stp\}$. Next we explain how different speeds and acceleration limits are handled in algorithm.

First of all, we call the function **preComputeSpeedTransitions** before we start planning paths for the agents. This function iterates over all pairs of speed values from V and for each pair (vel_i, vel_j) checks whether vel_j is reachable from vel_i w.r.t. distance travelled and given acceleration limits. If it is we add the corresponding speed change to the hash-table along with the associated cost, i.e. time needed to perform the move.

Specifically, let d be the distance between centers of two cells, and $vel_i \in V$, $vel_j \in V$ be two speeds which we want to check. We denote by t_{vel_i, vel_j} the time to traverse d by starting with vel_i and ending with vel_j using one fixed acceleration/deceleration. By definition this acceleration must satisfy Eq. 1. At the same time t_{vel_i, vel_j} can be written as Eq. 2. Thus, we get the condition 3. If this condition is satisfied then vel_j is achievable from vel_i.

$$- a_{max}^- \leq \frac{vel_j - vel_i}{t_{vel_i, vel_j}} \leq a_{max}^+, \tag{1}$$

$$t_{vel_i, vel_j} = \frac{2d}{vel_i + vel_j}, \tag{2}$$

$$- a_{max}^- \leq \frac{(vel_j - vel_i)(vel_i + vel_j)}{2d} \leq a_{max}^+. \tag{3}$$

There is one exclusion to the transitions described above, when $vel_i = 0$ and $vel_j = 0$, where we can not use one fixed acceleration. Instead, in this case the

transition is always available by using the maximum acceleration and deceleration for suitable periods of times and the move time can be calculated by the
formula $t_{0,0'} = (\frac{1}{a^+_{max}} + \frac{1}{a^-_{max}})\sqrt{\frac{2a^+_{max}a^-_{max}l}{a^-_{max}+a^+_{max}}}$.

In **Function getSuccessors()**, we have now two cases. The first case when
$v = 0$ in state s. In this case, the robot can wait and rotate, therefore the
robot can go to the four neighbor cells and try to arrive in all *safe intervals* but the only constraint is the speed of the agent, i.e. it can arrive only
with *achievableSpeeds*$[0]$. In the other case, when $v \neq 0$, the robot cannot
change its orientation or wait in place. Therefore, the agent can go only to the
next cell $nxtCell$ according to its orientation. The agent will try to arrive at
the next cell by all *achievableSpeeds*$[v]$ as follows. For every speed v' from
achievableSpeeds$[v]$ we calculate the time t' when the agent will arrive to
$nxtCell$ with v', then if t' is in an *safe interval* in $nxtCell$, then we add this
state to the returned result.

Statement 1. The proposed algorithm is complete in *well-formed infrastructures*.

Proof. It is assumed that the initial speed of the agent is always zero and the
initial cell is reserved for the agent for whole time. According to the mentioned
transitions, from a speed equals zero in an unlimited-free cell (from the upper
bound), we can always go to the latest safe interval in next cells (i.e. when the
cell is unlimited-free) with a speed also equals zero by waiting some time then
moving. In *well-formed* environments, we can apply this transition, beginning
from the start cell till the goal cell, as there exists a path which its cells are not
endpoints of other agents and therefore they will be unlimited-free after some
time. In result, the algorithm always finds a path to goal and hence is complete.

4.1 Heuristic Functions

The heuristic value in SIPP-MAPFKC is the estimation of the cost of moving
between two configurations i.e. from $cfg_1 = (p_1 = (x_1, y_1), \theta_1, v_1)$ to the configuration $cfg_2 = (p_2 = (x_2, y_2), \theta_2, v_2)$. In this work we assume that the final
orientation is not important and it could be any orientation, and the final speed
should zero. We propose the following heuristic functions for this case.

First, we propose a heuristic function H1 which estimates the time needed
to pass the Manhattan distance taking into account the kinematic constraints.
Specifically, H1 is the theoretical minimum time needed to pass each straight
segment in the Manhattan path respecting the maximum acceleration, maximum
deceleration and maximum speed constraints. If the Manhattan path consists of
more than one segment, a rotation time is added to H1. We also propose another
similar function H2 where we consider the speed discretization when accelerating
and decelerating at each cell the speed must be one of the discretized speeds.
We calculated H2 using dynamic programming. In tests, we also compare the
results using the heuristic function H3 from literature called *reversible* search. In

H3, we explore the whole map and calculate the minimum distance (e.g. using Dijkstra algorithm) from the goal state to all states in the map. In H3, we just consider the static obstacles of the map and we assume infinite acceleration (i.e. no speed in robot state) to not add any overwork to the original search.

5   Empirical Evaluation

5.1   Setup

We conducted tests on three different maps with different parameters for robots. The maps are warehouse-like environments of different sizes and have different numbers of obstacles. Figure 2 shows an example of one such map, **Map3**, which is of size 66×352 cells and has 15×15 symmetrically distributed obstacles of size 2×20 cells. The other maps are **Map1** with size of 24×46 cells with 5×5 blocks of obstacles of size 2×5 cells and **Map2** with size of 46×142 cells with 10×10 blocks of obstacles of size 2×10 cells.

Assuming that each cell on a map is $1\,\text{m}$ in width/height, we chose two different thresholds for maximum speed of the robots: $v_{max_1} = 2\,\text{m/s}$, $v_{max_2} = 3\,\text{m/s}$ with maximum acceleration and deceleration $a^+_{max_1} = a^-_{max_1} = 1\,\text{m/s}^2$, $a^+_{max_2} = a^-_{max_2} = 1.5\,\text{m/s}^2$. The robots themselves are modelled as disks with diameter equal to $1\,\text{m}$.

For each map, we randomly generated a set of start and goal points for agents, where for each agent either its start point or its goal point must be near the obstacle (simulating the case where the robot hold/release a warehouse-pod) or at one station (in the first vertical column of the map). The initial orientations were also generated randomly. For the instances where maximum speed $v_{max} = 3\,\text{m/s}$, we ran the algorithm with speed-steps of $\{0.1, 0.25, 0.5, 0.6, 1, 1.5\}\,\text{m/s}$. When the maximum speed was $v_{max} = 2\,\text{m/s}$ the speed-steps were $\{0.1, 0.25, 0.4\ 0.5, 0.66, 1\}\,\text{m/s}$. We regenerated the input set for the first map 50 times and for second and third maps, 25 times, and calculated the average value of each metric. We run the instances using our proposed algorithm with H1, H2 and H3. We also run the tests using the algorithm in [9] using fixed speeds equal $\{1, 1.5, 2, 3\}\,\text{m/s}$ with infinite acceleration (the robot can stop and move instantly) to compare the results.

5.2   Results and Discussion

The first set of results are conducted with $v_{max} = 2\,\text{m/s}$ and $a^+_{max} = a^-_{max} = 1\,\text{m/s}$ for all three maps. The results for the Map3 are shown on Fig. 3 (we got analogous results for Map1 and Map2 so we omit their graphs for space reasons). Considering running time, when using small speed-step, it is obvious and as expected that the branching factor in SIPP will be larger and therefore the running time of the algorithm is larger. From step $= 0.66\,\text{m/s}$, we notice increasing in the running time with increasing the step in H2 and H3 graphs and this is from the fact that from this speed and above the robot cannot get to the

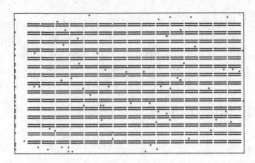

Fig. 2. The figure shows Map3 with one sample of the locations of start and goal points. **Black** segments denote to the obstacles, **green** circles are the start points and the **magnet** points are the goal points. (Color figure online)

maximum speed e.g. the robot cannot go from one cell with $v = 1.32\,\mathrm{m/s}$ to next cell with $v = 2\,\mathrm{m/s}$, and therefore these heuristic function do not give accurate estimations. On the other hand, considering the cost of the solutions, the cost increases with increasing the step. It is easy to notice that with increasing the discretization step, the decreasing slope of the running time for first small steps is very sharp in the opposite of the increasing slope of the cost for them. Therefore, searching for a medium step with balanced results is shown to be suitable and achievable (e.g. in our specific tests, step $= 0.5\,\mathrm{m/s}$ is the most balanced).

Observing the second set of results $v_{max} = 3\,\mathrm{m/s}$ and $a^+_{max} = a^-_{max} = 1.5\,\mathrm{m/s}$), we see that all previous notes are applicable. Comparing with the infinite acceleration, we can see that using an average fixed speed equals to the half of maximum speed or equals to maximum speed run the fastest. Considering the cost, the average fixed speed which is equal to the half of maximum speed gives more cost than most of the cases when we discretize the speed, but using maximum speed is also the ultimate winner here. However, as mentioned earlier, in this case additional post-processing to the solution is needed in real robotic setups to compensate for the infinite acceleration assumption and this actually will add cost.

Our final conclusion is that, given a MAPFKC problem, it is worth to test planning with our algorithm and choose the best step to discretize the maximum speed. Comparing between heuristic functions, we can notice that H2 gives the best results considering the running time, especially for bigger steps. While H3 accounts for all static obstacles, it less efficiently estimates the cost when the robot needs to stop or change its speed. It is also worth mentioning that in H3 we have preprocessing part (Reversible Dijkstra) which adds running time.

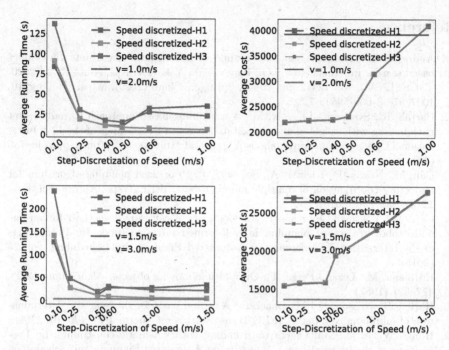

Fig. 3. The results of tests in Map3. The first row from the top shows the results when $v_{max} = 2\,\text{m/s}$, $a^+_{max} = a^-_{max} = 1\,\text{m/s}$. The second row shows the results when $v_{max} = 3\,\text{m/s}$, $a^+_{max} = a^-_{max} = 1.5\,\text{m/s}$. The left figures shows the average running time and the right figures shows the average cost of the solutions, against the speed-step. In all figures, the **Blue**, **orange** and **green** lines are the outputs when using speed-discretization while planning with heuristics functions H1, H2 and H2 respectively. **Red** line is the output of using fixed speed equal to $1\,\text{m/s}$ and infinite acceleration, and **purple** one when using fixed speed $= 2\,\text{m/s}$ and infinite acceleration. (Color figure online)

6 Conclusion

In this work we presented a method to solve the multi-agent path finding problem (with the focus on warehouse environment) taking into account the kinematic constraints of each agent i.e. the maximum speed and maximum acceleration. This method can be used to avoid post-processing of the paths produced by the conventional MAPF solvers (that do not take kinematic constraints into account). Empirical results show that the method works in acceptable time with acceptable cost if the parameters are chosen reasonably. Next, we are interested in applying the method on real robots.

References

1. Andreychuk, A.: Multi-agent path finding with kinematic constraints via conflict based search. In: Kuznetsov, S.O., Panov, A.I., Yakovlev, K.S. (eds.) RCAI 2020. LNCS (LNAI), vol. 12412, pp. 29–45. Springer, Cham (2020). https://doi.org/10.1007/978-3-030-59535-7_3

2. Barták, R., Švancara, J.Í., Vlk, M.: A scheduling-based approach to multi-agent path finding with weighted and capacitated arcs. In: Proceedings of the 17th International Conference on Autonomous Agents and MultiAgent Systems, pp. 748–756 (2018)

3. Čáp, M., Novák, P., Kleiner, A., Selecký, M.: Prioritized planning algorithms for trajectory coordination of multiple mobile robots. IEEE Trans. Autom. Sci. Eng. **12**(3), 835–849 (2015)

4. Čáp, M., Vokřínek, J., Kleiner, A.: Complete decentralized method for on-line multi-robot trajectory planning in well-formed infrastructures. In: Proceedings of the International Conference on Automated Planning and Scheduling, vol. 25 (2015)

5. Erdmann, M., Lozano-Perez, T.: On multiple moving objects. Algorithmica **2**(1), 477–521 (1987)

6. Hart, P.E., Nilsson, N.J., Raphael, B.: A formal basis for the heuristic determination of minimum cost paths. IEEE Trans. Syst. Sci. Cybern. **4**(2), 100–107 (1968)

7. Hönig, W., et al.: Multi-agent path finding with kinematic constraints. In: Proceedings of the International Conference on Automated Planning and Scheduling, vol. 26 (2016)

8. Hönig, W., Preiss, J.A., Kumar, T.S., Sukhatme, G.S., Ayanian, N.: Trajectory planning for quadrotor swarms. IEEE Trans. Rob. **34**(4), 856–869 (2018)

9. Ma, H., Hönig, W., Kumar, T.S., Ayanian, N., Koenig, S.: Lifelong path planning with kinematic constraints for multi-agent pickup and delivery. In: Proceedings of the AAAI Conference on Artificial Intelligence, vol. 33, pp. 7651–7658 (2019)

10. Phillips, M., Likhachev, M.: SIPP: safe interval path planning for dynamic environments. In: 2011 IEEE International Conference on Robotics and Automation, pp. 5628–5635. IEEE (2011)

11. Sharon, G., Stern, R., Felner, A., Sturtevant, N.R.: Conflict-based search for optimal multi-agent pathfinding. Artif. Intell. **219**, 40–66 (2015)

12. Sharon, G., Stern, R., Goldenberg, M., Felner, A.: The increasing cost tree search for optimal multi-agent pathfinding. Artif. Intell. **195**, 470–495 (2013)

13. Silver, D.: Cooperative pathfinding. AIIDE **1**, 117–122 (2005)

14. Standley, T.: Finding optimal solutions to cooperative pathfinding problems. In: Proceedings of the AAAI Conference on Artificial Intelligence, vol. 24 (2010)

15. Stern, R., et al.: Multi-agent pathfinding: definitions, variants, and benchmarks. In: Symposium on Combinatorial Search (2019)

16. Walker, T.T., Sturtevant, N.R., Felner, A.: Extended increasing cost tree search for non-unit cost domains. In: IJCAI, pp. 534–540 (2018)

17. Wang, K.H.C., Botea, A., et al.: Fast and memory-efficient multi-agent pathfinding. In: ICAPS, pp. 380–387 (2008)

18. Wurman, P.R., D'Andrea, R., Mountz, M.: Coordinating hundreds of cooperative, autonomous vehicles in warehouses. AI Mag. **29**(1), 9 (2008)

19. Yakovlev, K., Andreychuk, A.: Any-angle pathfinding for multiple agents based on SIPP algorithm. In: Proceedings of the International Conference on Automated Planning and Scheduling, vol. 27 (2017)

20. Yakovlev, K., Andreychuk, A., Stern, R.: Revisiting bounded-suboptimal safe interval path planning. In: Proceedings of the 30th International Conference on Automated Planning and Scheduling (ICAPS 2020), pp. 300–304 (2020)
21. Yakovlev, K., Andreychuk, A., Vorobyev, V.: Prioritized multi-agent path finding for differential drive robots. In: 2019 European Conference on Mobile Robots (ECMR), pp. 1–6. IEEE (2019)
22. Yu, J., LaValle, S.: Structure and intractability of optimal multi-robot path planning on graphs. In: Proceedings of the AAAI Conference on Artificial Intelligence, vol. 27 (2013)

DronePort: Smart Drone Battery Management System

Zdeněk Bouček[✉][ID], Petr Neduchal[ID], and Miroslav Flídr[ID]

Faculty of Applied Sciences, New Technologies for the Information Society,
University of West Bohemia, Univerzitní 8, 306 14 Plzeň, Czech Republic
{zboucek,neduchal,flidr}@kky.zcu.cz
http://fav.zcu.cz/en/, http://ntis.zcu.cz/en/

Abstract. This paper deals with the description of a drone management system for long-term missions called DronePort. First, the issue of long-term missions and possible approaches are outlined. Further, the individual components of proposed system, both hardware, and software are introduced. The DronePort system relies on battery swapping. By storing the battery in a battery compartment, the system is not strictly designed for one type of drone, but with simple modification, it is capable of maintaining a flight of various Vertical Take-Off and Landing (VTOL) drones. Afterward, more attention is paid to the simulation environment, which will greatly facilitate the development of the entire system. The simulation includes both drones equipped with a down-facing camera and a DronePort landing platform, which is fitted with an ArUco marker for precise landing. Next, the DronePort Traffic Control system is presented, which is tasked with communicating with the drones, scheduling battery swapping, and planning trajectories for the flight to and from the DronePort landing platform. The system uses the standard MAVLink protocol for communication, enabling use with a variety of MAVLink compatible drones. Finally, an example of collision-free trajectory planning considering battery capacity is presented. Trajectory was found in terms of Chebyshev pseudospectral optimal control.

Keywords: Aerial robotics · Drones · Battery management · Traffic control · Robot simulation

1 Introduction

Nowadays, one of the biggest challenges in the drone field is the long-term missions with multiple drones, which brings new demands for autonomy [9,17]. The vast majority of drones use Lithium-Polymer (LiPo) batteries, and usually, they last for only several tens of minutes in the air. In most applications, a hard-wired drone is out of the question because of the limited operating area and the increase in weight of the entire system due to cables.

There are applications with wireless charging such as [9], nevertheless, this solution is more time demanding than the standard battery swapping method

© Springer Nature Switzerland AG 2021
A. Ronzhin et al. (Eds.): ICR 2021, LNAI 12998, pp. 14–26, 2021.
https://doi.org/10.1007/978-3-030-87725-5_2

and requires staying on the ground. The standard method is to allocate the person who will operate the charging station. However, the employment of drones is usually considered to minimize the involvement of human operators to increase workplace safety and minimize personnel costs.

The state-of-the-art research shows that the most efficient method, which solves the power supply and charging issues, is autonomous battery swapping. Several experimental solutions are tightly adapted to specific drone models and batteries [11,22]. DronePort (DP) system proposed in this paper can operate various drones with Vertical Take-Off and Landing (VTOL) ability. It is capable of swapping batteries of various sizes and shapes.

The article is structured as follows. The subsequent section outlines the entire DP system with a description of its parts. Next, the simulation environment is described to streamline the development of the whole system. Then the DronePort Traffic Control system is introduced, and an example of trajectory planning is presented.

2   DronePort System

The DP system is an early-stage project with the goal of automating long-term drone missions. The development of the system involves the University of West Bohemia and SmartMotion, where SmartMotion is mainly responsible for the creation of the entire DP landing platform and battery storage. The system consists of two main parts. The first part is hardware, which consists of a landing platform and a battery compartment placed on the drone.

The landing platform is equipped with an ArUco code that allows safe and precise on-spot landing. It also includes battery storage and a smart multi-slot battery-charging station. The size and weight of the DP landing platform allow it to be moved by two people. A robotic manipulator is used to remove the battery from the drone, plug it into the charging station, and plug the charged battery into the drone. The battery compartment allows easy handling by a robotic manipulator and can be supplemented in the future with an NFC tag for easy identification of the battery by the system.

The DP system will also be equipped with a computer capable of connecting with the drones, downloading the necessary information, scheduling, and sending commands with battery swapping missions. In order to achieve wide usability of the system, it will use the standard MAVLink protocol [8] for communication. We intend to use drones equipped with Pixhawk PX4 autopilot for testing, but it is possible to interact with all drones communicating via MAVLink. So far, the PX4 software-in-the-loop (SITL) simulated drone in Gazebo has been successfully withdrawn from the mission to the desired coordinates, and the mission has been backed up in case of problems. Afterward, the simulated drone took off and successfully resumed its mission. The drone communication application was implemented in Python and was based on the pymavlink[1] library.

---

[1] https://github.com/ArduPilot/pymavlink.

Next, the software part of the project will be briefly described. Drone state estimation is not performed by the DP system. This fact makes the system very versatile and does not require a specific set of sensors. The only requirement is a down-facing camera due to the detection of the ArUco code on the landing platform. The system will estimate the battery's state, which will also be affected by the long-term behavior of the battery. This state will also be predicted based on drone and smart charger data for optimal scheduling of battery replacement.

Another software component is the landing controller, where the orientation and position data of the ArUco code is used. The next component is the DronePort Traffic Control system (DPTC), which, based on information received from the drones and the DP landing platform, decides on the scheduling of battery swapping and plans trajectories for an approach to the DP landing platform and subsequent return to the mission. DPTC will be discussed in more detail in Sect. 4. Another essential component is the simulation of the whole system, which serves as a tool for testing all parts of the DP system in a virtual environment and will be described in more detail in the following section.

3   Simulation

In order to reduce the cost and effort of the task, the simulation environment is used. In this section, we describe and discuss the design of the DronePort simulation. A brief overview of available simulators capable of simulating one or multiple drones will be presented in the first part. As will be mentioned, the Gazebo simulator, together with the PX4 controller, was chosen for our experiments. In the next part, DronePort simulation in Gazebo simulator [7] will be described. The third part of this section focuses on the unique DronePort model generation developed to reduce modeling effort.

3.1   Available Open-Source Simulation Software

Based on our research and several survey papers on this topic, such as [2, 3, 13, 20], we put together the following list of simulators capable of simulating missions of one or multiple drones. The well-known simulator is Gazebo which is based on Ogre 3D graphic engine. It can be easily extended using plugins written in the C++ programming language. Moreover, it can be connected to the PX4 controller using PX4-SITL_gazebo[2] plugin suite.

Several simulators are built on the top of the Gazebo simulator, such as RotorS [4] or BebopS [18]. It is a set of models, sensors, and controllers that can communicate with the Gazebo simulator.

There also exist simulators that are not built on the top of the Gazebo. The following projects can be mentioned. The first one is open source AirSim [16] simulator developed by Microsoft. Its interesting feature is the photorealistic graphics which enables to solve machine vision problems inside the simulation.

---

[2] https://github.com/PX4/PX4-SITL_gazebo.

Another interesting fact is that the AirSim can be run using Unreal Engine or Unity as its 3D graphics engine. Similar photorealistic graphics based on the Unity engine is available inside FlightMare [19] simulator developed by Robotics and Perception Group at ETH Zurich. Another option with photorealistic graphics is NVIDIA ISAAC [12] which is primarily intended to use NVIDIA Hardware.

Finally, more general simulators such as V-Rep [14] or Webots [10] can be mentioned. We chose the combination of the Gazebo simulator and PX4 controller for our experiments because it offers a well-known extensible environment with sufficiently simplified graphics to perform traffic control experiments with a DronePort model.

3.2   DronePort Simulation

DronePort model for simulation is simplified. The model's geometry is created using SDF[3] specification used by Gazebo simulator and consists of a blue block of model body and of the thin block textured using ArUco code. The model is shown in Fig. 1.

Fig. 1. Example of DronePort object and Iris drone in Gazebo simulator.

The software for the DronePort model is shown in Fig. 2. It consists of several parts that will be described in the following text. The main part is a DronePort Control Software that can be implemented in an arbitrary programming language. It handles the state of the DronePort device – either simulated or real. The control software is connected to the rest of the system and with a simulator using MAVLink protocol – see MAVLink Router block in the scheme. As visible from the scheme, MAVLink Router is connected with both the PX4 controller

---

[3] http://sdformat.org/spec.

for communication with drones and Gazebo Plugins to communicate with the simulated world in Gazebo. The last part of the scheme is a camera plugin connected to a simulated drone. It provides source image data for the ArUco code detector, which is used during the landing maneuver of the drone.

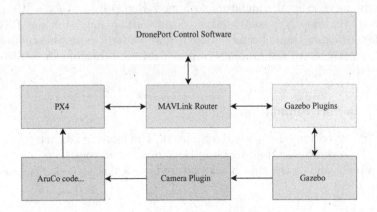

Fig. 2. DronePort simulation scheme.

The DronePort model in the Gazebo is equipped with a Gazebo plugin that broadcast its GPS coordinates using MAVLink message. This plugin is based on the gazebo_mavlink_interface plugin from the mentioned PX4-SITL_gazebo plugin suite.

3.3   Generation of a Unique DronePort Model

During the development of the DronePort model, the first intention was to create a unique DronePort during the initialization of the simulation. Unfortunately, it was discovered that it is no simple task to set texture with ArUco code on the fly. Thus, the generator of unique models from the template was developed in Python. Its purpose is to generate a model with particular properties such as ArUco code, size, color, and MAVLink protocol settings. Moreover, it can be connected to the simulation using software like Tmux and Tmuxinator, and thus, it can be launched before the simulation starts.

In practice, the simulation is based on the clear Gazebo without Robot Operating System (ROS). On the other hand, the support for ROS can be easily added to the model using a particular plugin. With a model generator, it is possible to run either simple or complex scenarios with one or multiple drones and one or multiple DronePort devices. Thus, a simulation of traffic control with DronePort can be performed. More about traffic control will be described in the following parts of the paper.

4   DronePort Traffic Control

This section describes the DronePort Traffic Control (DPTC) system, which is complemented by an example of collision-free drone trajectory planning concerning battery capacity is presented. The main task of the DPTC is to schedule the replacement and subsequent recharging of drone batteries at the DP platform. It will do so by monitoring and predicting the state of drone batteries and registering the number and state of batteries available on the DP platforms. Opposed to [22], the DPTC will optimally schedule the interruption and resumption of the current drone missions, considering the DP landing platforms availability, availability of charged batteries at the DP platforms, and minimizing mission interruption time. The DPTC will take care of the trajectory re-planning to the DP platform according to the current mission progress and the resumption of the original mission after battery replacement.

The functionality of the entire system can be inferred from the data flow for the DPTC API shown in Fig. 3. From DPTC's perspective, the whole system is divided into four parts. The first part is Ground Control (GC), which is not manipulated by DPTC and is only used to operate the drone. The second part is the drone itself which contains a battery compartment. The drone communicates with the GC and sends information to the DP platform. DPTC will be able to operate several drones at the same time. The drone contains low-level control and mission control, which executes commands from the GC and DPTC. The third part is the battery compartment, which contains an NFC tag to identify the battery. For each battery, the system makes a prediction of the state based on the measurement. The last part is the DronePort platform, which includes smart battery chargers that perform charging and measure battery status. The computer in the DP platform runs the DPTC, which schedules drone withdrawals from missions and handles communication with the drones. The activity of the DPTC from the drone's perspective is illustrated in Fig. 4.

The design of the data structure used to store the information used in the DPTC is shown in Fig. 5. The data should contain information about all the essential parts of the DP, i.e., drones, landing platforms, and charging stations. About the batteries, the current parameters and their history could be stored. In the case of drones, their battery ID, position, status, or mission plan could be stored. Data about a DP platform could include its location, geofence, and a list of components (batteries, chargers, assigned drones). For the time being, the system is considered fully centralized due to the fact that only one DP landing platform is considered. However, in the future, more platforms could be involved in the system, even with several DPTCs, where drones would be serviced, for example, based on airspace zoning and the occupancy of individual platforms.

Further, an example of collision-free drone trajectory planning will be demonstrated. The trajectory will be planned considering the State of Charge (SoC) of the battery [24]. The trajectory planning problem will be described as an optimal control problem (OCP) [6]. First, the Chebyshev pseudospectral method (PSM) will be introduced and employed to acquire the solution to the OCP. Subse-

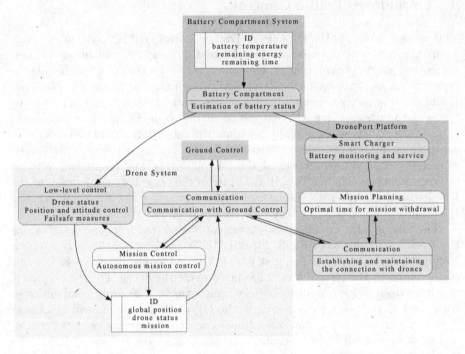

Fig. 3. Data flow of DronePort traffic control system API.

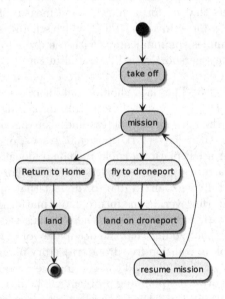

Fig. 4. Drone behavior.

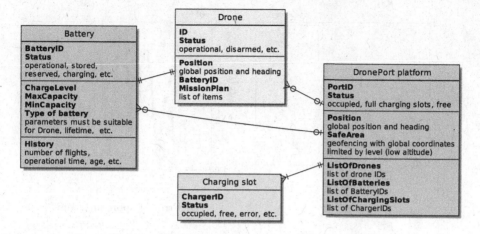

Fig. 5. Proposed data structure.

quently, the parameters of the problem will be described. Finally, the solution will be presented.

4.1 Chebyshev Pseudospectral Optimal Control

In this part, the Chebyshev pseudospectral method (PSM) [1,15,21] will be presented in the context of its utilization in solving the OCP. The PSM gives an exact solution to the problem at "grid" or so-called "collocation" points. It approximates the function outside these points by a basis set of functions usually composed of trigonometric functions or polynomials. Approximation of function and its error is clearly shown in Fig. 6. Each basis set has its unique set of optimal collocation points. The points are usually the roots of function, which can be augmented by boundary points. The presence of boundary points is essential for boundary value problems such as OCP.

The standard Chebyshev polynomial of the first kind [1] with a grid containing the boundary points is chosen. The integral objective is approximated with Clenshaw–Curtis quadrature, and the derivative which is needed for approximating dynamics is calculated using differential matrix. The Chebyshev approximation can be used on the interval $[-1, 1]$. Therefore, it is necessary to transform the problem coordinates according to the end-points of the time vector when solving the OCP.

PSM generally achieves higher accuracy at lower complexity than Finite Element Method or Finite Difference Method and better solution convergence than shooting methods [1]. Therefore, it is advantageous to use it for drone trajectories as it allows fast computation when re-planning is required and low complexity to be used even on a drone up-board computer.

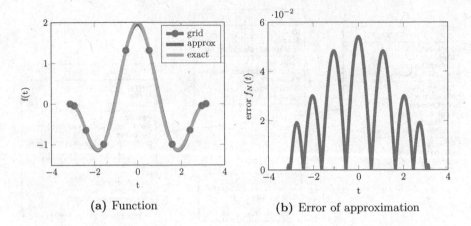

(a) Function   (b) Error of approximation

Fig. 6. Approximation of function with Chebyshev pseudospectral method.

4.2 Trajectory Planning

This part will describe the parameters of the trajectory planning problem and also provide implementation details. The state of the system consists of the position and speed of the drone and the State of Charge (SoC). The control vector is composed of the acceleration in the x, y, and z axis. The dynamics of the drone are described by a simple model. The x-axis motion is described as

$$\dot{r}_x = v_x, \quad \dot{v}_x = a_x, \tag{1}$$

where r_x, v_x, and a_x are position, velocity, and acceleration in x-axis, respectively. Movement in the other axes is described in the same way. State of battery is described in a standard manner using SoC which is given as 0.0 and 1.0 for empty and full battery, respectively. The dynamics of SoC is described as

$$\dot{b} = B_b \left(v_x^2 + v_y^2 + v_z^2 \right) + D_b, \tag{2}$$

where b is the battery SoC, the linear discharge versus time is represented by the parameter D_b and B_b is the coefficient of dependence on the square of the drone velocity. Each state is bounded by a box constraint. The problem contains fixed boundary points except for SoC b and end time t_f, which have a free end-points. Objective function includes SoC maximization.

The problem is further supplemented with constraints for obstacles in the form

$$- |r - c_i|_2 + R^2 \leq 0, \tag{3}$$

where r is position of drone, c_i is center of i-th obstacle and R is a radius of obstacle. Obstacles are sampled randomly through the whole space with uniform distribution.

4.3   Results

The trajectory planning problem was implemented in Python using the Pyomo optimization toolbox [5]. The apparatus for the Chebyshev polynomial approximation was rewritten based on the MATLAB implementation in [21]. The solution was sought on a standard desktop PC with Intel Core i9-9900 and Ubuntu 20.04 using well-known open-source NLP solver IPOPT [23]. The initial solution was obtained in 74 iterations, where IPOPT ran for 46 s. The subsequent solution was acquired in 16 iterations and took 8.2 s. The drone successfully avoided all obstacles and flew from the initial to the target point. The path of the drone is shown in Fig. 7, where the blue spheres are obstacles, the green point is the start, and red is the position of the goal. The SoC and other trajectory states, together with the control trajectory, are shown in Fig. 8.

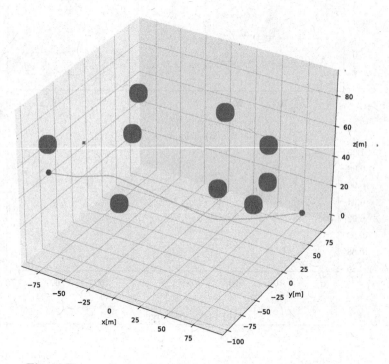

Fig. 7. Drone passage through an environment with obstacles.

The results show that the optimal trajectory that considers battery discharge has been successfully found. The problem could be extended in the future, for example, to reflect the temperature during battery discharge, scheduling battery replacement at service stations or the interaction of several drones simultaneously. Furthermore, the PSM could be extended by adaptive mesh refinement, segmentation, or more accurate initialization.

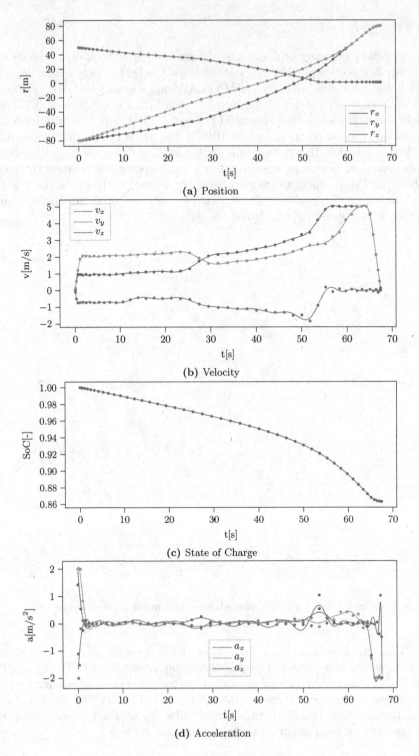

(a) Position

(b) Velocity

(c) State of Charge

(d) Acceleration

Fig. 8. Trajectory of state and control.

5 Conclusion

The paper presented the DronePort system for smart drone management during long-term missions. First, the purpose of the system was outlined, and its most important parts were introduced. Afterward, the simulation environment was described, which will significantly help to make the whole development more efficient and at the same time reduce costs. Finally, the DronePort Traffic Control system for controlling and scheduling the swapping of drone batteries was introduced. An example of collision-free trajectory planning considering battery capacity using a Chebyshev pseudospectral optimal control was presented within the Traffic Control.

Acknowledgements. This project has received funding from the ECSEL Joint Undertaking (JU) under grant agreement No 826610. The JU receives support from the European Union's Horizon 2020 research and innovation programme and Spain, Austria, Belgium, Czech Republic, France, Italy, Latvia, Netherlands.

References

1. Boyd, J.P.: Chebyshev and Fourier Spectral Methods. Dover Publications, New York (2000). https://doi.org/10.1007/978-0-387-77674-3
2. Castillo-Pizarro, P., Arredondo, T.V., Torres-Torriti, M.: Introductory survey to open-source mobile robot simulation software. In: 2010 Latin American Robotics Symposium and Intelligent Robotics Meeting, pp. 150–155. IEEE (2010)
3. Ebeid, E., Skriver, M., Terkildsen, K.H., Jensen, K., Schultz, U.P.: A survey of open-source UAV flight controllers and flight simulators. Microprocess. Microsyst. **61**, 11–20 (2018)
4. Furrer, F., Burri, M., Achtelik, M., Siegwart, R.: RotorS—a modular gazebo MAV simulator framework. In: Koubaa, A. (ed.) Robot Operating System (ROS). SCI, vol. 625, pp. 595–625. Springer, Cham (2016). https://doi.org/10.1007/978-3-319-26054-9_23
5. Hart, W.E., Watson, J.P., Woodruff, D.L.: Pyomo: modeling and solving mathematical programs in python. Math. Program. Comput. **3**(3), 219–260 (2011)
6. Kirk, D.E.: Optimal Control Theory: An Introduction. Dover Publications, New York (2004)
7. Koenig, N., Howard, A.: Design and use paradigms for Gazebo, an open-source multi-robot simulator. In: 2004 IEEE/RSJ International Conference on Intelligent Robots and Systems (IROS) (IEEE Cat. No. 04CH37566), vol. 3, pp. 2149–2154. IEEE (2004)
8. Koubaa, A., Allouch, A., Alajlan, M., Javed, Y., Belghith, A., Khalgui, M.: Micro Air Vehicle Link (MAVlink) in a nutshell: a survey. IEEE Access **7**, 87658–87680 (2019). https://doi.org/10.1109/ACCESS.2019.2924410
9. Malyuta, D., Brommer, C., Hentzen, D., Stastny, T., Siegwart, R., Brockers, R.: Long-duration fully autonomous operation of rotorcraft unmanned aerial systems for remote-sensing data acquisition. J. Field Robot. **37**(1), 137–157 (2020). https://doi.org/10.1002/rob.21898
10. Michel, O.: Cyberbotics Ltd. Webots^{TM}: professional mobile robot simulation. Int. J. Adv. Robot. Syst. **1**(1), 5 (2004)

11. Michini, B., et al.: Automated battery swap and recharge to enable persistent UAV missions. In: Infotech@Aerospace 2011, pp. 1–10. American Institute of Aeronautics and Astronautics, Reston, March 2011. https://doi.org/10.2514/6.2011-1405. https://arc.aiaa.org/doi/10.2514/6.2011-1405

12. Monteiro, F.F., Vieira, A.L.B., Teixeira, J.M.X.N., Teichrieb, V., et al.: Simulating real robots in virtual environments using NVIDIA's Isaac SDK. In: Anais Estendidos do XXI Simpósio de Realidade Virtual e Aumentada, pp. 47–48. SBC (2019)

13. Pitonakova, L., Giuliani, M., Pipe, A., Winfield, A.: Feature and performance comparison of the V-REP, Gazebo and ARGoS robot simulators. In: Giuliani, M., Assaf, T., Giannaccini, M.E. (eds.) TAROS 2018. LNCS (LNAI), vol. 10965, pp. 357–368. Springer, Cham (2018). https://doi.org/10.1007/978-3-319-96728-8_30

14. Rohmer, E., Singh, S.P., Freese, M.: V-REP: a versatile and scalable robot simulation framework. In: 2013 IEEE/RSJ International Conference on Intelligent Robots and Systems, pp. 1321–1326. IEEE (2013)

15. Ross, I.M., Karpenko, M.: A review of pseudospectral optimal control: from theory to flight. Ann. Rev. Control **36**(2), 182–197 (2012). https://doi.org/10.1016/j.arcontrol.2012.09.002

16. Shah, S., Dey, D., Lovett, C., Kapoor, A.: AirSim: high-fidelity visual and physical simulation for autonomous vehicles. In: Hutter, M., Siegwart, R. (eds.) Field and Service Robotics. Springer Proceedings in Advanced Robotics, vol. 5, pp. 621–635. Springer, Cham (2018)

17. Shakhatreh, H., et al.: Unmanned Aerial Vehicles (UAVs): a survey on civil applications and key research challenges. IEEE Access **7**, 48572–48634 (2019). https://doi.org/10.1109/ACCESS.2019.2909530

18. Silano, G., Oppido, P., Iannelli, L.: Software-in-the-loop simulation for improving flight control system design: a quadrotor case study. In: 2019 IEEE International Conference on Systems, Man and Cybernetics (SMC), pp. 466–471. IEEE (2019)

19. Song, Y., Naji, S., Kaufmann, E., Loquercio, A., Scaramuzza, D.: Flightmare: a flexible quadrotor simulator. In: Conference on Robot Learning (2020)

20. Staranowicz, A., Mariottini, G.L.: A survey and comparison of commercial and open-source robotic simulator software. In: Proceedings of the 4th International Conference on PErvasive Technologies Related to Assistive Environments, pp. 1–8 (2011)

21. Trefethen, L.N.: Spectral methods in MATLAB. Soc. Ind. Appl. Math. (2000). https://doi.org/10.1137/1.9780898719598

22. Ure, N.K., Chowdhary, G., Toksoz, T., How, J.P., Vavrina, M.A., Vian, J.: An automated battery management system to enable persistent missions with multiple aerial vehicles. IEEE/ASME Trans. Mechatron. **20**(1), 275–286 (2015). https://doi.org/10.1109/TMECH.2013.2294805

23. Wächter, A., Biegler, L.T.: On the implementation of an interior-point filter line-search algorithm for large-scale nonlinear programming. Math. Program. **106**(1), 25–57 (2006)

24. Zhang, D., Dey, S., Perez, H.E., Moura, S.J.: Real-time capacity estimation of lithium-ion batteries utilizing thermal dynamics. IEEE Trans. Control Syst. Technol. **28**(3), 992–1000 (2020). https://doi.org/10.1109/TCST.2018.2885681

Semantic Segmentation in the Task of Long-Term Visual Localization

Lukáš Bureš[✉] and Luděk Müller

Faculty of Applied Sciences, New Technologies for the Information Society,
University of West Bohemia, Univerzitní 8, 306 14 Plzeň, Czech Republic
{lbures,muller}@ntis.zcu.cz

Abstract. In this paper, it is discussed the problem of long-term visual
localization with a using of the Aachen Day-Night dataset. Our experiments confirmed that carefully fine-tuning parameters of the Hierarchical
Localization method can lead to enhance the visual localization accuracy.
Next, our experiments show that it is possible to find an image's area
that does not add any valuable information in long-term visual localization and can be removed without losing the localization accuracy. The
approach of using the method of semantic segmentation for preprocessing helped to achieve comparable state-of-the-art results in the Aachen
Day-Night dataset.

Keywords: Long-term visual localization · Semantic segmentation ·
SuperPoint · SuperGlue · HRNet-OCR

1 Introduction

The ability to effectively represent local visual information is the key to a vast
range of computer vision applications. The range of these applications may contain image alignment, which requires local image descriptors to be accurately
matched between different views of the same scene, image classification, and
image retrieval where massive descriptor collections are frequently scanned to
locate the ones most relevant to those of a query image. The recent summary
can be found in [20].

At the core of the problem, there is a challenge of extracting local representations at locations of keypoints. The keypoints are typically distributed sparsely
in the image in a discriminative and invariant manner to various image transformations. Additional requirements, often critical, are connected with an efficiency
of a representation in terms of the computational costs required to produce it,
the space required to store it, and the time required to search for matching
descriptors in large descriptor repositories.

The problem of the long-term visual localization can be described as follows:
estimating the 6 DoF camera pose from which a given image was taken relative
to a reference scene representation. Visual localization is a key technology for
augmented, mixed, and virtual reality, robotics, and self-driving cars.

© Springer Nature Switzerland AG 2021
A. Ronzhin et al. (Eds.): ICR 2021, LNAI 12998, pp. 27–39, 2021.
https://doi.org/10.1007/978-3-030-87725-5_3

To evaluate visual localization over time, a benchmark dataset is needed. It aims for evaluating 6 DoF pose estimation accuracy over large appearance variations caused by changes in seasonal and during different illumination conditions.

Long-term visual localization has multiple subtasks in the pipeline where the improvements to state-of-the-art can be made. A few open areas where is always space for improvement can be mentioned.

The first step in the pipeline it is usually the detecting of keypoints. End-to-end trained neural networks replaced the traditional approaches in which corners and similar points were considered to be keypoints. During the training process, there are multiple ways where the neural network can be improved, e.g., training data, the structure of the neural network, training procedure itself, optimizing function.

The next part is a keypoint descriptors which is used later for matching purposes. In traditional methods, the keypoint descriptor was represented by a feature vector describing a local window around the detected keypoint. The current describing approaches can be replaced by a neural network trained in an end-to-end manner. There are similar options, like in the case of keypoint detector, how to improve descriptor. However, the ultimate goal here is to get the most general descriptor unbiased to the given image.

The third area of improvement can be made in a keypoint matcher. Originally keypoint matchers like brute force or nearest neighbor were used. In the current state-of-the-art methods, the used matchers are based on neural networks which mostly outperform traditional matchers with a significant margin. The matcher has to be robust and match the right keypoints even if there are multiple instances of the same objects, e.g., tiles, windows, and fence.

Before the matching phase even starts, coarse matching is mostly used for speeding the process. The coarse matching helps to find the N most visually similar images and order them by a similarity value. It helps tremendously because the matching stage is not needed to match every possible query-dataset image combination exhaustively. Improving the global descriptor to find the most similar image to a given query image can help improve long-term visual localization overall.

Structure from motion (SfM) is also a part of the pipeline. It can be improved in a way, e.g., improve the number of keypoint co-occurrences, improve the robustness of co-occurrences or use a different type of data.

A carefully fine-tuning of a parameter of a method can improve the results of a given method. The importance is to do so without overlearning the training set and the test set.

Before the pipeline even starts to detect keypoints and process dataset, a preprocessing can be applied for enhancing input images. A similar approach can be applied to postprocessing images or keypoint descriptors before the data goes to the next stage of the pipeline.

This paper focuses on the last two points fine-tuning parameters of a method and preprocessing data.

2   Dataset

For the experiments, the Aachen Day-Night dataset was used [12]. It is a subset
of the original Aachen dataset [13] which contains 1.5M 3D points and 369 query
images. This Aachen Day-Night dataset consists of 4328 reference images and
922 query images. In sum, there are 824 images captured in the daytime and 98
ones taken in the nighttime.

The entire dataset was captured in the old inner city of Aachen, Germany,
by hand-held cameras and mobile phones over about two years. All of the query
images were captured during the nighttime and daytime and only using mobile
phone cameras. Therefore, this dataset is suitable for solving localization problems using mobile devices, e.g., Augmented or Mixed Reality. The 98 nighttime
query images were taken by using software HDR to obtain high-quality and
well-illuminated images.

The collection of images was publicly released, and it is not intended for
commercial use and should be applied primarily for research purposes.

The Aachen Day-Night dataset (see example in Fig. 1) was used to prove that
the proposed Structure from motion using dense convolutional neural network
features with the keypoint relocalization outperforms a state-of-the-art Structure
from motion (COLMAP[1] [14, 16], and [15] using RootSIFT) by a large margin
[8].

Fig. 1. The Aachen Day-Night dataset contains images taken by hand-held cameras in
the old city of Aachen, Germany. These two images were captured during the daytime.
The left images demonstrate the same scene in the summer and the right one represents
the same square during the winter season. Both images were taken during the daytime.

This dataset was also used to learn keypoint detection and description
together with a predictor of the local descriptor discriminativeness. The
detection-and-description approach simultaneously outputs sparse, repeatable,
and reliable keypoints that outperform state-of-the-art detectors and descriptors
on the HPatches dataset and the Aachen Day-Night localization benchmark [9].

---

[1] https://colmap.github.io/.

2.1 Benchmark for Dataset

For evaluation results, a benchmark is needed. A benchmark can play a role of validity and honesty of results and prevent not so scientifically correct results are considered a new state-of-the-art. On the other hand, methods specializing in the benchmark may be losing generalization power on other benchmarks/datasets.

Because the ECCV conference is one of the significant conferences in the computer vision community, then it is possible to assume the benchmark used during ECCV 2020 Workshop[2] with focus at the Long-Term Visual Localization under Changing Conditions Workshop fulfill the needs for benchmark objectivity and validity.

The submission page[3] for the benchmark allows to submit results to various benchmarking datasets that are commonly used in top-tier computer vision conferences for the problem of long-term visual localization. The benchmarking datasets, that can be evaluated there, include these: Aachen Day-Night and Aachen Day-Night v1.1 datasets, CMU Seasons dataset Localization and Extended CMU Seasons datasets, RobotCar Seasons and RobotCar Seasons v2 datasets, Symphony Seasons dataset, InLoc dataset, and SILDa Weather and Time of Day dataset.

Among many rules and recommendations for benchmark and challenge submission, there are a few which is worth mentioning here:

- Submissions show that existing methods can outperform methods with results published on the benchmarks, e.g., carefully tuning parameters or using a different training dataset.
- Combining
  existing methods with preprocessing or postprocessing approaches, e.g., using histogram equalization on the input images, building better 3D models (for example, through model compression or the use of dense 3D models), or integrating an existing localization algorithm into a (visual) Odometry/SLAM system.

The recommendations of **carefully tuning parameters** and **preprocessing approaches** are used and further expanded in this paper.

3 Used Methods in the Pipeline

In this section, there are briefly mentioned methods that were used in the experiments.

3.1 SuperPoint

The SuperPoint is a self-supervised framework for training interest point detectors and descriptors suitable for many multiple-view geometry problems in computer vision [5]. It is based on a fully convolutional model that operates on

---

[2] https://sites.google.com/view/ltvl2020/challenges.

[3] https://www.visuallocalization.net.

full-sized images and jointly computes pixel-level interest point locations and associated descriptors in one forward pass. It introduced Homographic Adaptation for boosting interest point detection repeatability. The SuperPoint keypoints and descriptors show excellent performance on the HPatches dataset.

The architecture of SuperPoint is designed as a fully-convolutional neural network architecture that operates on a full-sized image and produces interest point detections accompanied by fixed-length descriptors in a single forward pass.

The architecture is split into two "heads" after the encoder part. Each "head" learns task-specific weights – one for interest point detection and the other one for interest point description.

Most of the network's parameters are shared between these two tasks. That is the difference from traditional systems. The detection and description tasks are handled separately, and the description task needs keypoints locations for its calculation.

The Homographic Adaptation technique was used at training time to improve the base MagicPoint architecture generalization ability on real images. The process can be repeated iteratively to continually self-supervise and improve the interest point detector.

3.2 SuperGlue

SuperGlue [11] is a neural network that matches two sets of local features by jointly finding correspondences and rejecting non-matchable points. Assignments are estimated by solving a differentiable optimal transport problem, whose costs are predicted by a graph neural network.

It introduces a flexible context aggregation mechanism based on attention, enabling SuperGlue to reason about the underlying 3D scene and feature assignments jointly. SuperGlue performs matching in real-time on a modern GPU and can be integrated into modern SfM or SLAM systems.

SuperGlue presents a new way of thinking about the feature matching problem. Instead of trying to learn better features followed by simple heuristic matching (e.g., brute force matching), it learns matching from existing local features using a neural network architecture.

In the context of SLAM, which typically [1] decomposes the problem into the visual feature extraction front-end and the bundle adjustment or pose estimation back-end, the SuperGlue network lies in the middle.

3.3 Hierarchical Multi-scale Attention for Semantic Segmentation

The following semantic segmentation method is described in [18]. Whenever it is referred to the HRNet-OCR in this paper, this modified method is intended, and not the original one from [22].

The main goal of semantic segmentation is to label all pixels within an image as belonging to one of N classes. There are some specific types of predictions since some are best handled at a lower resolution, and other ones are better handled at a higher resolution.

The multi-scale inference is a commonly used practice for addressing this trade-off. The predictions (at a range of scales) are combined with averaging or max pooling. The results can be improved by using averaging to combine multiple scales. The drawback is the obvious problem of combining the best predictions with poorer ones.

For example, the best prediction for a given pixel comes from the 2× scale, and a much worse prediction comes from the 0.5× scale. Then averaging will combine these predictions, resulting in sub-par output. On the other hand, max-pooling selects only one of N scales to use for a given pixel, while the optimal answer may be a weighted combination across the different scales of predictions.

In multi-scale inference method, there are both the relation and multi-scale context methods [2–4,22] and use multi-scale evaluation to obtain the best results. There are two common approaches used for combining network predictions at multiple scales: average and max pooling. Average pooling involves equally weighting output from different scales which may be sub-optimal. The methods mentioned above share the trait that the network and attention "heads" are trained with a fixed set of scales. Only those scales may be used at run-time, else the network must be retrained.

The recent semantic segmentation work for the Cityscapes dataset has utilized the 20000 coarsely labeled images as-is for training state-of-the-art models [23]. However, a significant amount of each coarse image is unlabelled due to the coarseness of the labels. For achieving state-of-the-art results on the Cityscapes dataset, the method adopts an auto-labeling strategy motivated by [21]. The dense labels are generated for the coarse images in Cityscapes. Most image classification auto-labeling work uses continuous or soft labels but this method generates hard thresholded labels (for storage efficiency and training speed). With soft labels, a teacher network provides a continuous probability for each of N classes for each pixel of an image, whereas for hard labels, a threshold is used to pick a single top-class per pixel. Similar to [6,7] it generates hard and dense labels for the coarse Cityscapes images.

The used auto-labeling method is inspired by recent work on auto-labeling for classification tasks [19,21]. It uses auto-labeling for the Cityscape dataset to improve labeling quality. The Cityscape dataset contains 20000 coarsely labeled images and 3500 finely labeled images. The label quality of the coarse images is very modest and contains a large number of unlabelled pixels. The auto-labeling approach improves label quality.

The soft auto-labeling technique is commonly used. However, it would need to store many labeling data (3.2 TB for the Cityscape dataset). This amount of stored labels would slow the training process considerably.

The method uses the hard labeling strategy. The top class prediction of the teacher network is selected for a given pixel. The labels are based on teacher network output probability and are thresholded. Predictions that exceed the threshold are considered to be correct labels. The threshold is set to 0.9.

4   Evaluation and Ranking

4.1   Evaluation

The pose accuracy is evaluated for each submitted method in each dataset and challenge. The evaluation service follows [12] evaluation approach. It defines a set of thresholds on the position and orientation errors of the estimated pose. For each (X meters, Y degrees) threshold, it reports the percentage of query images localized within X meters and Y degrees of the ground truth pose.

More specifically for the selected Aachen Day-Night dataset, the camera pose estimations thresholds are defined for all conditions (day/night) as follows: the most precise threshold is set to 0.25 m and 2°, the follows threshold is set to 0.50 m and 5°, and the least precise threshold is set to 5.00 m and 10°. These thresholds define how precise the camera pose estimation is, e.g., if a pose estimation fits into the most precise threshold, it is also included in the other two, but when a pose estimation fits only under the least precise threshold, it is not included in the most precise threshold nor middle one.

4.2   Ranking Method

For ranking the methods, it is used the exact same method that was used for the Robust Vision Challenge CVPR 2018[4], Robust Vision Challenge CVPR 2020[5], and in ECCV 2020 Workshop[6].

For the dataset, the submitted results are ranked based on the percentages. The rankings are computed by using the Schulze Proportional Ranking method [17].

The Schulze Proportional Ranking method is based on a pairwise comparison of results. If the results of a method are not available for a dataset, the comparison will assume that it performs worse than a method for which the results are available.

5   Experiments

In this section, there are two main contributions to the state-of-the-art presented. The first contribution outperforms current methods in the selected dataset and the second one confirms that the images can contain information which is not needed for the task of long-term visual localization and can be removed by using semantic segmentation.

Based on selected benchmark in Sect. 2.1 and dataset in Sect. 2 a picking one of the top state-of-the-art performing approaches as a baseline seems to be obvious. One of the top-performing methods on the Aachen benchmarking dataset is the Hierarchical Localization (HLoc) pipeline [10] with Github source

---

[4] http://www.robustvision.net/rvc2018.php.
[5] http://www.robustvision.net.
[6] https://www.visuallocalization.net/workshop/eccv/2020/.

code[7]. It uses NetVLAD, SuperPoint, SuperGlue, and COLMAP[8]. The used pipeline is described in the paper [10] along with achieved results. The specific parameter settings are mentioned further in this section.

5.1   Parameter Tuning of Hierarchical Localization

If not stated otherwise the parameter was left unchanged and has its value equal to the Original HLoc from the paper [10].

The Aachen Day Images: for experiments with Aachen Day dataset the parameters were set to: NetVLAD: uses 50 most similar images. Image pre-processing: grayscale *True*, resize to 1600 pixels. SuperPoint: 2048 maximum keypoints, keypoint threshold 0.01, NMS radius 3 pixels. SuperGlue: outdoor weights, 100 Sinkhorn iterations. All other parameters were left unchanged and equal to the Original HLoc settings.

The obtained results can be seen in Table 1 in the Day column. The selected parameters helped to outperform previous state-of-the-art methods in the two most precise camera localization thresholds. In the most precise threshold, it was by 0.1% and the next by 0,4%. For the last, the least precise localization threshold, the fine-tuned parameters perform 0.1% worse.

Based on the results, it can be presumed (because ground truth camera poses estimations are unknown, and the evaluation service provides no more information about camera localization) that camera pose estimations for some images were refined (meets sticker thresholds). However, no more new images were localized successfully to pass the least sticker threshold.

The Aachen Night Images: for experiments with the Aachen Night dataset, the HLoc parameters were set to: NetVLAD: uses 50 most similar images. Image preprocessing: grayscale *True*, without any resizing. SuperPoint: 2048 maximum keypoints, keypoint threshold 0.01, NMS radius 3 pixels. SuperGlue: outdoor weights, 100 Sinkhorn iterations. The main difference between the Day and Night setting is that no resize was performed for Night images. All other parameters were left unchanged and equal to the Original HLoc settings.

The obtained results can be seen in Table 1 in the Night column. Results show that the new state-of-the-art results were achieved on the Aachen Night dataset. The improvement was made in the most precise two thresholds (the last one was already at 100% and can not be improved). The previous state-of-the-art results were surpassed by 1.0% in the first threshold and by 1.1% in the second one. Achieved results show that no resizing Aachen Night images can improve localization accuracy.

The Aachen Day-Night Images: the results from Day and Night experiments were combined and named Combined tuned HLoc. The results can be seen in Table 1.

---

[7] https://github.com/cvg/Hierarchical-Localization.
[8] https://colmap.github.io/.

Table 1. Comparsion of the Original HLoc results in the long-term visual localization benchmark on the Day-Night Aachen dataset compared with Combined tuned HLoc results.

Method	Day [%]	Night [%]
Combined tuned HLoc	**89.7/95.8**/98.7	**87.8/94.9/100.0**
Original HLoc [10]	89.6/95.4/**98.8**	86.7/93.9/**100.0**

5.2 Preprocessing for Semantic Segmentation

The main hypothesis that experiments should prove is that an image from the selected the Aachen dataset contains an area of the image that does not help in the task of long-term visual localization. The area can have associated semantic information from semantic segmentation.

In the case that the area would be removed (masked out and replaced by black color), the selected HLoc pipeline should perform at least as well as Original HLoc or better. If this area is found, it can be stated that the area does not improve the overall results. The moving and dynamic objects in the image could be selected as the area. The area of dynamic objects could be obtained by a semantic segmentation method. The dynamic object could have a high-level interpretation[9] from semantic segmentation classes. Then, groups of classes could be introduced to an aggregate number of classes into a lower number. Furthermore, groups of classes should be used for proving the primary hypothesis.

For long-term visual localization was used HLoc pipeline with the Aachen dataset. For semantic segmentation was used HRNet-OCR method. The performance of HRNet-OCR gives top results[10] in the Cityscape dataset[11] which is similar to the selected Aachen dataset. The implementation of HRNet-OCR was taken from the official Nvidia GitHub[12].

In the task of semantic segmentation multiple different classes can be segmented, e.g. human, bicycle, train, etc. The Cityscape dataset uses the following classes that were grouped into 4 groups. The **Nature** group consist of vegetation and terrain classes. Next, the **sky** group is represented only by sky class. The **Human** group is represented by person and rider classes. And finally, the **vehicle** group aggregates car, truck, bus, caravan, trailer, train, motorcycle, bicycle, and license plate classes. The Cityscape dataset has a few more classes that were omitted because they are rigid or void classes.

---

[9] For example, car, bus, and truck classes have vehicles (the group of classes) as high-level interpretations.

[10] https://paperswithcode.com/sota/semantic-segmentation-on-cityscapes.

[11] https://www.cityscapes-dataset.com.

[12] https://github.com/NVIDIA/semantic-segmentation.

Several experiments were performed with the Aachen Night dataset, but the current state-of-the-art semantic segmentation methods can not handle the night scenery well. Due to semantic segmentation methods' bad performance during night times, only the Aachen Day images were considered in the next experiments.

At first the semantic segmentations for all Aachen Day images were obtained for example see Fig. 2. From the image that contains all semantic segmentation classes were extracted 4 mentioned groups of classes. The segmented classes in every group were unified and one binary mask was created. The mask was used for masking the original image.

Fig. 2. Left: an original Aachen Day image. Right: semantic segmentation in the color palette of the Cityscape dataset.

All combinations of groups of classes was created, and specific experiments were done. The results can be seen in Table 2. Every experiment was rerun five times and averaged to eliminate randomness. From the table, the top performed result is with the human group of classes and the second best with the vehicle group of classes. Thus, the hypothesis was valid and confirmed.

On the other hand, the experiments that contain the nature group of classes performed poorly and are mostly at the bottom of Table 2. It may be caused because the segmented trees look different in every year season. During Fall, Winter, and Spring seasons, it is possible to see through the deciduous trees (where can buildings be located) and use the visual information that is impossible to see during the Summer season. But semantic segmentation labels not only branches of deciduous trees but also the buildings behind them as a tree class.

Table 2. The combinations of used groups of classes for masking input images of Aachen Day dataset and the precision of localizations.

Semantic Segmentation Groups of Classes	Day [%]
Human	**89.6**/95.5/**98.8**
Vehicle	89.4/95.4/**98.8**
Human, sky, vehicle	89.3/**95.8**/**98.8**
Human, sky	89.3/95.4/**98.8**
Nature, sky	89.2/94.7/98.5
Human, vehicle	89.1/95.4/**98.8**
Sky	89.0/95.4/**98.8**
Sky, vehicle	89.0/95.4/**98.8**
Human, nature, sky	88.6/94.5/98.5
Nature	88.5/94.9/98.5
Human, nature, vehicle	88.5/94.7/98.5
Human, nature, sky, vehicle	88.5/94.7/98.5
Human, nature	88.5/94.4/98.5
Nature, vehicle	88.3/94.8/98.5
Nature, sky, vehicle	88.3/94.5/98.5

6   Conclusion

The final comparison of obtained results is in Table 3 and can be checked on the official benchmark webpage[13]. From the results it can be stated that the experiment with semantic segmentation where a group of classes human was used (named: Masked human HLoc) performs similar to the current state-of-the-art base method Original HLoc. It outperforms Original HLoc by 0.1% in the second-best localization threshold on the Aachen Day dataset and matches results in other localization thresholds. The Combined tuned HLoc method outperforms both Masked human HLoc and Original HLoc methods on the Aachen Day dataset.

Table 3. The comparison of Combined tuned HLoc, Masked human HLoc, and Original HLoc precision.

Method	Day [%]	Night [%]
Combined tuned HLoc	**89.7**/**95.8**/98.7	**87.8**/**94.9**/**100.0**
Masked human HLoc	89.6/95.5/**98.8**	-/-/-
Original HLoc [10]	89.6/95.4/**98.8**	86.7/93.9/**100.0**

---

[13] https://www.visuallocalization.net/benchmark/.

In the future work we will perform experiments with semantic segmentation on other datasets and we will examine more semantic segmentation approaches that can lead us to more precise segmentation and thus enhance long-term visual localization precision.

Acknowledgements. This publication was supported by the project LO1506 of the Czech Ministry of Education, Youth and Sports.

References

1. Cadena, C., et al.: Past, present, and future of simultaneous localization and mapping: towards the robust-perception age. IEEE Trans. Rob. **32**(6), 1309–1332 (2016)
2. Chen, L., Papandreou, G., Schroff, F., Adam, H.: Rethinking atrous convolution for semantic image segmentation. CoRR abs/1706.05587 (2017)
3. Chen, L.C., Zhu, Y., Papandreou, G., Schroff, F., Adam, H.: Encoder-decoder with atrous separable convolution for semantic image segmentation. In: Proceedings of the European Conference on Computer Vision, February 2018
4. Cheng, B., et al.: Panoptic-deeplab: a simple, strong, and fast baseline for bottom-up panoptic segmentation. In: 2020 IEEE/CVF Conference on Computer Vision and Pattern Recognition, CVPR 2020, Seattle, WA, USA, 13–19 June 2020, pp. 12472–12482. IEEE (2020). https://doi.org/10.1109/CVPR42600.2020.01249
5. DeTone, D., Malisiewicz, T., Rabinovich, A.: Superpoint: self-supervised interest point detection and description. In: The IEEE Conference on Computer Vision and Pattern Recognition (CVPR) Workshops, June 2018
6. Lee, D.: Pseudo-label: the simple and efficient semi-supervised learning method for deep neural networks (2013)
7. Liu, L., Li, Y., Tan, R.T.: Decoupled certainty-driven consistency loss for semi-supervised learning (2020)
8. Widya, A.R., Torii, A., Okutomi, M.: Structure from motion using dense CNN features with keypoint relocalization. IPSJ Trans. Comput. Vis. Appl. **10**(1), 1–7 (2018). https://doi.org/10.1186/s41074-018-0042-y
9. Revaud, J., et al.: R2D2: repeatable and reliable detector and descriptor. CoRR abs/1906.06195 (2019)
10. Sarlin, P., Cadena, C., Siegwart, R., Dymczyk, M.: From coarse to fine: robust hierarchical localization at large scale. In: Conference on Computer Vision and Pattern Recognition (CVPR), pp. 12708–12717 (2019). https://doi.org/10.1109/CVPR.2019.01300
11. Sarlin, P.E., DeTone, D., Malisiewicz, T., Rabinovich, A.: Superglue: learning feature matching with graph neural networks. In: IEEE/CVF Conference on Computer Vision and Pattern Recognition (CVPR), June 2020
12. Sattler, T., et al.: Benchmarking 6DOF outdoor visual localization in changing conditions. In: Conference on Computer Vision and Pattern Recognition, pp. 8601–8610 (2018)
13. Sattler, T., Weyand, T., Leibe, B., Kobbelt, L.: Image retrieval for image-based localization revisited. In: British Machine Vision Conference, September 2012
14. Schönberger, J.L., Frahm, J.M.: Structure-from-motion revisited. In: Conference on Computer Vision and Pattern Recognition (CVPR) (2016)

15. Schönberger, J.L., Price, T., Sattler, T., Frahm, J.M., Pollefeys, M.: A vote-and-verify strategy for fast spatial verification in image retrieval. In: Asian Conference on Computer Vision (ACCV) (2016)

16. Schönberger, J.L., Zheng, E., Frahm, J.-M., Pollefeys, M.: Pixelwise view selection for unstructured multi-view stereo. In: Leibe, B., Matas, J., Sebe, N., Welling, M. (eds.) ECCV 2016. LNCS, vol. 9907, pp. 501–518. Springer, Cham (2016). https://doi.org/10.1007/978-3-319-46487-9_31

17. Schulze, M.: A new monotonic, clone-independent, reversal symmetric, and condorcet-consistent single-winner election method. Soc. Choice Welfare **36**, 267–303 (2011). https://doi.org/10.1007/s00355-010-0475-4

18. Tao, A., Sapra, K., Catanzaro, B.: Hierarchical multi-scale attention for semantic segmentation (2020)

19. Tarvainen, A., Valpola, H.: Mean teachers are better role models: Weight-averaged consistency targets improve semi-supervised deep learning results. In: Proceedings of the 31st International Conference on Neural Information Processing Systems, NIPS 2017, pp. 1195–1204 (2017)

20. Toft, C., et al.: Long-term visual localization revisited. IEEE Trans. Pattern Anal. Mach. Intell. 14 (2020)

21. Xie, Q., Luong, M.T., Hovy, E., Le, Q.V.: Self-training with noisy student improves ImageNet classification. In: Proceedings of the IEEE/CVF Conference on Computer Vision and Pattern Recognition (CVPR), June 2020

22. Yuan, Y., Chen, X., Wang, J.: Object-contextual representations for semantic segmentation. In: Vedaldi, A., Bischof, H., Brox, T., Frahm, J.-M. (eds.) ECCV 2020. LNCS, vol. 12351, pp. 173–190. Springer, Cham (2020). https://doi.org/10.1007/978-3-030-58539-6_11

23. Yuan, Y., Wang, J.: OCNet: object context network for scene parsing. CoRR abs/1809.00916 (2018)

Algorithm for Radio Survey of the Cyber-Physical Systems Operating Areas Using Unmanned Aerial Vehicles

Alexander Denisov and Dmitriy Levonevskiy(✉)

St. Petersburg Federal Research Center of the Russian Academy of Sciences (SPC RAS), St. Petersburg Institute for Informatics and Automation of the Russian Academy of Sciences, 39, 14th Line, 199178 St. Petersburg, Russia

Abstract. When configuring a cyber-physical system (CPS) for operating in large open areas and connecting distributed autonomous devices to it via wireless communication channels, it is necessary to take into account the threats that can disrupt the functioning of the CPS. This paper provides a classification of threats that directly affect the CPS operation. It was revealed that the most dangerous threats are associated with the influence of the environment. The paper proposes a solution to minimize the impact of the environment on the operation of the CPS. The growth in the number of heterogeneous devices with different properties and actual purposes, interacting over a wireless network, leads to the emergence of the problem of providing a speed-satisfactory method for configuring a wireless communication network between heterogeneous devices in a distributed CPS. To solve this problem, algorithm for the radio survey of the CPS territory using unmanned aerial vehicles (UAV) was developed.

Keywords: Cyber-physical systems · Robotics · Infrastructure management · Dynamic environment · UAV · Repeaters · Wireless communication

1 Introduction

A number of increased requirements are imposed on the infrastructure of cyber-physical systems (CPS) operating in open areas. This is due to the possibility of both accidental and deliberate destructive influences from the environment. Open areas have their own specifics: they are vast, have a complex structure and are subject to dynamic changes. Functioning in a dynamic environment is associated with increased risks of failure of individual components and the absence of stable communication channels between the elements of the system. For the trouble-free functioning of the CPS, it is necessary for them to be capable of reorganization. Standard centralized approaches to constructing CPSs with relative simplicity and ease of management have a number of disadvantages - in particular, limited scalability, the presence of bottlenecks and critical components, the failure of which can significantly disrupt the CPS connectivity, as well as problems with availability over large spaces [1]. Thus, there is a need to create stable, coherent, decentralized CPSs with the ability to dynamically connect and disconnect their components.

A. Ronzhin et al. (Eds.): ICR 2021, LNAI 12998, pp. 40–49, 2021.
https://doi.org/10.1007/978-3-030-87725-5_4

At the same time, one should take into account the limited computing power of CPS nodes, the need for effective energy management, the integration of the communication capabilities of the nodes, and the information security requirements [2].

Let us consider the problem of constructing and choosing strategies for the behavior of the CPS in the event of loss of system connectivity, as well as the problem of self-organization of the CPS in the event of failure of its individual components or component parts. To do this, we will construct a classification of situations (incidents) that can lead to failures in the CPS, investigate the known approaches to building a CPS resistant to such incidents, and analyze the compliance of the known solutions with the established requirements.

2 Related Work

The range of incidents is quite extensive, due to the distribution of CPS, heterogeneity and wide autonomy of their components, their large number and vulnerability separately, the use of wireless technologies, active interaction with the changing environment [3, 4].

Incidents that cause loss of connectivity in the CPS can be classified according to different criteria:

- by occurrence: accidental (malfunction of the CPS component; wrong strategy of the CPS behavior); related to the influence of the environment; intentional (attack by an intruder) [5];
- by level: physical, channel, network, transport, session, presentation level, application level (in this case, the ISO/OSI standard model [6] is used; in practical implementations, individual levels can be combined);
- by criticality for a specific task of the CPS: not affecting the performance of the task; reducing the efficiency of the task; excluding the execution of the task;
- by criticality for the functioning of the CPS as a whole: not affecting; reducing the effectiveness; making impossible the further functioning of the CPS;
- by information security aspect: integrity, availability, confidentiality, accountability, etc.

In the context of the problem under consideration, the most relevant threats are associated with the influence of the environment. The deployment of CPS over large areas can lead to the fact that individual components of the CPS will encounter difficulties in navigation, fail under the influence of the environment, leave the coverage area of wireless networks or the reachability of repeaters, which will lead to loss of connectivity.

To classify existing approaches, it is convenient to group them according to the levels of the ISO/OSI model. Solutions that are limited to the methods of data transmission over communication channels or the organization of these channels refer to the physical and data link layers. The network, transport, session layer includes solutions based on data routing and the creation of overlay networks and virtual communication channels. Solutions that take into account the applied tasks of the CPS and the roles of their nodes are assigned to the application and presentation levels.

On physical and link layers, a number of solutions are known based on the LoRaWAN protocol and its analogs, which improve the reliability, range and efficiency of communication between CPS nodes. So, in [7, 8], an assessment of the effectiveness of LoRa wireless networks is presented. The analyzed parameters are ToA (Time on Air), bit rate and spread factor (SF) affect the performance level. From the results obtained, it can be seen that with an increase in the SF parameter, the time during which a LoRa communication packet is transmitted over the air increases. If the bandwidth of the communication channel is increased, the ToA parameter will decrease significantly. The main LoRa modulation parameter is the multiplication factor (SF), which can range from 7 to 12. The maximum LoRaWAN payload depends on the SF factor selected at the application level, the maximum size is 256 bytes. The Gateway module serves multiple devices using a network topology. Thus, messages are re-transmitted from the LoRa module to the network server through the gateway module.

When designing CPSs operating in open areas, it is also necessary to take into account that the environment can have a significant impact on the propagation of a radio signal and thus hinder the communication of the CPS components. So, in [9, 10] it is indicated that the influence of the external environment on the radio signal is manifested both through changes in the transit time of radio signals from the transmitter to the receiver, and through the occurrence of multipath, caused by reflections of the mentioned radio signals from certain reflective surfaces located in the immediate vicinity from the receiver. The propagation of radio waves in the atmosphere is accompanied by their refraction, absorption, reflection and scattering. The intensity of these phenomena is determined by the properties of the spatial distribution of the refractive index of air, which is a function of pressure, temperature and humidity, as well as the presence and properties of hydrometeors (products of moisture condensation in the atmosphere - drops of rain, fog, clouds) and various impurities.

On network, transport, session layers, there are known solutions to improve the connectivity of the CPS by distributing the functions of data transmission between nodes and providing data routing. Such solutions allow self-organizing of CPS at the network, transport, session level and are usually based on the WSN (wireless sensor network) approach, the use of mesh networks and the establishment of multi-hop connections. Thus, in [11, 12], a data transmission system for constantly moving military mobile groups is considered. A mobile and wireless network platform capable of communicating with remote areas of military operations is being developed. A prototype of a military device based on the WSN approach has been successfully developed with the ability to use the device for search and rescue of victims. The prototype is capable of reading and sending status data to the base station, including death, user, location, and movement. The paper describes the use of a mesh network from the developed prototypes. Such a network allows nodes to act independently of each other to receive and transmit data.

The articles [13, 14] describe an approach to organizing communication, in which each agent in the system can leave the network or accept new connections by sending its information based on the transmission history of all nodes in the network. To this end, each agent must support 4 protocols to participate in the system, as well as an additional protocol for transmitting data to nearby nodes, which is based on a received signal strength indicator (RSSI) and data history.

Since the proposed system is heterogeneous, two types of agents are possible, based on the principle of WSN nodes. The first type of node is a robot-agent, which can be a UAV or an RM. The second type of agent is monitoring units and wireless sensors, which are static agents characterized by the presence of a wireless communication unit that accepts a special infrastructure mode to establish communication with the system, a processing unit for managing the received data, and either a sensor or a graphical user interface (GUI) to interact with the environment or the user, depending on whether it is a WSN or a monitoring agent.

At the application level, the roles and applied tasks of the CPS are taken into account, and the existing approaches allow the redistribution and management of these roles and tasks. So, in the article [15], the main methods of controlling groups of robots are considered, such as one-man, hierarchical, collective, herd, swarm, and the tasks that arise when organizing information exchange in groups of small-sized robots at different levels are described:

- information flow control and packet routing in the network;
- definition of a multipurpose tracking mode;
- creation of algorithms responsible for adaptive analog-discrete filtering;
- creation of an algorithm for optimized estimation of incoming information;
- creation of a secure channel (stable, hidden) information exchange between the operator and the group;
- creation of an algorithm that allows agents to learn;
- creation of an algorithm for optimal estimation, invariant to the time of arrival of measurements.

Each participant requires constant awareness of both their "neighbors" and the goals set - to solve this problem, a multipurpose escort mode (MDM) is used. The problem lies in a sufficiently long time interval between incoming measurement signals from one target, while control signals must be generated continuously. It should be noted that the method of processing incoming signals using standard algorithms for optimal estimation with simultaneous processing is unprofitable, since the processing time of signals by each sensor is different, and in addition, the location of the participants in space affects the time of signal arrival. Therefore, the capabilities of such a network are determined by the capabilities of the equipment used. Wireless technologies should be used to expand the scope of the algorithm.

It should be borne in mind that when using a wireless communication line, there are risks of secret receipt of information, unauthorized access and information compromise. For protection, it is proposed to use not hardware, but software encryption, which will reduce the weight and price of a small robot. The main problem of the proposed method is a large time interval between incoming signals from one target, while control signals must be generated continuously, which can lead to the failure of not only one device, but the entire network. This method is designed for a small number of devices on the network.

There are works that consider the issues of coordination of autonomous robots when performing various applied tasks. Thus, the contribution of work [16] consists in the analysis of communication protocols applied to the problem of UAV fleet management to fight against attacks of parasites on crops. Moreover, the study of different approaches aims to measure their performance and costs. In particular, different approaches to the problems of exploring the territory in the shortest possible time, in order to avoid studying the same area with the help of a large number of drones, detecting parasites and preventing their spread by spraying the required amount of pesticides. Drones equipped with limited amounts of fuel and pesticides may seek help from other drones to complete the pest control.

Networking small and mini UAVs has the potential to improve the performance and coverage of UAVs. Before the widespread introduction of heterogeneous flying special networks (FANETs) based on several UAVs, many new problems have to be solved, including the creation of a stable network structure. An efficient gateway selection algorithm and control mechanism are also required. However, monitoring the stability of the hierarchical UAV network ensures efficient interaction between drones. The article [17, 18] provides an overview of the FANET structure and architecture of its protocol. It then discusses various distributed gateway selection algorithms and cloud resiliency mechanisms, complemented by a number of open problems.

3   Materials and Methods

In this work, in order to reduce threats associated with the influence of the environment, it is proposed to use a radio survey of the territory of the CPS operation and algorithms for the optimal placement of radio elements of the system. To conduct a radio survey of the territory, it is proposed to use a UAV with a radio transceiver (radio module), a video camera, and a depth sensor installed on it. The radio transceiver is responsible for setting the signal level from the gateway throughout the CPS, determining the signal level from extraneous sources of radio wave propagation (calculating the level of radio noise). Also, the radio module allows you to determine the influence of obstacles in the territory of the CPS on the propagation of the radio signal. Attenuation of radio waves when passing through obstacles leads to the need for a closer location of repeaters to ensure data transmission at the required speed [19]. The total attenuation (dB) of radio waves in areas with green spaces was determined by the expression [20]:

$$W_n = V_\partial + M_1 + M_2, \tag{1}$$

where V_∂ is the diffraction component of the attenuation, $M_{1,2}$ are the interference factors of attenuation on the sections of the emitter-obstacle path, the obstacle-receiver.

$$M_{1,2} = \sqrt{1 + \Phi_{1,2}^2 - 2\Phi_{1,2}\cos\delta_{1,2}}, \tag{2}$$

where $\delta_{1,2} = 2kh_{1,2}\sin\Psi_{1,2}$, $k = 2\pi/\lambda$, λ is the length of the radio wave, $h_{1,2}$ are the heights of the transmitter and receiver antennas, $\Psi_{1,2}$ are the grazing angles in the sections of the diffraction paths, $\Phi_{1,2}$ are the reflection coefficients. According to [20], in a mixed forest with an average density of trees, the average seasonal linear attenuation of the radio signal is 0.1 dB/m for frequencies of 330 MHz.

In this work, to calculate the attenuation of propagation of radio waves in open areas and the effect of the surface features on the propagation of radio waves, we use the classical calculation formulas [21]. According to the Rayleigh criterion, we can get the acceptable height of the irregularities, i.e. the height of the irregularities at which the reflection can be considered mirror-like:

$$h < \frac{\lambda}{8\cos\theta} \tag{3}$$

where h is the permissible irregularity height, λ is the wavelength, θ is the angle of incidence of the wave.

Attenuation coefficient is calculated as follows:

$$|W| = \frac{1}{2p_1(r_1 + r_2)}\sqrt{1 + \frac{4}{\pi}p_1(r_1 + r_2)\frac{r_2}{r_1}}$$
$$p = \frac{\pi r}{\lambda\sqrt{\varepsilon_2^2 + (60\gamma_2\lambda)^2}} \tag{4}$$

r_1, r_2 are the path lengths, ε_2^2 is the dielectric constant, γ_2 is determined by the averaged electrical parameters of the soil on the path and the terrain.

Soil moisture also affects the propagation of the radio signal. With the help of a depth sensor on the UAV, a three-dimensional map of the area (depth map) can be built. Based on these data, it is possible to calculate soil moisture [22] and construct a table of soil moisture coefficients, which will allow calculating the transmission loss (attenuation) of the radio signal [23]:

$$L = h(\lambda + 5\lg(f) + 5\lg(r)) \tag{5}$$

where h is the value from the coefficient table, λ is the wavelength, f is the frequency, r is the distance from the transmitter to the receiver.

To ensure the possibility of using inexpensive UAVs to survey the territory, it is required to take into account their low carrying capacity and low volume of batteries. To solve this problem, an algorithm is proposed for the optimal movement of the UAV over the territory of the CPS, namely, the search for the shortest and fastest way to survey the entire territory (Fig. 1) [24].

The result of the UAV movement route calculation method to scan the territory is shown in Fig. 2.

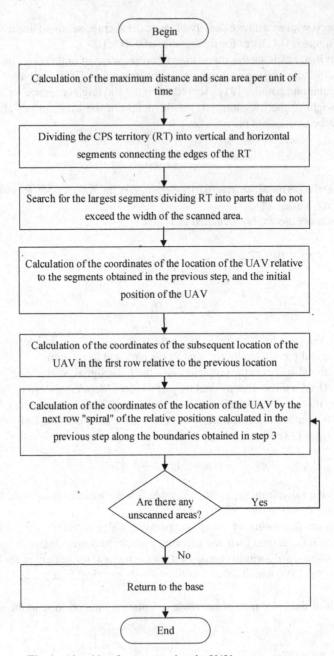

Fig. 1. Algorithm for constructing the UAV movement route.

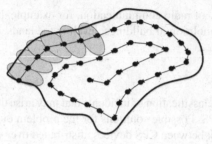

Fig. 2. The result of the algorithm for constructing the UAV movement route for scanning the territory.

4 Modeling

An area of \$ 27 × 27 was chosen for modeling with randomly located obstacles such as trees, small buildings and uneven terrain. According to the algorithm for constructing the route of movement of the UAV, the optimal trajectory of the movement of the UAV through the territory of the CPS was built. Analysis of the data from additional sensors on the UAV made it possible to construct a map of changes in the radio signal level in the surveyed area (Fig. 3), which will allow the most effective positioning of repeaters to cover the entire area with a signal.

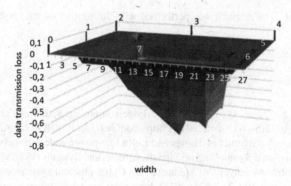

Fig. 3. The map of radio signal level changes in the surveyed area.

For clarity, radio modules (numbered 0–7 in the figure) were installed along the perimeter, being in line of sight and providing constant radio communication with each other. The figure shows the loss of data transmission in the territory of the CPS operation. As can be seen from the figure, along the edges of the territory under consideration, where the radio modules are located, the loss of the radio signal is minimal, since there are no obstacles. But in the center of the study area there are noticeable signal losses due to the presence of various obstacles (buildings, trees, water bodies).

Based on the modeling data, it is possible to determine the places with the greatest radio signal losses in the territory of the CPS operation, and use this data to improve and stabilize the quality of radio communication, for example, by adding repeaters, or removing obstacles (demolition of buildings, leveling the landscape, cutting trees etc.).

5 Conclusion

This paper represents a classification of incidents that may arise during the configuration and operation of the CPS. Possible solutions for the problem of configuring a wireless communication network between CPS devices, distributed over vast territories, are represented. An algorithm is proposed to solve one of the important threats in the formation and operation of the CPS - the threat associated with the influence of the environment, namely the influence of the environment on the propagation of the radio signal. It is proposed to use a radio survey of the territory of the CPS operation and algorithms for the optimal placement of radio elements of the system. To ensure the possibility of using inexpensive UAVs to survey the territory, it is required to take into account their low carrying capacity and low volume of batteries. To solve this problem, the paper proposes an algorithm for the optimal movement of the UAV over the territory of the CPS, namely, the search for the shortest and fastest way to survey the entire territory.

Further research will be aimed at improving the proposed algorithm for automating workflows and data exchange between CPS devices. Additional noise immunity of radio modules is also among the key objectives of the study, as well as work on eliminating collisions when relaying data packages.

Acknowledgement. The research was performed with the support of state budget (theme No. 0060-2019-0011).

References

1. Shi, W., Cao, J., Zhang, Q., Li, Y., Xu, L.: Edge computing: vision and challenges. IEEE Internet Things J. **3**(5), 637–646 (2016). https://doi.org/10.1109/JIOT.2016.2579198
2. Lavric, A., Popa, V.: Internet of Things and LoRa low-power wide-area networks: a survey. In: 2017 International Symposium on Signals, Circuits and Systems (ISSCS), pp. 1–5 (2017)
3. Alguliyev, R., Imamverdiyev, Y., Sukhostat, L.: Cyber-physical systems and their security issues. Comput. Ind. **100**, 212–223 (2018). https://doi.org/10.1016/j.compind.2018.04.017
4. Liu, C.H., Zhang, Y.: Cyber Physical Systems: Architectures, Protocols and Applications. CRC Press, Taylor Francis Group, Florida (2016)
5. ISO/IEC 27001 (2013)
6. ISO/IEC Standard 7498-1 (1994)
7. Lavric, A., Popa, V.: A LoRaWAN: long range wide area networks study. In: 2017 International Conference on Electromechanical and Power Systems (SIELMEN), pp. 417–420 (2017)
8. Cagatan, G.K.B., Magsumbol, J.A.V., Baldovino, R., Sybingco, E., Dadios, E.P.: Connectivity analysis of wireless sensor network in two-dimensional plane using Castalia simulator. In: 2017 IEEE 9th International Conference on Humanoid, Nanotechnology, Information Technology, Communication and Control, Environment and Management (HNICEM), pp. 1–8 (2017)
9. Shvetsova, A.A.: The influence of atmospheric conditions on the transmission of radio navigation signals. Appl. Electrodyn. Photonics Living Syst. 254–257 (2019)

10. Volkov, V.V., Gordyaskina, T.V.: Investigation of an analog radio-technical communication channel in the Mathcad software package. http://вф-река-море.рф/2020/PDF/9_6.pdf

11. Rabie, T., Suleiman, S.: A novel wireless mesh network for indoor robotic navigation. In: 2016 5th International Conference on Electronic Devices, Systems and Applications (ICEDSA), pp. 1–4. IEEE (2016)

12. Jawhar, I., et al.: Communication and networking of UAV-based systems: classification and associated architectures. J. Netw. Comput. Appl. **84**, 93–108 (2017)

13. Jiménez, A.C., García-Díaz, V., Bolaños, S.: A decentralized framework for multi-agent robotic systems. Sensors **18**(2), 417 (2018). https://doi.org/10.3390/s18020417

14. Kakamoukas, G.A., Sarigiannidis, P.G., Economides, A.A.: FANETs in agriculture-a routing protocol survey. Internet of Things 100183 (2020)

15. Petruchuk, E.V., Ivanov, D.Ya.: Organization of information exchange in decentralized swarm control systems for multi-robotic complexes using ZigBee technology. Vestnik BSTU named after V.G. Shukhov, no. 7 (2019)

16. Potrino, G., Serianni, A., Palmieri, N.: Drones coordination protocols in the precision agriculture context. In: Autonomous Air and Ground Sensing Systems for Agricultural Optimization and Phenotyping IV, International Society for Optics and Photonics, vol. 11008, p. 110080G (2019)

17. Wang, J., et al.: Taking drones to the next level: cooperative distributed unmanned-aerial-vehicular networks for small and mini drones. IEEE Veh. Technol. Mag. **12**(3), 73–82 (2017)

18. Tropea, M., et al.: Reactive flooding versus link state routing for FANET in precision agriculture. In: 2019 16th IEEE Annual Consumer Communications & Networking Conference (CCNC), pp. 1–6. IEEE (2019)

19. Kofnov, O.V., Lebedev, E.L., Mikhailenko, A.V.: Computer simulation of the diffraction of millimeter electromagnetic waves for detecting internal defects of products made using additive technology. In: Proceedings of SPIIRAS, vol. 1, no. 56, pp. 76–94 (2018)

20. Abarykov, V.N., Batoroev, A.: The influence of vegetation on the scattering and diffraction of radio waves at small grazing angles. In: All-Russian Scientific Conference on Radio Wave Propagation, pp. 9–12

21. Grudinskaya, G.P.: Propagation of radio waves. Higher School, Moscow, p. 280 (1975)

22. Florinsky, I.V.: Theory and applications of mathematical-cartographic modeling of relief. In: I.V. Florinsky, pp. 2010–2042 (2010)

23. Pishchin, O.N., Kalambatskaya, O.V.: Features of the propagation of UHF radio waves in the ground and drive tropospheric waveguide. In: Bulletin of the Astrakhan State Technical University. Series: Management, Computer Engineering and Informatics, no. 4 (2019)

24. Denisov, A.V.: Method of localization of agricultural robotic funds using AFAR, formed by the UAV complex. Rob. Tech. Cybern. **2** (2021)

Step Path Simulation for Quadruped Walking Robot

Dmitry Dobrynin[1]([✉]) [iD] and Yulia Zhiteneva[2]

[1] Federal Research Center for Computer Science and Control RAS, Moscow, Russia
[2] State University of Humanities and Technology, Orekhovo-Zuyevo, Russia

Abstract. This article discusses a model of a quadruped walking robot with 12 degrees of freedom. The trajectory of the robot's leg movement under the uniform rectilinear motion of the robot is synthesized. The trajectory consists of a reference phase and a transfer phase. In the transfer phase, elliptical foot trajectories are used. A mathematical model of the dependence of the drive parameters on time and geometric parameters of the trajectory is constructed. Numerical simulation of the obtained models is carried out. The dependences of accelerations, velocities, torques, and drive power on time and trajectory parameters are obtained. The article analyzes these dependencies. The possibility of optimizing the trajectory parameters for the specified drive parameters to obtain the maximum speed is shown. The dependence of the drive parameters on the geometric dimensions of the robot leg is analyzed. It is shown that the maximum speed is achieved at certain ratios of the geometric parameters of the leg. In conclusion, practical conclusions are given on optimizing the trajectory parameters in order to obtain the maximum speed.

Keywords: Walking robot · Simulation · Fast moving

1 Introduction

Currently, there is an increasing interest in developments in the field of walking robots all over the world. Commercial developments of Boston Dynamics and their analogues have shown the promise of using walking robots in various fields.

One of the main reasons for the development of a four-legged walking robot is to overcome the lack of mobility of wheeled vehicles on uneven terrain. Running mammals are able to cross uneven or changing terrain at high speeds, turn sharply, start moving suddenly, or stop.

The main problem in the field of creating walking robots is the need to get fast and smooth movement. Initially, a high speed of movement was hoped to be obtained with the help of mechanical step formation systems [1–3]. However, on an uneven surface, mechanical systems that form the same steps do not allow you to fully adapt to the surface. As a result, such systems can only reach high speeds on a flat surface.

Obtaining a high speed of the robot's movement on an uneven surface requires the use of active leg drives that can change the step parameters for each support point [4].

© Springer Nature Switzerland AG 2021
A. Ronzhin et al. (Eds.): ICR 2021, LNAI 12998, pp. 50–61, 2021.
https://doi.org/10.1007/978-3-030-87725-5_5

Some researchers try to obtain the step parameters using various types of training [5, 6]. In this case, it is possible to get a smooth movement. Some approaches to achieving high robot movement speed are given in [7, 8]. A good overview of crab-like robots and their gaits is given in [9].

This article deals with the simulation of the step of a quadruped robot by synthesizing the trajectory of the foot and optimizing its parameters.

2 Problem Statement

The robot has four legs, each of which has three degrees of freedom (Fig. 1a). The analytical model of the robot leg for the case of translational motion is shown in Fig. 1b. The drive 1 with torque M_1 moves the robot's leg to the side. The drive 2 with torque M_2 moves the entire robot leg back and forth. The drive 3 with torque M_3 moves the lower part of the robot's leg back and forth. The rotation angles of the drives θ_2 and θ_3, the lengths of leg parts L_2 and L_3 and the distances L_4, X, Y, L_s and h are shown in the Fig. 1b. Note that the drive 1 is not used for the forward movement of the robot. So, the model can be simplified and the parameters for this drive are not considered.

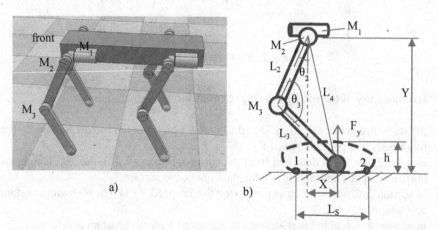

Fig. 1. Geometrical model of: a) robot; b) robot leg.

From the geometric dependencies (Fig. 1b), equations are obtained from which the angles θ_2 and θ_3 can be calculated depending on the coordinates of the point of contact of the foot (X, Y).

$$\theta_2(X, Y) = \arccos \frac{L_2^2 + L_4^2 - L_3^2}{2L_2L_4} - \arcsin \frac{X}{L_4},$$

$$\theta_3(X, Y) = \arccos \frac{L_2^2 + L_3^2 - L_4^2}{2L_2L_3},$$

$$L_4 = \sqrt{X^2 + Y^2}. \tag{1}$$

Let the robot move at a constant speed V_1. The trajectory of the robot's leg is a closed curve (Fig. 2). Section 1-2 corresponds to the reference phase, section 2-3-4-5-1 corresponds to the transfer phase. For various robot's gaits, the leg transfer time must be less than or equal to the duration of the reference phase. Since the length of the transfer trajectory 2-3-4-5-1 is greater than the length of the trajectory of the reference phase 1-2, the speeds and accelerations of the drives in the leg transfer phase reach their maximum values.

Therefore, the maximum speed of movement of the entire robot is determined by the restrictions on the maximum speeds and accelerations of the drives in the transfer phase.

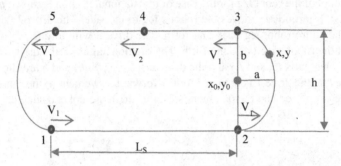

Fig. 2. Foot-end trajectory.

The trajectory of the robot's leg (Fig. 2) must meet several requirements:

1) the reference section 1-2 is a straight line on which the leg moves relative to the robot body at a constant speed V_1;
2) at point 2, the leg is detached from the surface. In section 2-3, the leg changes its horizontal speed and moves to a height h above the surface;
3) in section 3-4, acceleration is performed to the speed V_2 ($V_2 > V_1$) with constant acceleration;
4) in section 4-5, braking is performed to the speed V_1 with constant acceleration;
5) in section 5-1, the leg changes its horizontal speed and descends to the surface. At point 1, the surface is touched. The smoothness of the robot's gait depends on the speed at which the robot's leg will come to point 1. The presence of a vertical component of the speed will lead to dynamic disturbances.

The most critical areas on the trajectory of the robot's leg are sections 2-3 and 5-1, since these areas require maximum acceleration (deceleration) of all parts of the robot's leg. At point 4, a maximum speed of V_2 is required, which also needs to be taken into account.

Let's choose an elliptical trajectory for sections 2-3 and 5-1. The ellipse has the properties we need: at points 1 and 2, the vertical component of the velocity is zero. For an ellipse, there is a second derivative, hence the acceleration has no discontinuities, which is necessary for smooth movement. The maximum acceleration can be changed in a simple way by changing the eccentricity parameter of the ellipse a (Fig. 2). Note that this is one of the possible trajectories, and you can use other trajectories: pure ellipse, parabola, pendulum (modified pendulum), cardioid, and combined line segments [8]. Consideration of other types of trajectory is beyond the scope of this article.

To find the coordinates of a point on an ellipse, use the parametric definition of the ellipse:

$$x = x_0 + a \cdot \cos(w\,t),$$
$$y = y_0 + b \cdot \sin(w\,t),$$
$$b = \frac{h}{2}. \tag{2}$$

Here (x_0, y_0) is the center of the ellipse, a and b are the semi-axes of the ellipse, w is the angular velocity, and t is the time parameter.

To find the angular velocity w, we use the conditions at point 2:

$$\frac{dx}{dt} = V_1, \quad w\,t = -\frac{\pi}{2},$$
$$\frac{dx}{dt} = a \cdot w \cdot \left(-\sin\left(-\frac{\pi}{2}\right)\right), \tag{3}$$
$$V_1 = a \cdot w, \quad w = \frac{V_1}{a}.$$

By reducing Eqs. (2) to the robot coordinate system from Fig. 1, using (1) and (3), we obtain the equations for the angles θ_2 and θ_3 as a function of time t:

$$\begin{cases} \theta_2(X, Y) = \arccos \frac{L_2^2 + L_4^2 - L_3^2}{2 L_2 L_4} - \arcsin \frac{X}{L_4}; \\ \theta_3(X, Y) = \arccos \frac{L_2^2 + L_3^2 - L_4^2}{2 L_2 L_3}; \\ L_4 = \sqrt{X^2 + Y^2}; \\ X = \frac{L_s}{2} + a \cdot \cos\left(\frac{V_1}{a} t\right); \\ Y = H_0 - \frac{h}{2} \cdot \sin\left(\frac{V_1}{a} t\right) - \frac{h}{2}. \end{cases} \tag{4}$$

Here H_0 is the average height of the drive center 2 above the surface, h is the height of the step above the surface, L_s is the length of the step, $a = \mathrm{var}$ is the trajectory parameter to be optimized.

The equations for the moments of the drives in a simplified form (without taking into account the mutual influence of the drives) have the form:

$$M_2 = J_2 \cdot \theta_2'',$$
$$M_3 = J_3 \cdot \theta_3'',$$
$$J_2 = m_2 \cdot \left(\frac{L_2}{2}\right)^2 + m_3 \cdot \left(L_2^2 + \left(\frac{L_3}{2}\right)^2 - 2 \cdot L_2 \cdot \frac{L_3}{2} \cdot \cos(\theta_3)\right), \tag{5}$$
$$J_3 = m_3 \cdot \left(\frac{L_3}{2}\right)^2,$$

where m_2 is the mass of link 2, m_3 is the mass of link 3.

To determine the instantaneous power of the drives, you can use the formula for calculating the power for rotational motion:

$$P_2 = M_2 \cdot \theta_2',$$
$$P_3 = M_3 \cdot \theta_3'. \tag{6}$$

To determine the rate of change of angles and accelerations, it is necessary to find the first and second derivatives of the angles θ_2 and θ_3 from Eqs. (4). The formulas for the first and second derivatives of the angles of Eqs. (4) can be obtained analytically, but they have an unnecessarily cumbersome form. The search for the maxima and minima of the nonlinear dependences of the derivatives θ_2 and θ_3 can only be carried out numerically. As a result, further analysis will be carried out using numerical simulations - numerical differentiation and search for extremes.

3   Analysis of the Impact of Trajectory Parameters on the Drive Characteristics

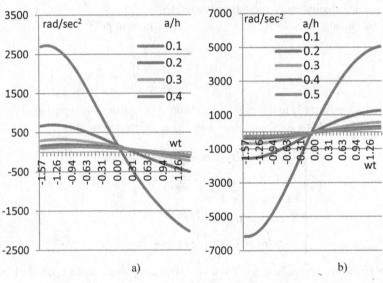

Fig. 3. Dependence of acceleration: a) θ_2'' (wt) from various a/h, b) θ_3''(wt) from various a/h.

The following parameters were used for numerical simulation of the robot's 2–3 step phase (Fig. 1b, Fig. 2):

$L_2 = 0.3$ m, $L_3 = 0.3$ m, $Ls = 0.2$ m
$m_2 = 0.2$ kg, $m_3 = 0.1$ kg
$H_0 = 0.5$ m, $h = 0.05$ m
$V_1 = 1.0$ m/s

Figure 3 shows the dependence of the accelerations of the second derivatives of the angles $\theta_2''(t)$ and $\theta_3''(t)$ at different values of a/h. The dependences were calculated from Eqs. (4) using numerical differentiation.

From Fig. 3 it is clearly seen that as the parameter of the ellipse a decreases, the absolute values of $\theta_2''(t)$ and $\theta_3''(t)$ grow non-linearly. The dependencies have maxima that shift to the right as a/h increases. The absolute maximum for link 3, corresponding to $\theta_3''(t)$, is about 2.3 times greater than for link 2 - $\theta_2''(t)$.

Figure 4 shows the dependence of the velocities - the first derivatives of the angles $\theta_2'(t)$ and $\theta_3'(t)$ at different values of a/h. It is clearly seen that the velocities have pronounced maxima. Figure 4 shows that the maximum speed for drive 3 is about twice as high as the maximum speed for drive 2 for small a/h. As the a/h value increases, the velocity ratio becomes smaller, approaching unity. Graph analysis of Fig. 4 shows that the maximum speed for drive 3 is always greater than for drive 2.

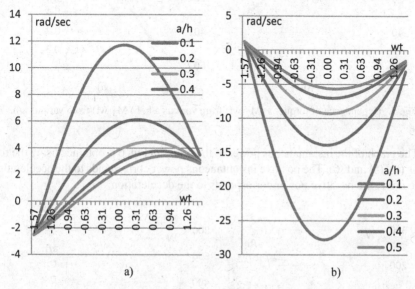

Fig. 4. Dependence of velocity: a) $\theta_2'(wt)$ from various a/h, b) $\theta_3'(wt)$ from various a/h.

The torque graph can be obtained using formulas (4) and (5). Figure 5 shows the torques $M_2(t)$ and $M_3(t)$ as a function of different a/h. Figure shows that as a/h decreases, the absolute torques grow non-linearly. The nature of the torque graphs Fig. 5 generally corresponds to the behavior of the second derivative angles, which is consistent with the formulas (5).

The dependence of the moments on the masses of the links is linear for M_3 and M_2, which follows from formulas (5). To reduce the moments according to formulas (5), it is necessary to reduce the mass of the links.

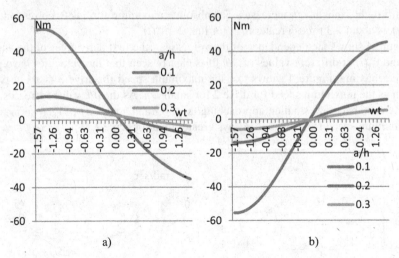

Fig. 5. Dependence of torque: a) $M_2(wt)$ from various a/h, b) $M_3(wt)$ from various a/h.

The graph of the instantaneous power of the drives in Fig. 6 is obtained using the formulas (4), (5) and (6). The positive instantaneous power corresponds to the acceleration of the drive, the negative power corresponds to the deceleration.

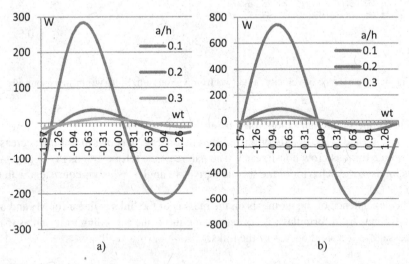

Fig. 6. Dependence of power: a) $P_2(wt)$ from various a/h, b) $P_3(wt)$ from various a/h.

The graphs show that the power of the drives increases sharply with a decrease in a/h. For small a/h the power ratio of P_3/P_2 is above 2.6. With an increase in a/h, the power ratio P_3/P_2 becomes smaller.

4 Optimization of Trajectory Parameters

To select the *a/h* ellipse parameter, it is convenient to find the dependences of the maximum accelerations, velocities, torques, and power on this parameter. Figure 7 shows the dependences of the maxima of accelerations and velocities on the ratio *a/h*. Figure 8 shows the dependences of the maxima of torques and instantaneous powers on the ratio *a/h*.

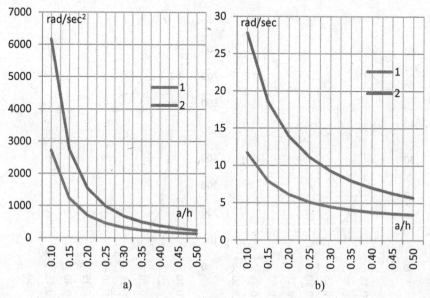

a)   b)

Fig. 7. Dependences of accelerations: a) 1 - max$|\theta_2''|$, 2 - max$|\theta_3''|$ from a/h, b) 1 - max$|\theta_2'|$, 2- max$|\theta_3'|$ from a/h.

The selection of the minimum allowable a/h value must be carried out according to several criteria:

- for maximum acceleration-according to Fig. 7a,
- for maximum speed-according to Fig. 7b,
- for maximum torque-according to Fig. 8a,
- for maximum power - according to Fig. 8b.

Consider a small example.

Let there be a drive GIM8008, which is used in MIT the Four Legged Robot dog [10]. It has parameters:

maximum output power – 250 W,
maximum torque – 17 Nm,
continuous torque – 6.9 Nm,
maximum output speed 40 rad/s.

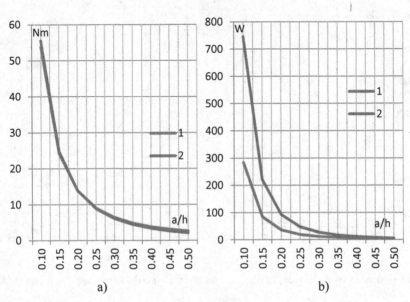

Fig. 8. Dependences of maximum: a) torque: 1 - max|M_2|, 2 - max|M_3| from a/h, b) 1 - max|P_2|, 2 - max|P_3| from a/h.

We estimate the *a/h* parameter for drive 3:

– at a maximum speed of 40 rad/s (Fig. 7b) $a/h \geq 0.1$;
– for a continuous moment of 6.9 Nm (Fig. 8a) $a/h \geq 0.3$;
– by power 250 watts (Fig. 8b) $a/h \geq 0.15$

From the estimates, it follows that the minimum value of $a/h = 0.3$, which is determined by the torque. To reduce this ratio, that is, to increase the speed, it is possible only by reducing the mass of links 2 and 3.

5   Analysis of the Influence of the Robot Leg Size on the Drive Characteristics

Let's analyze the influence of geometric parameters on the maximum torque.

Table 1. Parameter L_2 and L_3 for Fig. 9.

№	L_2, m	L_3, m
1	0,1	0,5
2	0,2	0,4
3	0,3	0,3
4	0,4	0,2
5	0,5	0,1

Figure 9a shows the dependence of the maximum torque $max\,|M_2|$ on a/h for different link lengths L_2 and L_3, which are presented in Table 1. The sum of the link lengths remains constant, the ratio L_2/L_3 changes.

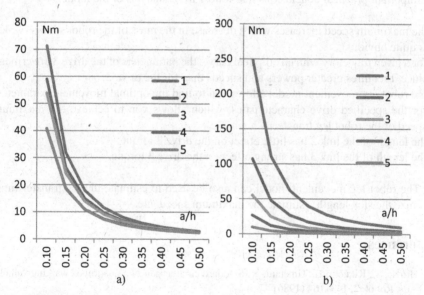

a)   b)

Fig. 9. Dependence of maximum: a) torque max$|M_2|$ from a/h for various L_2 and L_3 (Table 1), b) torque max$|M_3|$ from a/h for various L_2 and L_3 (Table 1).

From the graph of Fig. 9a it is clearly seen that the moment M_2 changes slightly with a decrease in the length of L_2. Lines 2 and 3 (4 and 5) in Fig. 9a are practically merged. As the length of the link decreases, the range of angles that should work out in the same time increases, so the acceleration should increase. However, the moment arm also decreases, so their product (5) changes slightly.

This leads to the practical conclusion that the length of the link 2 weakly affects the torque M_2.

Figure 9b shows the dependence of the maximum torque $max|M3|$ on a/h for different lengths of links L_2 and L_3, which are presented in Table 1. As the length of the L_3 link decreases, the moment decreases greatly. For $a/h = 0.1$, when L_3 decreases from 0.5m to 0.1m, the torque M_2 decreases from 71 Nm to 40 Nm, and the torque M_3 decreases from 248Nm to 10 Nm. According to the formula (5), the moment M_3 decreases according to the quadratic law.

An important practical conclusion that follows from this is that to reduce the moment M_3, it is necessary to make the link 3 as short as possible. Since drive 3 requires higher power values than drive 2, this rule is more important for increasing the maximum speed than for link 2.

6   Conclusion

The constructed model of the robot leg movement allows evaluating the drive parameters to obtain the maximum speed of the robot movement. The movement of the robot's leg is smooth, there are no acceleration gaps.

Important practical conclusions that follow from analysis of the model:

– the maximum speed increases with a decrease in the mass of the robot's links (which is quite obvious);
– for a given trajectory with an elliptical curve, the parameters of the drive 3 are critical, since it requires greater powers and speeds than for the drive 2;
– the robot leg movement model allows you to find the optimal movement parameters for the specified drive characteristics, which allows you to achieve the maximum speed of the robot leg transfer;
– the length of the link 2 has little effect on the drive 2 torque;
– the length of the link 3 has strong effect on the drive 3 torque.

The robot leg movement model can also be used to estimate the leg transfer time, optimize the step length, estimate the maximum speed, etc.

References

1. Hirose, S., Kikuchi, H., Umetani, Y.: Standard circular gait of a quadruped walking vehicle. Adv. Robot. **2**, 143–164 (1986)
2. Jindrich, D.L., Full, R.J.: Many-legged maneuver-ability: dynamics of turning in hexapods. J. Exp. Biol. **202**, 1603–1623 (2005)
3. Kim, J.Y., Yang, U.J.: Mechanical design of powered prosthetic leg and walking pattern generation based on motion capture data. Adv. Robot. **29**(16), 1061–1079 (2015)
4. Hereid, A., Ames, A.D.: Frost: fast robot optimization and simulation toolkit. In: IEEE/RSJ International Conference on Intelligent Robots and Systems (IROS), Vancouver, BC, Canada. IEEE/RSJ (2017)

5. Beranek, R., Ahmadi, M.A.: Learning behavior based controller formaintaining balance in robotic locomotion. Intell. Robot. Syst. **82**, 189–205 (2016)
6. Jatsun, S.F., et al.: Control the movement of the exoskeleton of lower limbs when walking. Yugo-Zapadnyy universitet: monographiya. Kursk, p. 185 (2016)
7. Kim, S., Park, F.C.: Fast robot motion generation using principal components: framework and algorithms. IEEE Trans. Ind. Electron. **55**(6), 2506–2516 (2008)
8. Sakakibara, Y., Kan, K., Hosoda, Y., Hattori, M., Fujie, M.: Foot trajectory for a quadruped walking machine. In: IEEE International Workshop on Intelligent Robots and Systems, Towards a New Frontier of Applications, vol. 1, pp. 315–322 (1990). https://doi.org/10.1109/IROS.1990.262407
9. Santos, P.G., Garcia, E., Estremera, J.: Quadrupedal Locomotion. Springer, London (2006)
10. Documentation GIM8008. http://brushlessgimbal.ca/Servo-Actuator/Mini-Cheetah-Act uator-Motor-Gear-Motor-Module-V3-Driver

The Problem Statement of Cognitive Modeling in Social Robotic Systems

Galina Gorelova[1], Eduard Melnik[2], and Irina Safronenkova[2(✉)]

[1] Engineering and Technology Academy of the Southern Federal University, 44, Nekrasovsky Lane, GSP-17, 347922 Taganrog, Russian Federation
[2] Federal Research Centre the Southern Scientific Center of the Russian Academy of Sciences, 41, Chekhov Street, 344006 Rostov-on-Don, Russian Federation

Abstract. In connection with the rapid development of robotics, the problems of interaction between humans and robots, considered as social interaction problems, are becoming more and more urgent. The problems of interaction of robots with people at the social level require versatile interdisciplinary research to identify and exclude their possible negative consequences. Practical information about such consequences in different areas of robot use may be considered insufficient. In this paper, it is proposed to use an approach to research based on simulation modeling to obtain additional information about the object, which is defined as the "Social Robotic System" (SRS). It is proposed to apply the methodology of cognitive simulation of complex systems as a methodology that uses the capabilities of cognitive processes in subjects in their interaction with objects. The toolkit for cognitive modeling of complex systems is also proposed to use for the development and substantiation of management decisions in the field of interaction between robots and humans. Two formulations of the problem for social robotic systems are considered. The models of these systems are in the form of cognitive maps. The results of the study of the SRS structural properties and stability properties on its cognitive maps are presented. The final stage of cognitive modeling is the development of scenarios for the possible development of situations in the system with internal and external environmental changes. All this research makes it possible to conclude the consistency of the models with possible real situations of human-robot interaction and to justify the necessary management decisions.

Keywords: Digital humanities · Complex system · Social robotics · Interaction · Imitation · Cognitive modeling

1 Introduction

The emergence of a new type of robots which are capable to communicate with people interactively at a social level, theoretical searches and practical implementation of the ideas of social robotics have become one of the promising directions in the development of digital humanities. With the proliferation of robotic systems, the level of their intellectualization (in the context of information technologies development) began to increase. A further stage in the development of robotic systems is that robots become subjects

© Springer Nature Switzerland AG 2021
A. Ronzhin et al. (Eds.): ICR 2021, LNAI 12998, pp. 62–75, 2021.
https://doi.org/10.1007/978-3-030-87725-5_6

of social life, which is facilitated by the growth of technologies for intelligent control and information processing in various areas of human activity. The social aspects and problems of the development of intelligent robotics, involving the interaction of people and robots, are increasingly manifested. This is associated with the emergence of a whole series of problems of the humanitarian, legal, technical and other order. They are especially acute in the field of cyber-physical systems at the level of smart enterprises, houses, cities, territories [1]. Therefore, the interaction of people and robots in order to prevent possible negative consequences gives rise to the need to study it, create and study cultural interfaces of social robots. Practical information on the negative consequences of using robots in various fields of activity is rather limited, most often in the field of assumptions and concerns. As you know, in conditions of information uncertainty, it is possible to obtain the necessary information about the system using the idea of simulation modeling, using the appropriate models and methods of simulation. This work uses just such an approach to the study of a complex system of interaction between humans and robots, and as one of the possible methodological foundations of digital humanities, it is proposed to apply the methodology of cognitive simulation of complex systems [2–15]. With the help of cognitive modeling tools, it is possible to model and study artificial cognitive systems that have a cognitive function (including the construction of an interactive space-time model of events).

In the process of cognitive research of complex systems [8–14, 16, 17], a number of problems of interaction of different objects have already been considered, for example, interregional economic interaction, counteraction of conflicting parties, etc. [10, 11].

The purpose of this work is to show the possibility and necessity of applying the apparatus of cognitive modeling to the study of a complex system of interaction between humans and robots and designated in this case as the "Social Robotic System" (SRS), as well as to consider possible formulations of tasks in the study of SRS and present the results of their cognitive modeling.

On cognitive modeling of complex systems. The direction of cognitive modeling of economic, social, political systems in Russia began to develop in the 90s of the last century, initially in Moscow by the works of the staff of the Institute of Control Sciences of the Russian Academy of Sciences ("Cognitive modeling and situation management") and then in the form of "Cognitive modeling of complex systems" in Taganrog employees of the SFedU [8–14, 16, 17]. Unlike many cognitive studies and methods of cognitive modeling "Cognitive modeling of complex systems" as a direction of artificial intelligence in the field of cognitive sciences, the object of research is complex social, economic, ecological, socio-technical, political systems, and other systems, and does not include in the research methodology only the development of cognitive maps (and more mathematically complex cognitive models) of the system, but also methods of formal analysis of the properties of the system on its model, and the study of the possible future development of processes in the system. Cognitive modeling is supported by the author's software system CMCS (Cognitive Modeling Complex Systems) [16]. Cognitive models of a complex system display diverse causal chains of connections between the vertices of the graph - objects ("concepts", "entities", "subjects", "factors") of the system, describe the structure of the system as it is understood, set or designed by the researcher. A significant advantage of such models is that they contain not only quantitative, but also qualitative, verbally defined factors (causes, effects) and relationships between them, which is necessary for a more complete, close to reality, display of a complex system. A convenient moment in cognitive modeling is the possibility and necessity of a visual representation of the structure of the system in the form of a graph, which serves as an essential tool in the process of understanding the object of research. Cognitive models can determine the structure of the knowledge base of an intelligent decision support system (IDSS).

Without repeating previously published material, let us refer, for example, to works [2, 8–14], which present various forms of cognitive models.

Cognitive modeling of complex systems occurs in stages, this process can be cyclical. The main stages include: the first stage - the development of a cognitive model (cognitive map - sign digraph, weighted sign digraph, functional vector graph, etc.); the second stage is the analysis of the properties of the cognitive model (stability, complexity, coherence, controllability, sensitivity, etc.) and returning, if necessary, to the first stage; the third stage is scenario analysis (impulse modeling for solving forecasting problems, scientific foresight) and returning, if necessary, to the first and second stages. The scheme of all stages of cognitive modeling is presented in works [11, 12] and can vary when adapting it to the peculiarities of the studied subject area.

To carry out cognitive modeling of interaction in social robotic systems, we will consider several possible formulations of tasks when developing an appropriate cognitive model.

2 Statement of the Problem of Cognitive Modeling of Interaction in Social Robotic Systems

In the process of cognitive research of complex systems, a number of interaction problems have already been considered, for example, interregional economic interaction, counteraction of conflicting parties, etc. To carry out cognitive modeling of interaction in social robotic systems, we will consider several possible formulations of tasks when developing a cognitive model.

Let us represent an element (Fig. 1) as a single elementary structure of a cognitive map, which we denote

$$g_0 = \langle V, E \rangle, \tag{1}$$

where $V = \{v_1, v_2\}$ is a set of two vertices "robot" and "human", $E = \{e_{12}, e_{21}\}$ is a set of two edges denoting the fact of relations between v_1 and v_2.

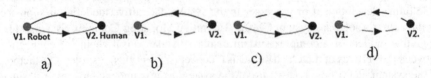

Fig. 1. Unit elementary structures g0.

Figure 1 is made in the CMCS software system [16]. The edges between the vertices can display both a positive "+1" (solid line in Fig. 2) and a negative "−1" (dashed line in Fig. 1) relationship between them. A positive relationship " +1" means that amplification/attenuation of the signal at the vertex of v_1 leads to an increase/decrease in the signal at the vertex of v_2. A negative relationship "−1" means that amplification/attenuation of the signal at the vertex of v_1 leads to an attenuation/amplification of the signal at the vertex of v_2. Figures 1(a) and (d) show the elementary contours of positive feedback, Fig. 2(b) and (c) - negative (stabilizing).

Figure 2 shows examples of simple positive (all edges in the cycle are positive or there is an even number of negative edges) and negative cycles (there is an odd number of negative edges in the cycle) connections of three vertices.

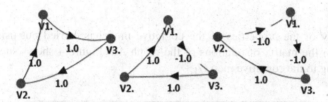

Fig. 2. Simple g_1 loops of positive and negative feedback.

In real social robotic systems, there are both individual single elements (for example, at the level of a person and his smart home), and a large number of elements and subsystems interacting with each other under conditions of, say, cooperation, or opposition to each other (if we consider competing, conflicting systems). In this case, the model in the form of a cognitive map is mathematically represented by a sign-oriented graph:

$$G = \langle V, E \rangle, \tag{2}$$

where $V = \{v_i\}$ is the set of vertices, i = 1, 2, ... k, $E = \{e_{ij}\}$ is the set of edges. The digraph G can contain both elementary elements g_0 and cycles g_1, and more complex causal chains of relations between vertices.

Task 1. Consider a variant of the formal formulation of the problem of interaction of partially interconnected robots with a person. Figure 3 shows an illustrative example of a system consisting of 8 vertices: a human and 7 robots. The type G_1 cognitive map is developed at the first stage of cognitive modeling. Moreover, all the vertices and the relationship between them, naturally, should have a meaningful meaning.

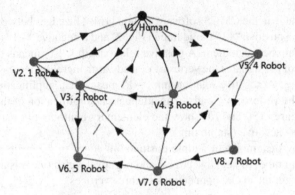

Fig. 3. Cognitive map G_1, Example 1.

The study of the properties of the cognitive model is carried out using various operations on the matrix of relations of the graph A_G. Figure 4 shows such a matrix corresponding to the cognitive map G_1.

Connectivity matrix

- Infl./ Dep.	V1	V2	V3	V4	V5	V6	V7	V8
V1	X	1.0	1.0	1.0	-1.0			
V2	1.0	X	1.0					
V3			X		1.0			
V4	-1.0		1.0	X			1.0	
V5	1.0			1.0	X			1.0
V6	-1.0	1.0				X		
V7			1.0		-1.0	1.0	X	
V8							1.0	X

Save   Export data   Close

Fig. 4. G_1 cognitive map relationship matrix.

At the second stage of cognitive modeling, the properties of the developed model are analyzed. Let's look at some of them using this example. So, Fig. 5 shows the results of determining the degree of cognitive map vertices. Figure 6 shows two of the 27 cycles of the cognitive map, one negative g_1 and one more complex positive one. A negative feedback loop (stabilizing) is a loop with an odd number of negative arcs. A positive (amplifying) feedback loop is a loop that does not contain or contains an even number of negative edges. Based on the results of the analysis of the properties of the cognitive map G_1, one can come to the following conclusions.

1. Analysis of the degrees of vertices: the vertex V_1. Human with the highest degree (p = 8), in this model, can be considered as the most significant, most of all influencing the other vertices. The next most important are the vertices with degree p = 5, and so

on. The least significant peak is V_7; in this case, the $V_{3.2}$ Robot vertex can have the least effect on the other vertices, its positive half-degree p+ $= 4$ (incoming edges) is greater than in other vertices, except for V_1. The vertices with p$- = 4$ and p$- = 3$ are least susceptible to external influence. Such information can be used, among other things, when choosing the vertices, which will be changed during the simulation of impulse processes.

Graph properties			
Vertices: 8. Edges: 19.			
Vertex	**p**	**p+**	**p-**
V1. Human	8	4	4
V2. 1 Robot	4	2	2
V3. 2 Robot	5	4	1
V4. 3 Robot	5	2	3
V5. 4 Robot	5	2	3
V6. 5 Robot	4	2	2
V7. 6 Robot	5	2	3
V8. 7 Robot	2	1	1

Fig. 5. Analysis of the vertices of the cognitive map G_1.

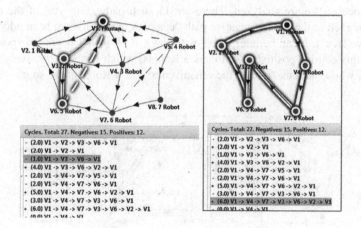

Cycles. Total: 27. Negatives: 15. Positives: 12.
- (2.0) V1 -> V2 -> V3 -> V6 -> V1
+ (2.0) V1 -> V2 -> V1
- (1.0) V1 -> V3 -> V6 -> V1
+ (4.0) V1 -> V3 -> V6 -> V2 -> V1
- (2.0) V1 -> V4 -> V7 -> V5 -> V1
- (2.0) V1 -> V4 -> V7 -> V6 -> V1
+ (5.0) V1 -> V4 -> V7 -> V6 -> V2 -> V1
- (3.0) V1 -> V4 -> V7 -> V3 -> V6 -> V1
+ (6.0) V1 -> V4 -> V7 -> V3 -> V6 -> V2 -> V1

Cycles. Total: 27. Negatives: 15. Positives: 12.
- (2.0) V1 -> V2 -> V3 -> V6 -> V1
+ (2.0) V1 -> V2 -> V1
- (1.0) V1 -> V3 -> V6 -> V1
+ (4.0) V1 -> V3 -> V6 -> V2 -> V1
- (2.0) V1 -> V4 -> V7 -> V5 -> V1
- (2.0) V1 -> V4 -> V7 -> V6 -> V1
+ (5.0) V1 -> V4 -> V7 -> V6 -> V2 -> V1
- (3.0) V1 -> V4 -> V7 -> V3 -> V6 -> V1
+ (6.0) V1 -> V4 -> V7 -> V3 -> V6 -> V2 -> V1

Fig. 6. G_1 cognitive map cycles.

2. Analysis of the cycles of a cognitive map allows judging the structural stability of the system by the ratio of its negative and positive cycles. In this case, the model under consideration is structurally stable, according to the condition [15]: for structural stability, it is necessary that the system has an odd number of negative cycles. In our case, out of 27 cycles, there are 15 negative cycles. This means that "small" changes in the structure of the model should not affect the tendencies of the processes taking place in it.
3. Model G_1 can be used as an element of a more complex system of interaction between humans and robots.

Task 2. Interaction of two robotic systems. Figure 7 shows a cognitive map G2 showing the relationship between two human-controlled systems.

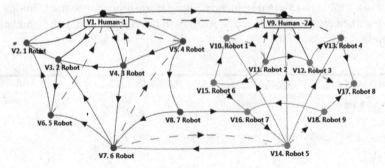

Fig. 7. Cognitive map G2 of SRS interaction.

Cognitive map path analysis G_2. Using the CMCS software system [16], it is easy to analyze all possible paths from any vertices of the graph. Figure 8 shows one of the variants of paths from the top V_1. Human-1 to the top V_9. Human-9, i.e. the paths of V_1 influence on V_9 are analyzed. There are 11 such paths, only one of the negative paths is marked in the figure (negative path "is a path in which there is an odd number of negative arcs"). It can be interpreted as follows. If Human-1 begins to "positively" act, then this action "positively" initiates 3 Robots, which further "positively" affects 6 Robots, whose actions "reduce the effectiveness" of 4 Robots, and so on. along the

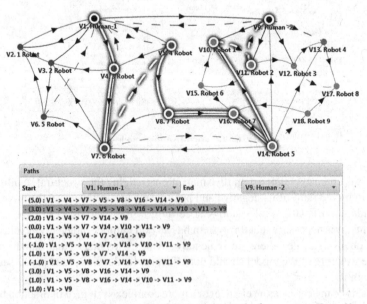

Fig. 8. Illustration of the results of determining paths from vertex V_1 to V_9.

entire chain of causation. As a result, the considered path is a negative path, weakening the efforts of Human-9. Similarly, it is possible to analyze all the paths of interest to the researcher on the nature of their causal effects, as well as on the consistency of their theoretical and practical considerations.

Analysis of the cycles of the cognitive map G2. Figures 9 and 10 show the results of determining the cognitive map G2 by the cycle and highlight one of its positive and negative cycles. In total, there are 67 cycles in this model, of which 37 are negative and 30 are positive.

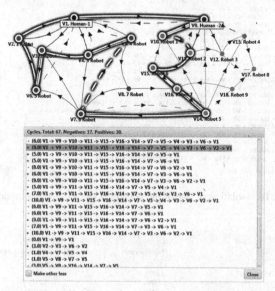

Fig. 9. Isolation of one of the positive cycles of the G_2 model.

Analysis of the stability of the model to disturbances. The analysis of resistance to disturbances and by the initial value is carried out according to the result of calculating the roots of the characteristic equation of the matrix of relations of the cognitive map [6, 12, 15]. For stability, it is necessary that the largest in modulus number of the characteristic equation of the matrix of relations be less than one (Fig. 11).

Modeling of scenarios of possible development of situations is carried out by means of impulse modeling (a model of an impulse process on cognitive maps was originally given in [5, 15]). The CMCS software system allows for impulse modeling by introducing perturbations into one, two or more vertices of the model; the impulse value can be greater or less than 1 (at the beginning of the study it is recommended to set the impulse q = + 1 or q = −1) and be applied at the initial or any other simulation cycle. Before starting this stage of simulation, it is recommended to think over an experiment plan, the design of which is also influenced by the results of previous cognitive modeling. In this case, we present the results of impulse modeling for two "simple" scenarios.

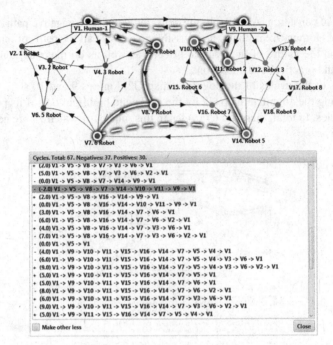

Fig. 10. Isolation of one of the negative cycles of the G_2 model.

#	Real part	Imaginary part	Module (1.7478)
0	-1.0262	1.0771	1.0771
1	-1.0262	-1.0771	1.0771
2	0.4735	1.7478	1.7478
3	0.4735	-1.7478	1.7478
4	-0.8302	0.4487	0.8302
5	-0.8302	-0.4487	0.8302
6	0.04	1.2581	1.2581
7	0.04	-1.2581	1.2581
8	0.4718	0.7485	0.7485
9	0.4718	-0.7485	0.7485
10	0.5806	0.7456	0.7456
11	0.5806	-0.7456	0.7456
12	-0.419	0.0	0.419
13	1.0	0.0	1.0
14	0.0	0.0	0.0
15	0.0	0.0	0.0
16	0.0	0.0	0.0
17	0.0	0.0	0.0

Fig. 11. Calculation of the roots of the characteristic equation of the matrix AG_2.

Scenario №. 1. Suppose that active actions begin at the vertex V_1, which is modeled in this case by introducing a disturbing action into it - impulse +1. The rest of the vertices are in the initial zero state. The results of the computational experiment are presented in Fig. 12, according to which some of the graphs of impulse processes in Fig. 13 are constructed. In Fig. 13, in order to facilitate a visual analysis of the trends in the development of processes in the system, only a part of the graphs is shown, which are built according to the results of the computational experiment in Fig. 12 for 7 cycles of modeling. In this case, the vertices are selected, including the results of the analysis of their degrees and half-degrees (as the largest for V_1.Human-1: $p = 10$, $p+ = 5$, $p- = 5$; for V_9.Human-2: $p = 8$, $p+ = 3$, $p- = 5$; for $p+ = 5$, $p- = 5$; for V_7.6 Robot: $p = 7$, $p+ = 3$, $p- = 4$; for V14. Robot 5: $p = 7$, $p+ = 2$, $p- = 5$). As can be seen from Fig. 13, initiation of actions at the vertex V_1 leads to the initiation of the vertex V_9 at the second step of the simulation, at the 3rd and 4th steps V_7 and V_{14} come into play. At the same time, the tendencies in the system develop in an increasing oscillatory mode, i.e. the system is not stable to disturbances, which is consistent with the previous analysis of the roots of the characteristic equation (Fig. 11). This is one of the possible, but not the only, scenario for the development of events in the analyzed system.

Step / Vertex	0.0	1.0	2.0	3.0	4.0	5.0	6.0	7.0	8.0	9.0	10.0
V1. Human-1	0.0	1.0	1.0	-1.0	-1.0	1.0	9.0	6.0	-29.0	-31.0	51.0
V2. 1 Robot	0.0	0.0	1.0	1.0	0.0	3.0	1.0	1.0	4.0	-8.0	14.0
V3. 2 Robot	0.0	0.0	1.0	3.0	1.0	-4.0	-1.0	12.0	28.0	-10.0	-103.0
V4. 3 Robot	0.0	0.0	1.0	0.0	-2.0	-1.0	3.0	12.0	-2.0	-44.0	-19.0
V5. 4 Robot	0.0	0.0	-1.0	-1.0	0.0	2.0	3.0	-8.0	-15.0	12.0	51.0
V6. 5 Robot	0.0	0.0	0.0	1.0	4.0	0.0	-8.0	-2.0	21.0	45.0	-30.0
V7. 6 Robot	0.0	0.0	0.0	1.0	-1.0	-4.0	-1.0	9.0	17.0	-20.0	-77.0
V8. 7 Robot	0.0	0.0	0.0	-1.0	-1.0	0.0	2.0	3.0	-8.0	-15.0	12.0
V9. Human -2	0.0	0.0	1.0	1.0	-2.0	-2.0	4.0	13.0	2.0	-47.0	-36.0
V10. Robot 1	0.0	0.0	0.0	1.0	1.0	-2.0	-2.0	5.0	15.0	-2.0	-57.0
V11. Robot 2	0.0	0.0	0.0	1.0	0.0	-3.0	0.0	6.0	8.0	-13.0	-45.0
V12. Robot 3	0.0	0.0	0.0	1.0	2.0	-2.0	-5.0	4.0	19.0	10.0	-60.0
V13. Robot 4	0.0	0.0	0.0	-1.0	0.0	3.0	0.0	-5.0	-7.0	7.0	39.0
V14. Robot 5	0.0	0.0	0.0	0.0	-1.0	0.0	4.0	2.0	-10.0	-18.0	16.0
V15. Robot 6	0.0	0.0	0.0	0.0	1.0	0.0	-3.0	0.0	6.0	8.0	-13.0
V16. Robot 7	0.0	0.0	0.0	0.0	-1.0	0.0	1.0	-1.0	-1.0	-4.0	3.0
V17. Robot 8	0.0	0.0	0.0	0.0	-2.0	-2.0	6.0	5.0	-13.0	-28.0	7.0
V18. Robot 9	0.0	0.0	0.0	0.0	0.0	1.0	0.0	-4.0	-2.0	10.0	18.0

Fig. 12. Calculation of impulse values corresponding to Scenario No. 1.

Scenario №. 2. Suppose that two vertices V_1 and V_9 are initiated by introducing perturbing unit positive impulses into them. q1 + 1 and q9 + 1. The results of impulse modeling are shown in Figs. 14, 15 and 16.

Figure 15 shows graphs of impulse processes corresponding to scenario No. 2, displaying a "conflict" at the level of vertices V_1 and V_9. As can be seen from Fig. 15, the tendencies of an increase in oscillatory processes in the system exist as in the case of scenario No. 1, but their intensity is weaker. This can also be seen, for example, from the histograms in Fig. 16 at the 7th step of the simulation.

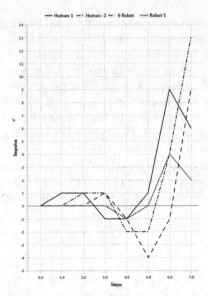

Fig. 13. Impulse processes at the vertices V_1, V_9, V_6, V_{14}, Scenario No. 1.

Step / Vertex	0.0	1.0	2.0	3.0	4.0	5.0	6.0	7.0	8.0	9.0	10.0
V1. Human-1	0.0	1.0	0.0	-2.0	1.0	2.0	5.0	-4.0	-32.0	11.0	83.0
V2. 1 Robot	0.0	0.0	1.0	0.0	-1.0	4.0	-2.0	-2.0	6.0	-13.0	21.0
V3. 2 Robot	0.0	0.0	1.0	2.0	-2.0	-4.0	5.0	11.0	8.0	-38.0	-74.0
V4. 3 Robot	0.0	0.0	1.0	-1.0	-2.0	2.0	3.0	6.0	-14.0	-36.0	41.0
V5. 4 Robot	0.0	0.0	-1.0	0.0	1.0	1.0	1.0	-10.0	-4.0	30.0	25.0
V6. 5 Robot	0.0	0.0	0.0	1.0	3.0	-4.0	-7.0	10.0	19.0	10.0	-74.0
V7. 6 Robot	0.0	0.0	0.0	1.0	-2.0	-3.0	5.0	8.0	2.0	-36.0	-40.0
V8. 7 Robot	0.0	0.0	0.0	-1.0	0.0	1.0	1.0	1.0	-10.0	-4.0	30.0
V9. Human -2	0.0	1.0	2.0	0.0	-2.0	3.0	8.0	5.0	-13.0	-39.0	30.0
V10. Robot 1	0.0	0.0	1.0	2.0	1.0	-2.0	3.0	9.0	5.0	-20.0	-43.0
V11. Robot 2	0.0	0.0	1.0	1.0	-2.0	-3.0	5.0	5.0	-4.0	-18.0	-19.0
V12. Robot 3	0.0	0.0	1.0	3.0	1.0	-4.0	0.0	13.0	10.0	-17.0	-57.0
V13. Robot 4	0.0	0.0	-1.0	-1.0	3.0	2.0	-5.0	-4.0	3.0	11.0	22.0
V14. Robot 5	0.0	0.0	0.0	0.0	-1.0	2.0	4.0	-5.0	-12.0	0.0	36.0
V15. Robot 6	0.0	0.0	0.0	1.0	1.0	-2.0	-3.0	5.0	5.0	-4.0	-18.0
V16. Robot 7	0.0	0.0	0.0	0.0	0.0	1.0	0.0	-4.0	2.0	0.0	4.0
V17. Robot 8	0.0	0.0	0.0	-2.0	-4.0	2.0	7.0	-7.0	-21.0	-2.0	40.0
V18. Robot 9	0.0	0.0	0.0	0.0	0.0	1.0	-2.0	-4.0	5.0	12.0	0.0

Fig. 14. Calculation of impulse values corresponding to scenario no. 2.

Based on the results of the analysis of the properties of the cognitive map G2, including those illustrated in Figs. 8, 9, 10, 11, 12, 13, 14, 15 and 16, one can come to the following conclusions.

1. Analysis of stability to disturbances showed it to be unstable both in initial value and in disturbance: the largest modulus number of the characteristic equation of the matrix of relations is greater than one (Fig. 11). This fact is confirmed by the results of the third stage of cognitive modeling - scenario modeling, which can be seen from

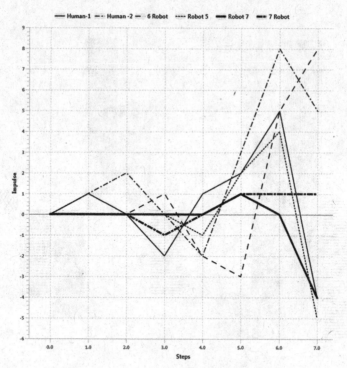

Fig. 15. Impulse processes, scenario no. 2.

Figs. 12 and 14, as well as from Figs. 13 and 15, which show the results of impulse modeling for Scenarios 1 and 2.

2. As can be seen from the results of impulse modeling, the processes in the considered model system have a tendency to increasing fluctuations. If such a result can be considered unsatisfactory (but for this it is first necessary to enter acceptance criteria - deviations of possible scenarios for the development of situations on the model), it is possible to refine, rebuild the structure of the model, introduce weight coefficients on the corresponding arcs, carry out scenario modeling by introducing perturbations in one, two in any combination of cognitive map vertices.

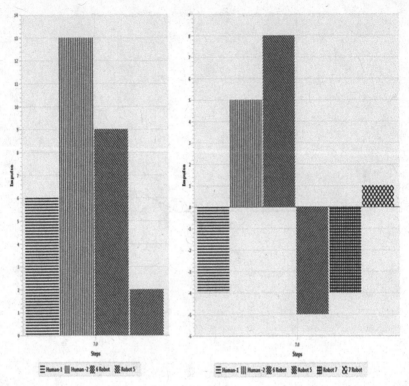

Fig. 16. Histograms of impulse values at the 7th step of modeling according to scenarios No. 1 and No. 2.

3 Conclusion

The methodology of cognitive modeling of complex systems and the corresponding tools proposed for research in the subject area of social robotics can contribute to a deeper understanding and disclosure of problems in this area. Imitation cognitive modeling helps to justify various management decisions, anticipating the possible development of processes in complex systems and preventing undesirable consequences - scenarios.

The two simple tasks considered in the work and the corresponding cognitive modeling of the "Social Robotic System" represent the main idea and possibilities of studying such systems. The transition from model to real problems may require a significant increase in the number of system elements and relationships between them, as well as the use of not only cognitive maps for simulation modeling, but also more complex models such as functional graphs.

Acknowledgement. This study is supported by the by the RFBR project 18-29-22086 and the GZ SSC RAS N GR project AAAA-A19-119011190173-6.

References

1. Gorelova, G.V.: Cognitive modeling of complex systems in the aspect of socio-cyber-physical systems. Manage. Econ. Soc. Syst. **2**, 10–19 (2019)
2. Abramova, N.A., Avdeeva, Z.K.: Cognitive analysis and management of the development of situations: problems of methodology, theory and practice. Probl. Manage. **3**, 85–87 (2008)
3. Avdeeva, Z.K., Kovriga, S.V., Makarenko, D.I., Maksimov, V.I.: Cognitive approach to management. Manage. Probl. **3**, 2–8 (2007)
4. Axelrod, R.: The Structure of Decision: Cognitive Maps of Political Elites. Princeton University Press, Princeton (1976)
5. Atkin, R.H.: Combinatorial connectivies in social systems. An application of simplicial complex structures to the study of large organisations. Interdisc. Syst. Res. (1997)
6. Casti, J.: Connectivity, Complexity, and Catastrophe in Large-scale Systems. A Wiley – Interscience Publication International Institute for Applied Systems Analysis. Wiley, Chichester, New York, Brisbane, Toronto (1979)
7. Eden, C.: Cognitive mapping. Eur. J. Oper. Res. **36**, 1–13 (1998)
8. Gorelova, G.V., Pankratova, N.D.: Scientific foresight and cognitive modeling of socio-economic systems. IFAC-PapersOnLine **51**(30), 145–149 (2018)
9. Gorelova, G.V., Pankratova, N.D., Borisova, D.V.: Problems of interregional integration, cognitive modeling. IFAC-PapersOnLine **52**(25), 168–173 (2019)
10. Gorelova, G.V., Borisova, D.V.: Cognitive tools for the inter-regional economic integration study. Sustain. Dev. Mount. Territ. **11**(1), 65–78 (2019)
11. Gorelova, G.V.: On the development of cognitive modeling in the study of complex systems. Manage. Econ. Soc. Syst. **1**, 11–26 (2019)
12. Gorelova, G.V., Pankratova, N.D.: Innovative development of socio-economic systems based on foresight and cognitive modeling methodologies. Collective monograph. Naukova Dumka, Kiev (2015)
13. Klimenko, A., Gorelova, G., Korobkin, V., Bibilo, P.: The cognitive approach to the coverage-directed test generation. In: Silhavy, R., Silhavy, P., Prokopova, Z. (eds.) CoMeSySo 2017. AISC, vol. 662, pp. 372–380. Springer, Cham (2018). https://doi.org/10.1007/978-3-319-67621-0_34
14. Langley, P., Laird, J.E., Rogers, S.: Cognitive architectures: research issues and challenges. Cogn. Syst. Res. **10**(2), 141–160 (2009)
15. Roberts, F.: Graph Theory and its Applications to Problems of Society. Society for Industrial and Applied Mathematics, Philadelphia (1978)
16. Program for cognitive modeling and analysis of socio-economic systems at the regional level. Certificate of state registration of computer programs no. 2018661506 dated 09 July 2018
17. Abramova, N.A., Ginsberg, K.S., Novikov, D.A.: The Human Factor in Management. KomKniga, Moscow (2006)

Adaptive Event Triggered Control
of Nonholonomic Mobile Robots

Mehmet Güzey$^{(\boxtimes)}$ ⬤

Erzurum Technical University, 25050 Erzurum, Turkey
mehmet.guzey@erzurum.edu.tr

Abstract. In this paper, the design of adaptive regulation control of mobile robots in the presence of uncertain robot dynamics and with event-based feedback is presented. Two-layer neural networks (NN) are utilized to represent the uncertain nonlinear dynamics of the mobile robots, which is subsequently employed to generate the control torque with event-sampled measurement update. Relaxing the perfect velocity tracking assumption, control torque is designed to minimize the velocity tracking error, by explicitly taking into account the dynamics of the robot. The Lyapunov's stability method is utilized to develop an event-sampling condition and to demonstrate the regulation performance of the mobile robot. Finally, simulation results are presented to verify theoretical claims and to demonstrate the reduction in the computations with event-sampled control execution.

Keywords: Event-triggered control · Adaptive control · Mobile robot · Robot dynamics

1 Introduction

Initially, the event-triggered techniques from the literature [1, 4, 5] were designed for ensuring stable operation of the closed-loop system by assuming that a stabilizing controller exists for the system under consideration. Developing an event-triggering condition and establishing the existence of positive inter-event time with the proposed event-sampling condition was the main focus in these works [1, 4, 5]. The traditional optimal control problem under the event-sampled framework is studied in [6] while in [2], the event-sampled adaptive controller design was presented for physical systems with uncertain dynamics.

Event-sampled adaptive dynamical regulation controls are proposed for mobile robots. The velocity tracking errors which are due to robot dynamics are considered as well. Using the NN-based representation of the mobile robot dynamics, the control inputs are obtained to minimize this velocity tracking error with event-sampled feedback. It is worth mentioning that the velocity tracking errors of the robot acts as a virtual controller for the regulation error system. Thus, using the back-stepping controller design, if the velocity tracking errors reduced, the robot reaches the desired set point. It should to noted that, in contrast to the existing event-triggered controller of mobile robots and [7,

---

A. Ronzhin et al. (Eds.): ICR 2021, LNAI 12998, pp. 76–87, 2021.
https://doi.org/10.1007/978-3-030-87725-5_7

8] the dynamics of the mobile robot is explicitly taken into account, relaxing the perfect velocity tracking assumption.

For the non-holonomic robot, an adaptive event-sampling condition is required to determine the sampling instants to generate the feedback information in order to update the controllers. Since unknown parameters are tuned at the event sampled instants, the computations are reduced when compared to traditional adaptive control schemes, but it introduces aperiodic parameter updates. Therefore, an event-sampling condition is derived using the stability conditions directly to ensure that the performance of the adaptive controller is not deteriorated due to the intermittent feedback. Finally, the extension of the Lyapunov's direct method is used to prove the local uniform ultimate boundedness (UUB) of the tracking errors and the parameter estimation error with event-sampled feedback. In our previous work, [13], stability proof of the controllers was omitted. Main contribution of the work is proving stability of the event-triggered adaptive regulation controller of mobile robot through Lyapunov stability analysis.

2   Controller with Periodic Update

Let ρ be the distance of the point (x, y) of the robot to the goal point (x_d, y_d). Let α be the angle of the pointing vector to the goal with respect to the robot's main axis, and define β to be the angle of the same pointing vector with respect to the orientation error [10]. That is,

$$
\begin{aligned}
\rho &= \sqrt{\Delta x^2 + \Delta y^2}, \\
\alpha &= -\theta + \mathrm{atan2}(\Delta y, \Delta x) + \pi, \\
\beta &= \alpha + \theta - \theta_d,
\end{aligned}
\tag{1}
$$

where $\Delta x = x_d - x$ and $\Delta y = y_d - y$.

Then, the polar coordinate kinematics of a mobile robot can be given as discussed in [10], and expressed as

$$
\begin{bmatrix} \dot{\rho} \\ \dot{\alpha} \\ \dot{\beta} \end{bmatrix} =
\begin{bmatrix} -\cos(\alpha) & 0 \\ \sin(\alpha)/\rho & -1 \\ \sin(\alpha)/\rho & 0 \end{bmatrix}
\begin{bmatrix} v \\ \omega \end{bmatrix}.
\tag{2}
$$

From (2), it is observed that the input vector field associated with v is singular for $\rho = 0$, thus satisfying Brockett's Theorem. To drive mobile robots from any initial position to a goal position, a nonlinear control law is given as [10]:

$$
\begin{aligned}
v_d &= k_\rho \rho \cos \alpha, \\
\omega_d &= k_\alpha \alpha + k_\rho \left(\frac{\sin \alpha \cos \alpha}{\alpha} \right)(\alpha + k_\beta \beta),
\end{aligned}
\tag{3}
$$

where k_α and k_β are positive design constants. As shown in [10], the controller (3) provides asymptotic converge to the constant desired posture.

However, the results are obtained by assuming the perfect velocity tracking (assuming that $v_d = v$ and $\omega_d = \omega$) which does not hold in practice. To relax the perfect velocity tracking assumption, the backstepping technique was employed in [11].

Define the velocity tracking error as

$$e_v^R = \begin{bmatrix} e_{v1}^R \\ e_{v2}^R \end{bmatrix} = \overline{v}_d - \overline{v}, \tag{4}$$

where $\overline{v}_d = [v_d \omega_d]^T$. Rearranging (4) gives $\overline{v} = \overline{v}_d - e_v^R$, and substituting this expression into the open loop system (2) while using (7) reveals

$$\begin{bmatrix} \dot{\rho} \\ \dot{\alpha} \\ \dot{\beta} \end{bmatrix} = \begin{bmatrix} -k_\rho \rho \cos^2 \alpha + e_{v1}^R \cos \alpha \\ -k_\alpha \alpha - k_\rho \left(\frac{\sin \alpha \cos \alpha}{\alpha}\right) k_\beta \beta + e_{v2}^R - \frac{\sin \alpha}{\rho} e_{v1}^R \\ k_\rho \sin \alpha \cos \alpha - \frac{\sin \alpha}{\rho} e_{v1}^R \end{bmatrix}. \tag{5}$$

The closed loop kinematic system (5) explicitly considers the velocity tracking error (4). Therefore, the backstepping technique ensures the robot tracks the design velocities (3). Consider the mobile robot dynamics

$$\overline{M}\dot{\overline{v}} + \overline{V}_m(q, \dot{q})\overline{v} + \overline{F}(\overline{v}) + \overline{\tau}_d = \overline{\tau}, \tag{6}$$

where $\overline{M} \in \Re^{\rho \times \rho}$ is a constant positive definite inertia matrix, $\overline{V}_m \in \Re^{\rho \times \rho}$ is the bounded centripetal and Coriolis matrix, $\overline{F} \in \Re^\rho$ is the friction vector, $\overline{\tau}_d \in \Re^\rho$ represents unknown bounded disturbances such that $\|\overline{\tau}_d\| \leq d_M$ for a known constant, d_M, $\overline{B} \in \Re^{\rho \times \rho}$ is a constant, nonsingular input transformation matrix, $\overline{\tau} = \overline{B}\tau \in \Re^\rho$ is the input vector, and $\tau \in \Re^\rho$ is the control torque vector. For complete details on (6) and the parameters, refer to [9].

Differentiating (3) and using (6), the mobile robot velocity tracking error system as

$$\overline{M}\dot{e}_v^R = -\overline{V}_m(q, \dot{q})e_v^R - \overline{\tau} + f(z) + \overline{\tau}_d, \tag{7}$$

where $f(z) = \overline{M}\dot{\overline{v}}_d + \overline{V}_m(q, \dot{q})\overline{v}_d + \overline{F}(\overline{v})$ and contains the mobile robot parameters such as masses, moments of inertia, friction coefficients, and so on. When the robot dynamics are known, the control torque applied to the robot system (6), which ensures the desired velocity (3), is achieved and is written as

$$\overline{\tau} = K_v e_v^R + f(z) + \lambda(\rho, \alpha, \beta), \tag{8}$$

where $\lambda(\rho, \alpha, \beta) = \begin{bmatrix} \cos \alpha \left(\rho + 0.5\left(a^2 + k_\beta \beta^2\right)\right) - \sin \alpha_i(\alpha + k_\beta \beta) \\ \rho \alpha \end{bmatrix}$ is a function of the polar coordinate error system (1) and is required for stability. Substituting (8) into (7) reveals the closed loop velocity tracking error dynamics:

$$\overline{M}\dot{e}_v^R = -K_v e_v^R - \overline{V}_m(q, \dot{q})e_v^R + \overline{\tau}_d - \lambda(\rho, \alpha, \beta). \tag{9}$$

Lemma 1: Given the mobile robot system described by (6) and (8), let the velocity tracking error and its dynamics for driving the nonholonomic system to the goal configuration, q_d, be given by (4) and (7), respectively, and let the control torque vector be defined by (8). Then, in the absence of disturbances $\overline{\tau}_d = 0$, the velocity tracking error system (7) and kinematic system (2) converge to the origin asymptotically, and the robot reaches its desired velocity and converges to its desired posture. That is, $e_v^R(t, t_0) \to 0$ and $q \to q_d$.

Proof: See [11] for the proof.

Next, event sampled regulation controller is developed.

3 Event Sampled Controller Design

In this section, the NN controller design with event-sampled feedback, for the nonholonomic mobile robots will be presented and the aperiodic NN weight adaptation law will be derived from the Lyapunov stability analysis. The event-sampling mechanism is designed using stability analysis such that the event-sampling error

$$e_{ET}(t) = x(t) - \breve{x}(t),\ t_k < t \le t_{k+1},\ \forall k = 0, 1, \cdots, n, \tag{10}$$

satisfies a state-dependent threshold for every inter-event period for each robot, which is of the form

$$\left\| \bar{E}_{ET} \right\| \le \sigma \mu_k \left\| \breve{E} \right\|, \qquad t_k \le t < t_{k+1},\ k = 1, 2, 3 \ldots \tag{11}$$

with $0 < \sigma < 1$, and μ_k is a positive design parameter and $E_{ET}, \breve{E}$ are functions of event-sampling error and the formation, and velocity tracking errors respectively. By using the event-sampled feedback, the objective is to reduce the computations from periodic parameter adaptation without compromising the stability while ensuring acceptable velocity tracking performance.

Definition 1: Define first, $\forall i = 1, 2, \ldots, N$, $t_k \le t < t_{k+1}$

$$\breve{\rho}(t) = \rho(t_k),\ \breve{\alpha}(t) = \alpha(t_k),\ \breve{\beta}(t) = \beta(t_k),\ \varepsilon_\rho = \rho(t) - \rho(t_k),$$
$$\varepsilon_\alpha = \alpha(t) - \alpha(t_k),\ \varepsilon_\beta = \beta(t) - \beta(t_k). \tag{12}$$

Now, to define the regulation error dynamics with event-sampled measurement error, consider (3), during the kth inter-event period, the desired virtual control equations are obtained as

$$\breve{\bar{v}}_d = \begin{bmatrix} \breve{v}_d \\ \breve{\omega}_d \end{bmatrix} = \begin{bmatrix} k_\rho \breve{\rho} \cos \breve{\alpha} \\ k_\alpha \breve{\alpha} + k_\rho \left(\dfrac{\sin \breve{\alpha} \cos \breve{\alpha}}{\breve{\alpha}} \right) \left(\breve{\alpha} + k_\beta \breve{\beta} \right) \end{bmatrix},\ t_k \le t < t_{k+1} \tag{13}$$

After defining the event-sampled signals, (13) can be rewritten with the measurement errors as

$$\dot{\bar{v}}_d = \begin{bmatrix} \breve{v}_d \\ \breve{\omega}_d \end{bmatrix} = \begin{bmatrix} k_\rho \rho \cos \alpha + \varepsilon_v \\ k_\alpha \alpha + k_\rho \left(\dfrac{\sin \alpha \cos \alpha}{\breve{\alpha}} \right) \left(\alpha + k_\beta \beta \right) \\ + \varepsilon_\omega \end{bmatrix},\ t_k \le t < t_{k+1}, \tag{14}$$

where ε_v, ε_ω are given by $\varepsilon_v = k_\rho \breve{\rho} \cos \breve{\alpha} - k_\rho \left(\breve{\rho} + \varepsilon_\rho \right) \cos \left(\breve{\alpha} + \varepsilon_\alpha \right)$ and

$$
\varepsilon_\omega = k_\alpha \breve{\alpha} + k_\rho \left(\frac{\sin \breve{\alpha} \cos \breve{\alpha}}{\breve{\alpha}} \right) \left(\breve{\alpha} + k_\beta \breve{\beta} \right) - k_\alpha \alpha
$$

$$
+ k_\rho \left(\frac{\sin \left(\breve{\alpha} + \varepsilon_\alpha \right) \cos \left(\breve{\alpha} + \varepsilon_\alpha \right)}{\breve{\alpha}} \right) \left(\begin{matrix} \left(\breve{\alpha} + \varepsilon_\alpha \right) \\ + k_\beta \left(\breve{\beta} + \varepsilon_\beta \right) \end{matrix} \right).
$$

Remark 1: Realize that the event triggering errors ε_v, ε_ω are the functions of the event triggering errors of the each state ε_ρ, ε_α, ε_ρ as well as the last measured state values $\breve{\rho}, \breve{\alpha}, \breve{\beta}$ which is available for the controller in the interval $t_k < t \leq t_{k+1}$.

To get the closed-loop formation error dynamics in the presence of measurement error, use (14) in (2), which reveals the event-sampled regulation error dynamics as

$$
\begin{bmatrix} \dot{\rho} \\ \dot{\alpha} \\ \dot{\beta} \end{bmatrix} = \begin{bmatrix} \left(-k_\rho \rho \cos^2 \alpha + e_{v1}^R \cos \alpha - \cos \alpha \varepsilon_v \right) \\ \left(-k_\alpha \alpha - k_\rho \left(\frac{\sin \alpha \cos \alpha}{\alpha} \right) k_\beta \beta + e_{v2}^R - \frac{\sin \alpha}{\rho} e_{v1}^R + \frac{\sin \alpha \varepsilon_v}{\rho} - \varepsilon_\omega \right) \\ \left(k_\rho \sin \alpha \cos \alpha - \frac{\sin \alpha}{\rho} e_{v1}^R + \frac{\sin \alpha \varepsilon_v}{\rho} \right) \end{bmatrix}. \tag{15}
$$

The closed loop regulation error dynamics in the presence of event trigger errors are obtained in (15). Similar to that, the velocity tracking errors in the event sampled framework will be derived next.

The unknown NN weights can be estimated as $\hat{\Theta}$, and an estimate of the unknown dynamics with event sampled feedback can be obtained as

$$
\hat{f}(z) = \hat{\Theta}^T \psi \left(\breve{z} \right), \quad t_k \leq t < t_{k+1}, \tag{16}
$$

with $\breve{z} = z + \varepsilon_z$, being the event-sampled signals of the mobile robot. The unknown NN weight estimation error is defined as $\tilde{\Theta} = \Theta - \hat{\Theta}$ and the estimation error dynamics can be given as $\dot{\tilde{\Theta}} = -\dot{\hat{\Theta}}$. The event-sampled control torque, using (16), is obtained as

$$
\bar{\tau} = -K_v \breve{e}_v + \hat{f} \left(\breve{z} \right) - \breve{\gamma} \left(\breve{\rho}, \breve{\alpha}, \breve{\beta} \right), \quad t_k \leq t < t_{k+1}, \tag{17}
$$

With

$$
\breve{e}_v = e_v + e_{ET}, \tag{18}
$$

where the event triggered velocity tracking error $\breve{e}_v(t) = e_v(t_k)$ is defined similar to the event triggered formation errors and $\breve{\gamma}$ is the stabilizing term with measurement error due to event-sampled mechanism.

Substituting (17) into (7) reveals the closed-loop velocity tracking error dynamics

$$
\bar{M} \dot{e}_v = -K_v e_v + \bar{\tau}_d - \breve{\gamma} \left(\breve{\rho}, \breve{\alpha}, \breve{\beta} \right) + \tilde{f} \left(\breve{z} \right) - K_v e_{ET}
$$

$$+ \; [f(z_i) - f\left(\breve{z}_i\right)] - \overline{V}_{mi}(q_i, \dot{q}_i)e_{iv}^F, \quad t_k \leq t < t_{k+1}, \tag{19}$$

where $\tilde{f}\left(\breve{z}\right) = \tilde{\Theta}\psi\left(\breve{z}\right) + \chi$. With the regulation error dynamics (15) and the velocity tracking error dynamics (19) driven by the event-sampling errors, the stability results for mobile robots are presented in the theorem statements.

Next the definition for UUB is introduced.

Definition 2: An equilibrium point x_e is said to be uniformly ultimately bounded (UUB) if there exists a compact set $S \subset \mathfrak{R}^n$ so that for all $x_0 \in S$ there exists a bound B and a time $T(B, x_0)$ such that $\|x(t) - x_e\| \leq B$ for all $t \geq t_0 + T$.

Theorem 1 (Input-to-state stability): Given the regulation error dynamics (15) and the velocity tracking error dynamics (19) of the robot, let the regulation controller (17) be applied to the robot. Define the control torque by (17) with

$$\breve{\gamma}\left(\breve{\rho}, \breve{\alpha}, \breve{\beta}\right) = \begin{bmatrix} \cos\breve{\alpha}\left(\breve{\rho} + 0.5\left(\breve{\alpha}^2 + k_\beta\breve{\beta}^2\right)\right) - \sin\breve{\alpha}_i(\breve{\alpha} + k_\beta\breve{\beta}) \\ \breve{\rho}\breve{\alpha} \end{bmatrix}. \tag{20}$$

Further, tune the unknown NN weights using the adaptation rule

$$\dot{\hat{\Theta}} = \Lambda_1\psi(z)e_v^T - \Lambda_1\kappa\hat{\Theta}, \tag{21}$$

where $\Lambda_1 > 0, \kappa > 0$ are small positive design parameters and with the measurement error satisfying the inequality $\|E_{ET}\| \leq \overline{B}_{ETM}$, with $\overline{B}_{ETM}$ being a positive constant. Consider Assumptions 1, 2 and 3 hold. The velocity tracking (19) and regulation errors (15) are UUB and a) the robot reach any desired posture in the presence of bounded measurement error and b) the closed-loop system is input-to-state stable (ISS), with the input being a function of the measurement error e_{ET}.

Proof: See Appendix.

In the following theorem, the event-sampling mechanism is designed, and stability of the robot formation is analyzed by using the Lyapunov stability theory in the presence of disturbance torque input and NN reconstruction error.

Theorem 2: Given the regulation error dynamics (19) for the robot with the disturbance torque and the NN approximation error $\overline{\tau}_d \neq 0, \chi_i \neq 0$, respectively. Consider the Assumptions 1 holds. Let the regulation control input, (17) with (20), be applied to the mobile robot at the event-based sampling instants and the event-sampling condition be defined by (11). Further, consider the unknown NN weights are tuned at the event sampling instants using the aperiodic tuning rule (21). Then the velocity tracking error (19) and regulation error systems (15) are UUB and a) the mobile robot reaches any desired posture.

Proof: See Appendix.

4 Simulation Results

The desired and initial positions, initial bearing angles and the initial velocities of the non-holonomic mobile robot are given by

$$x(t_0) = 157 \ x^d = 192 \ y(t_0) = -126 \ y^d = -108 \ \theta(t_0) = \pi, \ \theta^d = \pi/6.$$

The controller gains are selected as $K_v = 80 k_\rho = 2, k_\alpha = 1, k_\beta = 0.5$. The parameters for the robot dynamics are selected as $m = 5\,\text{kg}, I = 3\,\text{kg}^2, R = 0.15\,\text{m}, r = 0.08\,\text{m}, d = 0.4\,\text{m}$ and the mass matrix is calculated as $\overline{M} = \begin{bmatrix} 810 & 0 \\ 0 & 133.02 \end{bmatrix}$, and $\left\|\overline{M}^{-1}\right\| = 0.0075$. Figure 1 depicts the motion of the non-holonomic mobile robot.

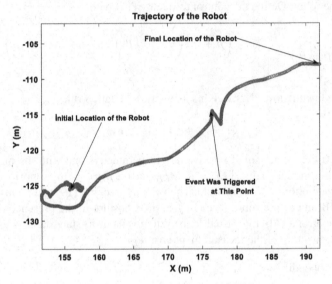

Fig. 1. Mobile robot moving to its desired location.

The initial movements of the robots are oscillatory (till the 400th second) because of the unknown dynamics. With the parameter adaptation using $\Lambda = 0.2, \kappa = 0.01$ the controllers of the robot learn the unknown parameters. Once the uncertain parameters are tuned, the robot starts moving toward its desired location on x, y.

The difference between the desired linear and angular velocities and the actual linear and angular velocities, which is the velocity tracking error, is plotted in Fig. 2 (Fig. 3).

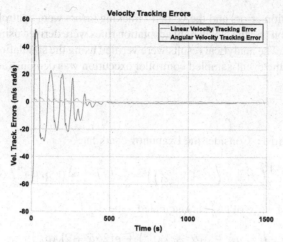

Fig. 2. Velocity tracking errors.

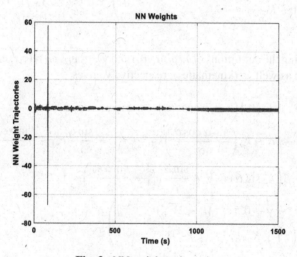

Fig. 3. NN weight trajectories.

5 Conclusions

In this paper, the event-based control implementations for the robotic system were presented. The adaptive event-sampled regulation torque control for the nonholonomic mobile robot was able to drive the robot to its desired location with bounded error due to event sampled measurement errors. The bounds are also found to be a function of the disturbance bounds. The event-sampling mechanism was able to generate additional events so that the velocity tracking error remains bounded in the presence of disturbance.

The uncertain friction and Coriolis terms were adaptively tuned by the controller at event-sampled instants. Using the dynamics as well as the kinematics of the mobile robot, the regulation errors and the velocity tracking errors were controlled. The event-sampling condition and the NN weight adaptation rules were derived using the Lyapunov stability analysis. The analytical results were verified using the simulation examples and the efficiency of the event-sampled controller execution was demonstrated.

Appendix

Proof of Theorem 1: Consider the Lyapunov candidate

$$L = \frac{1}{2}\left(\rho^2 + \rho\left(\alpha^2 + k_\beta\beta^2\right)\right) + \frac{1}{2}e_v^T \bar{M} e_v^T + 0.5tr\{\tilde{\Theta}^T \Lambda \tilde{\Theta}\}. \tag{A1}$$

Then, the derivative of (A1) is calculated to be

$$\dot{L} = \rho\dot{\rho} + \dot{\rho}\left(\alpha^2 + k_\beta\beta^2\right) + \rho\left(2\alpha\dot{\alpha} + 2k_\beta\beta\dot{\beta}\right) +$$
$$- e_v^T \left(\begin{array}{c} K_v e_v - \check{\gamma}(e) + 0.5\,e_v^T(\dot{\bar{M}} - 2\bar{V}_m)e_v + \bar{\tau}_d \\ +\tilde{f}\left(\bar{z}\right) + K_v e_{ET} \end{array} \right) + [f(z) - f\left(\bar{z}\right)]) + tr\{\tilde{\Theta}^T \Lambda \dot{\tilde{\Theta}}\}. \tag{A2}$$

Next, applying the definitions of $\lambda(\rho_i, \alpha_i, \beta_i)$ and $\gamma(e_{i1}, e_{i2}, e_{i3})\gamma(e_{i1}, e_{i2}, e_{i3})$ defined in (13) and (22) as well as (kinematics), respectively, gives

$$\dot{L} = \left(\rho + \alpha^2 + k_\beta\beta^2\right)\left(-k_\rho\rho\cos^2\alpha + e_{v1}^R\cos\alpha - \cos\alpha\varepsilon_v\right)$$
$$+ \rho\left(\begin{array}{c} 2\alpha\left(-k_\alpha\alpha - k_\rho\left(\dfrac{\sin\alpha\cos\alpha}{\alpha}\right)k_\beta\beta + e_{v2}^R - \dfrac{\sin\alpha}{\rho}e_{v1}^R + \dfrac{\sin\alpha\varepsilon_v}{\rho} - \varepsilon_\omega\right) \\ +2k_\beta\beta\left(k_\rho\sin\alpha\cos\alpha - \dfrac{\sin\alpha}{\rho}e_{v1}^R + \dfrac{\sin\alpha\varepsilon_v}{\rho}\right) \end{array} \right)$$
$$- e_v^T\left(\begin{array}{c} K_v e_v - \check{\gamma} + 0.5\,e_v^T(\dot{\bar{M}} - 2\bar{V}_m)e_v + \bar{\tau}_d \\ +\tilde{f}\left(\bar{z}\right) + K_v e_{ET} \end{array} \right)$$
$$+ [f(z) - f\left(\bar{z}\right)]) + tr\{\tilde{\Theta}^T \Lambda \dot{\tilde{\Theta}}\}. \tag{A3}$$

After using the skew symmetry property, $\dot{L}$ becomes

$$\dot{L} = \left(\rho + \alpha^2 + k_\beta\beta^2\right)\left(-k_\rho\rho\cos^2\alpha + e_{v1}^R\cos\alpha - \cos\alpha\varepsilon_v\right)$$
$$+ \rho\left(\begin{array}{c} 2\alpha\left(-k_\alpha\alpha - k_\rho\left(\dfrac{\sin\alpha\cos\alpha}{\alpha}\right)k_\beta\beta + e_{v2}^R - \dfrac{\sin\alpha}{\rho}e_{v1}^R + \dfrac{\sin\alpha\varepsilon_v}{\rho} - \varepsilon_\omega\right) \\ +2k_\beta\beta\left(k_\rho\sin\alpha\cos\alpha - \dfrac{\sin\alpha}{\rho}e_{v1}^R + \dfrac{\sin\alpha\varepsilon_v}{\rho}\right) \end{array} \right)$$
$$- e_v^T\left(K_v e_v - \check{\gamma} + \bar{\tau}_d + \tilde{f}\left(\bar{z}\right) + K_v e_{ET}\right) + [f(z) - f\left(\bar{z}\right)]) + tr\{\tilde{\Theta}^T \Lambda \dot{\tilde{\Theta}}\}. \tag{A4}$$

By following the similar steps done in 11 without the blending functions yields (A4)

$$\dot{L} = -\rho^2 \cos^2 \alpha - \rho \alpha^2 - \rho \cos^2 \alpha \left(\alpha^2 + k_\beta \beta^2 \right) \Big/ 2 - \cos \alpha \left(\rho + \alpha^2 + k_\beta \beta^2 \right) \varepsilon_v$$

$$+ 2\alpha \sin \alpha \varepsilon_v - 2\alpha \rho \varepsilon_\omega + \sin \alpha \varepsilon_v - e_v^T (K_v e_v - \breve{\gamma} + \bar{\tau}_d + \tilde{f}\left(\breve{z} \right) + K_v e_{ET})$$

$$\text{(A5)}$$

$$+ [f(z) - f\left(\breve{z} \right)]) + tr\left\{ \tilde{\Theta}^T \Lambda \dot{\tilde{\Theta}} \right\}.$$

Using defining of the bound $\| \psi(z) \| \le \psi_M$, we obtain

$$\dot{L} \le -\rho^2 \cos^2 \alpha - \rho \alpha^2 - \rho \cos^2 \alpha \left(\alpha^2 + k_\beta \beta^2 \right) \Big/ 2 - \cos \alpha \left(\rho + \alpha^2 + k_\beta \beta^2 \right) \varepsilon_v$$

$$+ 2\alpha \sin \alpha \varepsilon_v - 2\alpha \rho \varepsilon_\omega + \sin \alpha \varepsilon_v - (K_v - 0.5) \| e_v \|^2 + e_v^T \tilde{\Theta}^T \psi \left(\breve{z} \right) + e_v^T K_v e_{ET}$$

$$\text{(A6)}$$

$$+ 2\psi_M^2 \| \Theta \|^2 + e_v^T (\bar{\tau}_d) + tr\left\{ \tilde{\Theta}^T \Lambda \dot{\tilde{\Theta}} \right\}.$$

Utilizing the parameter adaptation rule defined in (21) and the definition of the NN weights estimation error, we have

$$\dot{L}_i \le -\rho^2 \cos^2 \alpha - \rho \alpha^2 - \rho \cos^2 \alpha \left(\alpha^2 + k_\beta \beta^2 \right) \Big/ 2 - \cos \alpha \left(\rho + \alpha^2 + k_\beta \beta^2 \right) \varepsilon_v$$

$$+ 2\alpha \sin \alpha \varepsilon_v - 2\alpha \rho \varepsilon_\omega + \sin \alpha \varepsilon_v. - (K_v - 0.5) \| e_v \|^2 + e_v^T \tilde{\Theta}^T \psi \left(\breve{z} \right) + e_v^T K_v e_{ET}$$

$$+ 2\psi_M^2 \| \Theta \|^2 + e_v^T (\bar{\tau}_d) - tr\left\{ \tilde{\Theta}^T \Lambda \left(\Lambda_1 \psi(z) e_v^T - \Lambda_1 \kappa \hat{\Theta} \right) \right\}.$$

$$\dot{L}_i \le -\rho^2 \cos^2 \alpha - \rho \alpha^2 - \rho \cos^2 \alpha \left(\alpha^2 + k_\beta \beta^2 \right) \Big/ 2$$

$$+ \left[-\cos \alpha (\rho + \alpha^2 + k_\beta \beta^2) + 2\alpha \sin \alpha + \sin \alpha - 2\alpha \rho \right] \begin{bmatrix} \varepsilon_v \\ \varepsilon_\omega \end{bmatrix}$$

$$- (K_v - 0.5) \| e_v \|^2 + e_v^T \tilde{\Theta}^T \psi \left(\breve{z} \right) + e_v^T K_v e_{ET} + 2\psi_M^2 \| \Theta \|^2$$

$$+ e_v^T (\bar{\tau}_d) - tr\left\{ \tilde{\Theta}^T \Lambda \left(\Lambda_1 \psi(z) e_v^T - \Lambda_1 \kappa \hat{\Theta} \right) \right\}.$$

Combining the similar terms and using the Young's inequality once again yields

$$\dot{L} \le -KE + K_{ET} E_{ET} + B \tag{A7}$$

where $B = 2\psi_M^2 \| \Theta \|^2$ with $\psi_M > \psi(t)$ is the upper bound for the activation function, $\Xi_i = [\rho^2 \ \alpha^2 \ \| e_v \|^2 \ \| \tilde{\Theta} \|^2]$, $K_i = [\bar{k}_1 \ \bar{k}_2 \ \bar{k}_3 \ \kappa]$ with $\bar{k}_1 = \cos^2 \alpha \ \bar{k}_2 = \rho \bar{k}_3 = K_v$.

$$K_{ET} = \begin{bmatrix} -\cos \alpha \left(\rho + \alpha^2 + k_\beta \beta^2 \right) & -2\alpha \rho \\ +2\alpha \sin \alpha + \sin \alpha & \end{bmatrix}, E_{ET} = \begin{bmatrix} \varepsilon_v \\ \varepsilon_\omega \end{bmatrix}.$$ Using the assumption that

the measurement errors are bounded, $\| E_{ET} \| \le \bar{B}_{ETM}$ we can claim that the regulation and velocity tracking errors and NN weight estimation errors are bounded.

Proof of Theorem 2: Consider the Lyapunov candidate in (A1) follow the similar steps done in the proof of the first theorem and obtain

$$\dot{L} \leq -KE + K_{ET}E_{ET} + B, \tag{A8}$$

where $B = 2\psi_M^2 \|\Theta\|^2$ with $\psi_M > \psi(t)$ is the upper bound for the activation function, $\Xi_i = [\rho^2 \ \alpha^2 \ \|e_v\|^2 \ \left\|\tilde{\Theta}\right\|^2]$, $K_i = [\bar{k}_1 \ \bar{k}_2 \ \bar{k}_3 \ \kappa]$ with $\bar{k}_1 = \cos^2\alpha$, $\bar{k}_2 = \rho$, $\bar{k}_3 = K_v$:

$$K_{ET} = \begin{bmatrix} -\cos\alpha\left(\rho + \alpha^2 + k_\beta\beta^2\right) & -2\alpha\rho \\ +2\alpha\sin\alpha + \sin\alpha & \end{bmatrix}, E_{ET} = \begin{bmatrix} \varepsilon_v \\ \varepsilon_\omega \end{bmatrix}.$$

Using the event-sampling condition (11) in (A7), we get $\dot{L} \leq -KE + K_{ET}\mu E + B$ Choosing $\mu = 1/K_{ET}$, the Lyapunov derivative is further simplified such that $\dot{L} \leq -(K-1)E + B$. It can be seen that the regulation and velocity tracking errors and NN weight estimation errors are bounded during the inter-event period since the unknown NN weights are not updated, they remain constant during the inter-event period.

References

1. Tabuada, P.: Event-triggered real-time scheduling of stabilizing control tasks. IEEE Trans. Autom. Control **52**(9), 1680–1685 (2007)
2. Sahoo, A., Xu, H., Jagannathan, S.: Near optimal event-triggered control of nonlinear discrete-time systems using neuro-dynamic programming. IEEE Trans. Neural Netw. Learn. Syst. **27**(9), 1801–1815 (2016)
3. Zhong, X., Ni, Z., He, H., Xu, X., Zhao, D.: Event-triggered reinforcement learning approach for unknown nonlinear continuous-time system. In: International Joint Conference on Neural Networks (IJCNN), pp. 3677–3684 (2014)
4. Guinaldo, M., Lehmann, D., Sanchez, J., Dormido, S., Johansson, K.H.: Distributed event-triggered control with network delays and packet losses. In: Annual Conference on Decision and Control (CDC), pp. 1–6 (2012)
5. Wang, X., Lemmon, M.D.: Event-triggering in distributed networked control systems. IEEE Trans. Autom. Control **56**(3), 586–601 (2011)
6. Molin, A., Hirche, S.: On the optimality of certainty equivalence for event-triggered control systems. IEEE Trans. Autom. Control **58**(2), 470–474 (2013)
7. Chen, X., Hao, F., Ma, B.: Periodic event-triggered cooperative control of multiple non-holonomic wheeled mobile robots. IET Control Theory Appl. **11**(6), 890–899 (2017)
8. Yilong, Q., Fei, C., Linying, X.: Distributed event-triggered control for coupled nonholonomic mobile robots. In: 34th Chinese Control Conference (CCC), pp. 1268–1273 (2015)
9. Lewis, F.L., Dawson, D.M., Abdallah, C.T.: Robot Manipulator Control: Theory and Practice. CRC Press (2003)
10. Miah, S., Chaoui, H., Sicard, P.: Linear time-varying control law for stabilization of hopping robot during flight phase. In: 23rd International Symposium on Industrial Electronics (ISIE), pp. 1550–1554 (2014)
11. Guzey, H.M., Dierks, T., Jagannathan, S., Acar, L.: Hybrid consensus based control of nonholonomic mobile robot formation. J. Intell. Rob. Syst. **88**(1), 181–200 (2017)

12. Dierks, T. and Jagannathan, S.: Neural network output feedback control of robot formations. IEEE Trans. Syst. Man Cybern. Part B (Cybern.) **40**(2), 383–399 (2010)
13. Güzey, H.M.: Adaptive event-triggered regulation control of nonholonomic mobile robots. In: Ghommam, J., Derbel, N., Zhu, Q. (eds.) New Trends in Robot Control. SSDC, vol. 270, pp. 177–188. Springer, Singapore (2020). https://doi.org/10.1007/978-981-15-1819-5_9

Development of a Multi-sensor Emotional Response System for Social Robots

Estilla Hefter[1], Charlotte Perry[1], Nicholas Coiro[1], Harry Parsons[1], Shuo Zhu[1], and Chunxu Li[1,2(✉)]

[1] Center for Robotics and Neural Systems, Plymouth University, Plymouth, UK
{estilla.hefter,charlotte.perry,nicholas.coiro,
harry.parsons}@students.plymouth.ac.uk,
{shuo.zhu,chunxu.li}@plymouth.ac.uk
[2] College of Automation and Electronic Engineering,
Qingdao University of Science and Technology, Qindgao, China

Abstract. Loneliness is a significant and prevalent public health issue. To combat this, many social intervention agents have been developed the majority of these systems limit themselves to one emotional categorization system and as a result, lack a complex emotional understanding of the user. This paper has created a novel system for use in companion robots. By using sensor fusion of touch-sensitive fur and computer vision technology it determines the emotional state of the user. Combining these sensor inputs help deepen the estimate of the emotional state of the user and allows for the system to predict more complex emotions. This paper is aimed to help create a companion robot that responds to the user in a sympathetic way that will best create a positive response in the user. As an additional result, the achieved touch classification accuracy was found high enough to show promise for this innovative approach to touch sensing in the future.

Keywords: Social robotics · Sensor fusion · Emotion recognition · Fur sensor · Empathetic response

1 Introduction

Loneliness has become a major public health issue. Demographic trends show that the number of people aged 50 and over who are experiencing loneliness is increasing. The number is predicted to reach 2.03 million in 2025/26 compared to the 1.36 million measured in 2016/17, showing a 49% increase in the UK, over the last 10 years [22]. While it is not a direct cause, loneliness has been shown to have a correlation with malnutrition [9], sleep problems and depression [20]. Loneliness in older adults has been an important issue long before this year but with the lockdowns and social isolation measures, the scientific community is expecting an increase in the number of people experiencing loneliness [7]. Many kinds of social support intervention methods have been developed but these

A. Ronzhin et al. (Eds.): ICR 2021, LNAI 12998, pp. 88–99, 2021.
https://doi.org/10.1007/978-3-030-87725-5_8

may not always be available or desirable. One method that has been suggested is Animal Assisted therapy (AAT) and Pet Ownership (PO). Studies showed that petting animals can reduce anxiety and spending regular time with pets has long-term mental health benefits [21]. This method, however, raises multiple patient safety issues [16]. Infections, phobias, allergies, or other animal-caused injuries are the four main issues surrounding pet therapy [5,6]. Care homes that have allergic patients might have to op-out of this method completely to guarantee no allergic reactions due to cross-contamination. Artificial agents can present an innovative alternative to these issues in social care.

Studies showed that social intervention or companion robots can help reduce the feeling of loneliness either through direct interactions or by initiating conversations between the users themselves [19]. It is important that a robot like this is able to recognize the user's emotional state and respond accordingly. By doing this, the robot can avoid making the user feel uncomfortable, help avoid conflicts and work towards creating meaningful connections with the user. Many companion robots exist currently on the market. One notable example is Paro^{TM} [2], a companion intended for a medical environment in the form of a baby seal. The unfamiliarity of a seal's appearance offers enough of a barrier to prevent the robot from entering the uncanny valley but does not offer any expressive features due to its realism. The robot is equipped with tactile and posture sensors that allow its behaviour to change based on user input and handling, but the software is focused on mimicking basic animalistic behaviour rather than predicting the user's emotional state and responding to it. This is an issue many other social robots have on the market today. Most of them only rely on tactile/touch sensors [1] and while the most commonly used types of touch sensors, Force Sensitive Resistors, are great for detecting the presence of the user's touch, it in itself is unable to categorize different types of gestures. While some applications utilise different methods like facial emotion detection [8] or sound analysis [14] and combine the inputs, these systems tend to limit themselves to a handful of basic emotions such as positive or negative user state [14].

With these limitations in place, the robots are unable to predict the user's emotions and provide an accurate socio-emotional response the user would expect. This work presented seeks to offer a subsystem as a solution to these issues. The contribution of this paper could be concluded as follows:

1. The Multi-sensor Emotional Response System (MERS) offers a modular solution to allow artificial social agents to combine incoming user data from multiple sensors and thus recognize complex user emotions.
2. This also allows future robots to provide more empathetic responses to the users and help create connections with them.
3. The integration of different techniques, e.g. deep learning, computer vision, sensing processes, touch feedback and object detection, should never be underestimated.

2   Methodologies

The proposed system is built upon 3 subsystems: a facial emotion detection system, a touch recognition system, and a sensor fusion system that outputs appropriate responses. This system combines information gained from a vision-based emotion recognition system and a fur fabric that recognises when and how it's being touched. Combining this information, the robot will be able to decide on an empathetic response and express that to the user. The sensor systems will be discussed to demonstrate how they work, how the systems were validated, and the considerations made in their development.

2.1   Emotion Detection

The facial emotion detection system is a core part of sensor processing in this overall system. It takes a camera input and parses the data, detecting a human face (if present), recognising the emotion the face displays, and outputting the detected emotion. The emotion detection system is adapted from Github user Atul Balaji's system [4]. With the emotion recognition system remaining largely intact, the output and file reading systems were changed to allow for the easy addition of new emotions and training data, as well as easier integration with the output middleware. The recognition process involves a series of steps. The first step is facial detection, followed by emotion estimation, and finally, emotion classification.

In order to track the user's emotion, the software has to track the user's face. The software uses a Haar cascade to do this. Haar cascades have the benefits of being very lightweight and almost real-time in processing, however, they have the drawback of only recognizing front-on images. However, for a social system that will be used for interaction, front on eye contact can be assumed. In addition to this, in future applications, integrated into a social robot, the robot will be able to move the camera. After the Haar cascade detects a face, it draws a rectangle around it. The pixels within this rectangle are made grayscale and dropped to the resolution of 48 × 48, the resolution that the emotion classifier uses, and fed into the emotion classifier. In an attempt to generate a dataset for this application, the Flickr-Faces-HQ dataset of 70,000 faces was used [15].

The emotion classifier is a sequential neural network model from the tensorflow library. It is trained and validated from 48 × 48 grayscale images. The data can be changed by modifying the folders and contents within the training and testing folders. The emotions classified are labelled by the folder names in the training folder. The model stores its weights externally, meaning the model can be pre-trained before use. When a face is fed in from the Haar cascade, the classifier outputs a series of confidences for each emotion. Each confidence is a percentage that represents how closely the input image matches the model's internal structure of what that emotion is. The main output of this system is the emotion with the highest confidence. Figure 1 shows the proposed emotion detection system using CNN.

Fig. 1. Emotion detections.

2.2 Touch Detection

Touch is an important interaction type in social robotics. The use of the touch sensor can be used to help interpret the emotional state of the user by the use of determining aggressiveness or passivity of the user. The ability to touch the robot allows the user to build more of a connection with it and can increase their happiness while interacting [10,11,13]. The touch-sensitive fur is based on and inspired by Perner-Wilson and Satomi's design [12,18] and it's constructed from 3 materials; fur fabric, conductive thread and conductive fabric (shown in Fig. 2). Different prototypes of the fur were constructed and tested to determine the best format for this paper. Some of the different changes tested were density of the conductive threads, length of the threads and length of the fur strands on the fabric. The final fur touch sensor chosen and developed for this paper had a density of conductive threads of 1 thread bundle per cm^2. Each bundle is created by 3 threads looped through the fur material creating a 6 strand thread cluster.

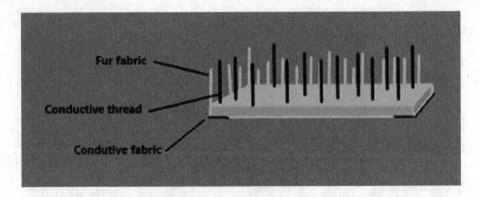

Fig. 2. Fur touch sensor construction.

The sensor created works by comparing changes in resistance from its resting position to when it is touched. When the user interacts with the sensor, the overlapping threads complete the circuit, giving a measurable current. This layout of the fur gave the most similar results each time it was tested and provided a system that allowed the identification of 5 types of touch with an additional "no interaction" state. The types of touch used in this paper were single directional stroke, multi-directional stroke, poke, pat and scratch. The final fur hardware is shown in Fig. 3.

A kind of microcontroller Arduino nano was selected as the device to measure the current and transmit the data to a PC. Using a known value resistor as a shunt, the Arduino measures the voltage across the fur sensor and converts that into a current value. As values are read, they are sent to the PC via Serial. PC integration software is modular in design. It had functions that would find the address of a given board, the next starts a serial link with the board, and finally reads an input number of samples and returns them as a list. The fur material used in this paper however was not ideal, as due to its density and static it tended to stick to and clump around the conductive threads, meaning they were unable to make contact with each other. For future development in this paper, different fur materials will need testing to determine the most appropriate kind. To classify the type of touch the user is giving, the gesture recognition module uses a Convolutional Neural Network (CNN). This type of network is generally used for image processing or classification. The network was highly inspired by Robinson et al. [12], used supervised learning and has been provided with a labelled data set consisting of 30+ recorded samples for each touch type. Each sample was recorded over 2 s, consisting of 400 recordings of the calculated current (mA) across the hardware. The data frame was collected using the fur touch sensor and a Python script.

Instead of using time series categorization, this module turns the data into the frequency domain. As the module's goal is to categorize periodic data with re-occurring patterns which are not limited to specific time frames, using the frequency domain, the module can highlight the patterns better and avoid over-

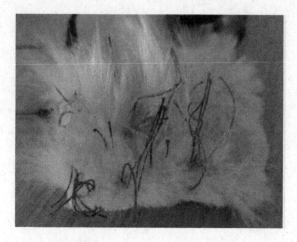

Fig. 3. Finalised touch detection hardware.

fitting the system. To do this, the system performs a Fourier transform in the samples before feeding them into either the training or the categorization module. Examples of the extracted, transformed and averaged touch patterns are shown in Fig. 4.

The network consists of 3 subsequent layer sets, each of which contain a convolution, batch normalisation and dense (ReLu) layer. The architecture is inspired by and based on Bagnall et al.'s paper [3]. The network uses a $1 \times 1 \times 400$ input layer. The number of epochs is set to 300 and batch size to 8. The output is an array of the confidence level of each case/touch type. After training the network had 99% of training and 93% of validation accuracy. The confidence graph is shown in Fig. 5.

2.3   Sensor Fusion System

The system developed in this study computes all of the data input via the touch detection and facial emotion recognition modules to produce an output that corresponds to the input. For a social robot the response of the robot is key to aiding interaction between the end user and the robot [17]. In the case of this system, this means programming an emotional response to the data received. The current system reads appropriate responses to inputs from a lookup table. The facial recognition algorithm inputs one part of the lookup table and the touch detection produces the other part. Each square of the table represents a response that will be output. An example of this would be that if the facial recognition noticed an angry look on the users face, and the touch recognition registered a harsh touch, it implies that the user is angry or annoyed. In this case, it is best for a social robot to attempt to calm the user. Therefore the output of the robot would be a calming response.

As the system developed during this paper is not a full working robot, the current output is simply an indication of what sort of response should be given.

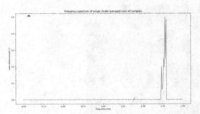

(a) : Frequency spectrum of the single stroke averaged over all samples

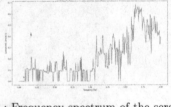

(b) : Frequency spectrum of the scratch averaged over all samples

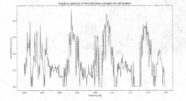

(c) : Frequency spectrum of the multi stroke averaged over all samples

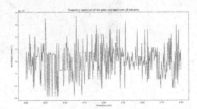

(d) : Frequency spectrum of the poke averaged over all samples

Fig. 4. Examples of the extracted and averaged touch patterns.

This is output, via terminal, and means that in future it will be possible to simply program a set of instructions to a robot with regards to each of the different responses. At this stage, the paper is ready to be built upon, there are several things that could be done. The main options are to build further upon this system in order to make it more reliable or suitable for a specific application not considered in this paper. The other is to use this system as a starting point to build a robot that can interact with humans with consideration for their emotional state (Table 1).

Table 1. The lookup table used by the middleware of MERS.

	Enjoy	Anger	Sadness	Neutral	Surprise	Fear	Disgust	None
Single Stroke	Playful	Confused	Nuzzle	Happy	Interest	Calm	Happy	Pleased
Multi-stroke	Contented	Confused	Nuzzle	Happy	Content	Calm	Happy	Pleased
Pat	Curious	Submissive	Comforting	Happy	Curious	Comforting	Curious	Nuzzle
Poke	Playful	Scared	Confused	Happy	Playful	Curious	Playful	Confused
Scratch	Happy	Scared	Nuzzle	Happy	Pleased	Relaxed	Happy	Relaxed
None	Enjoy	Submissive	Curious	Neutral	Surprise	Sad	Upset	No response

Systems that could be built on top of this one include new methods to detect emotion or other improvements such as detection of different emotions. These could be used to prepare the system for use in other types of social robots or for a specific use. The system could be modified for use with a different target audience, for example. It might be programmed to comprehend spoken instructions

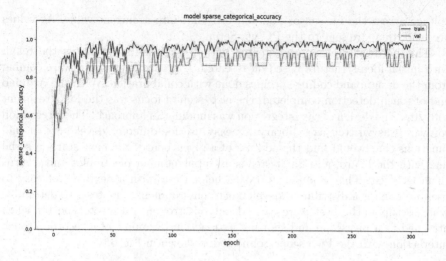

Fig. 5. Training and validation accuracy graph.

as well or understand tone of voice to more accurately detect emotion. Robots built on top of this system would need to be programmed with suitable actions allocated to each of the system's outputs. A basic design considered during this paper was a hamster with enlarged human-styled eyes, to avoid "the uncanny valley", and to allow for better emotional expressions, as humans comprehend a lot of emotion from the eyes. Other types of robots could also be built, using different animals as inspiration, or using different features to exhibit the emotions.

3   Experimental Studies

3.1   System Setup

The proposed final result of this paper is a system that combines two separate sensor inputs to determine the users emotional state and give an appropriate response to it. The two sensors consist of an emotion recognition system that uses a trained neural network to detect the facial emotion of the user and a fur touch sensor to determine the type of touch the user is applying. These combine in a logic table to produce an appropriate response to the inputs. While one part of the authors focused on the fur hardware and carried out the necessary testing, the other part could start development on the full modular sensor. A microcontroller was selected as the device to measure the current and transmit the data to a PC. The Arduino nano was the microcontroller selected as it offered a form factor smaller than the Lilypad used in our reference material and had the same capabilities of analogue voltage measuring. The Arduino code itself is simple. Using a known value resistor as a shunt, the Arduino measures the voltage across the fur sensor and converts that into a current value. As values are read, they are sent to the PC via Serial.

This hardware sensor was created with work distributed across the team, with initial idea structure based off research, reference for fur hardware coming from the design, and coding specifics done with collaboration. With the Arduino end of touch detection completed, the next step of focus was the PC's recipient software. The design of the integration was modular in approach. The integration software was written as a library for easy use for different developers. It had functions that would find the address of a given board, the next starts a serial link with the board, and finally reads an input number of samples and returns them as a list. This modular approach helped establish a flexible, yet easy to use, toolbox for a distributed development environment. The tests to determine which setup is the best were carried out by stroking the prototype fur when attached to a picoscope and showing its reaction. Example of a recorded touch interaction with the Pico scope connected is shown in Fig. 6.

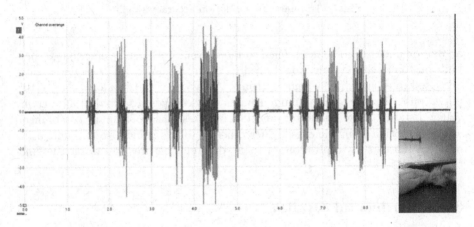

Fig. 6. Pico-scope measurements during a user interaction.

3.2   Analysis and Discussion

MERS brings together two forms of detection to create a robust and multifaceted system for generating responses to the user's emotional state. This section seeks to discuss the successes and limitations of MERS, discussing each component system and the integration of the two. As well as briefly discuss the future works that can be taken to further improve this approach to human-computer interaction. The touch sensor that MERS uses is a synthetic fur with conductive thread woven in at a density of 1 conductive thread per cm^2. The current across the thread is measured at a frequency 200 Hz over a 2 s interval. These 400 samples are transmitted as a table to a CNN to classify the touch types detected. The findings show the CNN to be a reliable way of classifying touch-type with a

99% training accuracy. Although, the training data has to be of good quality, and over a large number of samples to ensure that the classes can be properly defined. The fur sensor itself was capable of measuring touch types. The current was the best metric to measure touch type with the conductive thread method of touch sensing. However, the fur medium chosen was rather soft and delicate and had an issue with shedding, meaning the fur had to be brushed to clean the conductive threads. Further research into base fur material may help determine an optimal medium. The emotion recognition system uses a Haar cascade to detect a user's face and a CNN to classify the expression on the detected face. Using a pre-made solution has allowed for a functional framework that satisfactorily detects a user's emotion. The use of a Haar cascade offer's a low impact, high-speed solution for facial detection, allowing for very fast image processing for a live video feed. However, this form of facial detection is position and lighting dependant. With the speed of the touch sensor, a higher accuracy form of facial detection may be optimal. The data set used accurately measures many emotions but used some non-human faces. Further works into a natural expression data set may improve the accuracy of this system. The integration software works as a multi-threaded sampling process that gathers touch and expression data simultaneously. Gathering the 400 samples from the touch system and classifying them, and averaging the detected facial emotions detected over the two second window. The highest confidence result from each component system is applied to a truth table to determine the optimal response for the imaged emotional state. This system applies a simple solution to the problem of integration, but serves its purpose sufficiently. Relying on a two second window gives a more gradual response time to a change in emotional state, this allows for a more naturalistic response. A system rapidly adapting to changing emotional state, especially in the case of a false positive or negative, would give a robotic and unnatural feel to the system. **Future Work:** future work involving a social interaction robot could be used to generate bespoke datasets for emotion detection, touch detection and sensor fusion would allow for data gathered from real use cases. This data would benefit: (1)the overall accuracy of the system; (2) to gather emotion detection data, such as recognition rate/detection time, and touch detection data, such as touching gesture and duration, from the same source to give a single basis for labels in a sensor fusion.

4   Conclusion

In order to give meaningful responses to a user's emotional state, MERS integrates multiple systems of computer interactions. The computer vision system detects the visual expressions of the user, giving an estimate of the expressed emotions. The artificial fur sensor gives a deeper insight into the current state of the user, via their interactions with it. This combination gives a companion robot a more in-depth method for responding to a user. This approach can function if either system's input is unavailable, allowing for a robust system even if a more complex response is unavailable at the time. A demo video of the proposed MERS could be found from: https://youtu.be/m4qw6NatzPI.

References

1. Nao. robot (2008). https://www.softbankrobotics.com/emea/en/nao
2. AIST: Paro. robot (2001). http://www.parorobots.com/
3. Bagnall, A., Lines, J., Bostrom, A., Large, J., Keogh, E.: The great time series classification bake off: a review and experimental evaluation of recent algorithmic advances. Data Min. Knowl. Disc. **31**(3), 606–660 (2016). https://doi.org/10.1007/s10618-016-0483-9
4. Balaji, A.: Emotion detection using deep learning. https://github.com/atulapra/Emotion-detection (2020)
5. Bert, F., Gualano, M.R., Camussi, E., Pieve, G., Voglino, G., Siliquini, R.: Animal assisted intervention: a systematic review of benefits and risks. Eur. J. Integr. Med. **8**(5), 695–706 (2016). https://doi.org/10.1016/j.eujim.2016.05.005
6. Brodie, S.J., Biley, F.C., Shewring, M.: An exploration of the potential risks associated with using pet therapy in healthcare settings. J. Clin. Nurs. **11**(4) (2002). https://doi.org/10.1046/j.1365-2702.2002.00628.x
7. Brooke, J., Jackson, D.: Older people and COVID-19: Isolation, risk and ageism (2020)
8. Castellano, G., Leite, I., Pereira, A., Martinho, C., Paiva, A., Mcowan, P.: Affect recognition for interactive companions: challenges and design in real world scenarios. J. Multimodal User Interfaces **3**, 89–98 (2009). https://doi.org/10.1007/s12193-009-0033-5
9. Ferry, M., Sidobre, B., Lambertin, A., Barberger-Gateau, P.: The solinut study: analysis of the interaction between nutrition and loneliness in persons aged over 70 years. J. Nutr. Health Aging **9**, 261–268 (2005)
10. Field, T.: Touch for socioemotional and physical well-being: a review. Dev. Rev. **30**(4), 367–383 (2010). https://doi.org/10.1016/j.dr.2011.01.001
11. Field, T., et al.: Massage theraphy for infants of depressed mothers. Infant Behav. Dev. **19**(1), 107–112 (1996). https://doi.org/10.1016/s0163-6383(96)90048-x
12. Flagg, A., Tam, D., MacLean, K., Flagg, R: Conductive fur sensing for a gesture-aware furry robot. In: 2012 IEEE Haptics Symposium (HAPTICS) (2012). https://ieeexplore.ieee.org/document/6183776
13. Henricson, M., Berglund, A.L., Määttä, S., Ekman, R., Segesten, K.: The outcome of tactile touch on oxytocin in intensive care patients: a randomised controlled trial. J. Clin. Nurs. **17**(19), 2624–2633 (2008). https://doi.org/10.1111/j.1365-2702.2008.02324.x
14. Le Tallec, M., Antoine, J.Y., Villaneau, J., Duhaut, D.: Affective interaction with a companion robot for hospitalized children: a linguistically based model for emotion detection. In: 5th Language and Technology Conference (LTC 2011), Poznan, Poland, p. 6 p., November 2011. https://hal.archives-ouvertes.fr/hal-00664618
15. Lehtinen, J., Luebke, D., Kynkäänniem, T., Hellsten, J., Kuosmanen, T., Jänis, P.: Flickr-Faces-HQ Dataset (FFHQ)—Kaggle. Technical report (2017)
16. Li, C., Yang, C., Giannetti, C.: Segmentation and generalisation for writing skills transfer from humans to robots. Cogn. Comput. Syst. **1**(1), 20–25 (2019)
17. Li, C., Yang, C., Wan, J., Annamalai, A., Cangelosi, A.: Neural learning and Kalman filtering enhanced teaching by demonstration for a baxter robot. In: 2017 23rd International Conference on Automation and Computing (ICAC), pp. 1–6. IEEE (2017)
18. Perner-Wilson, H., Satomi, M.: Diy wearable technology (2009). http://agamanolis.com/distancelab/database/publications/Perner-Wilson.09.DIY.ISEA.pdf

19. Robinson, H., MacDonald, B., Kerse, N., Broadbent, E.: The psychosocial effects of a companion robot: a randomized controlled trial. J. Am. Med. Direct. Assoc. **14**(9), 661–667 (2013). https://doi.org/10.1016/j.jamda.2013.02. 007. https://www.sciencedirect.com/science/article/pii/S1525861013000972

20. Singh, A., Misra, N.: Loneliness, depression and sociability in old age. Ind. Psychiatry J. **18**(1) (2009). https://doi.org/10.4103/0972-6748.57861

21. Souter, M., Miller, M.: Do animal-assisted activities effectively treat depression? A meta-analysis. Anthrozoos: Multidisc. J. Interact. People Animals **20**, 167–180 (2007). https://doi.org/10.2752/175303707X207954

22. Varrenti, E.: All the lonely people. Big Issue Aust. **560**, 22–23 (2018)

A Technique to Provide an Efficient System Recovery in the Fog- and Edge-Environments of Robotic Systems

Anna Klimenko[1]([⊠]) and Igor Kalyaev[2]

[1] Scientific Research Institute of Multiprocessor Computer Systems of Southern Federal University, 2, Chekhov Street, 347928 Taganrog, Russian Federation
[2] Southern Federal University, 105/42 Bolshaya Sadovaya Street, 344006 Rostov-on-Don, Russia

Abstract. Considering the issues of the fog- and edge-robotics, a problem of the computations in the dynamic environment is quite relevant. Due to the dynamics of the devices, which perform computations (e.g., edge learning for assistive robots), frequent application migrations take place (in this paper they are considered as system recovery procedure). We consider a problem of such migrations as the reliability one: when the time of system recovery increases, the less time remains for the functional tasks processing under the conditions of the fixed operation time. It leads to the reliability or QoS degrading. The reducing of the recovery time by means of the workload increase leads to the nodes reliability degrading as well. Also, due to the dynamics of the computational environment there is no possibility to plan the reconfiguration procedures relating to the functional tasks processing. In the current paper a novel technique is proposed to improve the reliability function of the computational nodes by means of the choice of the nodes monitoring and control strategy. According to the environmental peculiarities, the appropriate monitoring and control method is chosen, which provides the minimum of the time and workload for the nodes.

Keywords: Edge robotics · Fog robotics · Reconfiguration · Efficiency

1 Introduction

Nowadays the fog- and edge-robotics have become an efficient mechanism to provide robots with low-latency computational data processing services. The low-latency data preprocessing is of a high importance for such robotics areas as assistive robots, mobile robots, robot swarms and many others.

The transformation from the cloud robotics to the fog- and edge- robotics has emerged from the intersection of fog-computing and the robotics. It enhances the capabilities of the end-point robots, improves the system latency, network load and security. Besides, the intersection of the robotics and MEC (multi-access edge computing) and the robotics relates to such concept, as the "Follow Me" one. "Follow me" concept [1] considers terms such as Follow Me Cloud, Follow Me Edge, Follow Me Edge Cloud, Follow Me

A. Ronzhin et al. (Eds.): ICR 2021, LNAI 12998, pp. 100–112, 2021.
https://doi.org/10.1007/978-3-030-87725-5_9

Fog, Move with Me, Companion Fog Computing. The key idea of this field is that the migration of the virtual machines, or containers, or processes are presupposed to the appropriate nodes of the edge (fog) to follow the end-point application in the angle of its geographical position.

The concepts mentioned, as well as the feature of high dynamics of the edge and of the fog, have brought a novel peculiarity to the computational processes in such environments: the reconfiguration processes become more frequent, because of the need to relocate the data processing services not due to the fog- or edge- nodes failures, but due to the new requirements to the node resources, or due to the lack of energy on the mobile node, or due to the turning the device off or being out of the data transmission range, etc.

The frequency of the reconfigurations in the fog is emphasized in studies [2–4], as well as the problem, which emerges under these new conditions. Considering possibly high frequency of the reconfigurations in the fog (edge), and the application down-times, which accompany the application relocations, the issue of the Quality of Service provisioning is relative and up-to-date [4].

It must be mentioned that in some studies the question of the system reconfiguration is considered as well as some comprehensive reviews on the problem are presented. Yet, the question of the fog- and edge nodes reliability is out of the consideration.

The current paper considers the reconfiguration in the fog/edge as a computational procedure, which emerges spontaneously and brings some extra computational workload on the nodes. Besides, the time of reconfiguration is important in the focus of the QoS for the user(robot) application. Considering the reconfiguration task as the computational one, which has to choose the new nodes for processes relocation, such task includes the workload distribution task with the input data as some nodes, which must be chosen in the fog. The time of these procedures could be reduced by the workload increase on the other nodes, but such approach decreases the reliability function dramatically and potentially leads to the nodes failure rate increase.

In this paper a new technique is presented to improve the reconfiguration efficiency from the reliability angle. It is based on the choice of the appropriate methods of the nodes monitoring and control, which can reduce the system recovery time and so to improve the reliability function of the nodes, meeting the QoS requirements.

2 Edge- and Fog-Computing Applications in the Robotics Field

Edge computing or Multi-Access Edge Computing (MEC) generally handles the processing of data where data is created, avoiding the need to process the data in the cloud. Edge-computing provides advantages in the following example cases [5]:

- Autonomous connected vehicles functioning. Self-driving cars learn without constant connection to the cloud to process data, but use the computational capabilities of other edge-nodes nearby.
- Predictive maintenance in the robot complexes. Edge computing can help detect machines that are in danger of breaking, and find the right fix before they do and in the shortest time delay.

- Supporting of the fog architecture. Fog computing refers to a distributed computing model, in which edge (peripheral) devices are used as terminals for computing.

Fog computing is an architecture that defines how edge computing should be organized, and delivers the data preprocessing, as well as data storage.

Fog computing extends the concept of cloud computing to the network edge and utilizes the local computer resources rather than accessing remote computer resources causing a decrease of latency issues and performance further making it more powerful and efficient.

Fog computing delivers the following advantages [6]:

- The Reduce of data volume which should be sent to cloud.
- The network latency reduce.
- Supports mobility.
- Conserves network bandwidth.
- Improves system response time.

Another important example of the edge- and fog-computing application to the robotics is the concept of the Internet of Robotic Things [7, 8]. This concept concerns the integration of two areas: Smart Space and Robotics. Smart Space considers such subareas as Smart Room, Smart Factory, Smart City, etc. The applications mentioned are used to monitor states and processes in the defined areas. Also some other functions are used: temperature and air humidity correction, managing power consumption, controlling the human presence, etc.

Yet, despite of having simple sensors and actuators, Smart Space does not consider mobile agents presence, which could perform some service actions. The mobile agents considered are the assistive robots, manipulators, service robots. It must be mentioned, that the Smart Space and Robotics integration expands the capabilities of those considerably: robots have the access to the sensors environment of the Smart Place, while the latter expands its functional variability.

Also, a lot of other examples of fog- and edge- computing integration with the robotics do exist:

- In [9], a cost-efficient strategy is proposed to implement a deep learning at the edge.
- In [10], the robots learning procedure is implemented by means of the edge computing concept.
- And many others, including such areas, as Human-robot interaction, which needs the modeling of the human-robot space interaction [11, 12].

Summing up, the integration of the robotics field and the fog- and edge-computing paradigms, on the one hand extends the capabilities of the robots, on the other hand, involves the edge and fog computational nodes to the intensive computational tasks processing (e.g., learning procedures). From this moment the reconfigurations among the computational edge- and fog-nodes plays quite an important role: as the reconfigurations are frequent and unpredictable in the dynamic environments, the consumed time can affect the quality of the computational tasks results, user's Quality of Service and nodes reliability, when the time of the functional tasks processing reduces increasing the nodes workload. So, the reduce of the reconfiguration time can improve the efficiency of the computations.

3 Reconfiguration and Its Effect on the Nodes Reliability Function

Consider a reconfiguration as a computational procedure, which implements the tasks relocation from the faulted nodes to the operational ones. In this paper, we consider the node failure as a particular state, when the node cannot participate the task processing due to any reasons. Failure detection procedure precedes the reconfiguration. The sum of the failure detection and of the reconfiguration times determines the time of system recovery.

The frequency of the reconfigurations in the fog- and edge-environments can be quite high. Although there are little live examples in the literature, we found some. For instance, a good example of possible reconfigurations frequency is given in [1]: "The street environment is based on a linear highway scenario of 3.6 km long with three road segments; each segment is two-lane and 1 km long. For the mobile network environment, the eNodeBs are located along the highway and are separated by a distance of 0.35 km in such a way that each eNodeB covers a zone of 0.5 km of the highway". So, assuming the speed of vehicle movement as 60 km/h, the reconfiguration within the concept of the "Follow-me-edge" can take place approximately 5 times per 3,6 min, and, hence, up to 1583 times per 24 h. It must be mentioned that in the paper [1] the example which relates to the Virtual Machine Migration problem is considered, yet this is an example of the cases when the reconfiguration takes place not due to the nodes failure only, but because of the highly dynamic environment.

Consider then that some computational tasks are processed on the fog- or edge-nodes, and there is a predetermined time period, in which the computational tasks must be solved to provide the appropriate level of the QoS. So, the reducing of the system recovery time affects the task solving time and, consequently, the solution quality. Also, if the workload generated by the computational tasks can be distributed through the available time, the possibility of the nodes workload decrease emerges, which causes a positive effect on the nodes reliability functions. Further we presuppose that the efficiency of the reconfiguration procedure is determined by the reliability function value in the end of the operation time period.

Yet, the time of system recovery can be reduced in different ways:

- by the intensive computations in a shorter time periods;
- by the parallelization of the computations;
- and, as it is proposed in the current paper, by the usage of combinations of particular methods of the system monitoring and reconfiguration, which allows to improve the efficiency of the system recovery in the angle of the nodes reliability function.

Indeed, consider the situation when configuration tasks are processed by computational nodes with high workload, while the remainder of the time the nodes work in operational regime. Then, the process can be described by the following scheme (Fig. 1):

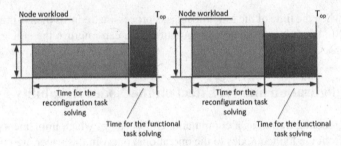

Fig. 1. Reconfiguration and functional tasks time distribution.

Consider the reliability function of the node in a way presented by the Eq. (1).

$$P(t) = e^{\int_o^t -\lambda(t)dt} = e^{\int_0^{xTop} -\lambda_1 dt + \int_{xTop}^{Top} -\lambda_2 dt} = e^{-\lambda_1 xTop} \cdot e^{-\lambda_2(1-x)Top}, \quad (1)$$

where λ_1 is the failure rate of the node with the workload of the reconfiguration task solving; λ_2 is the failure rate of the node with the workload of the functional task solving; x is the share of time for the reconfiguration task solving; T_{op} is the declared operation time. Consider W_1 and W_2 as the computational complexities of the reconfiguration and of the functional task. Then, the reliability function of the node is described as:

$$P(T_{op}) = e^{-\lambda_1 xTop} \cdot e^{-\lambda_2(1-x)Top} = e^{-\lambda_0 \cdot 2^{\frac{dW_1}{xTop*p*10}} *xTop} * e^{-\lambda_0 \cdot 2^{\frac{dW_2}{(1-x)Top*p*10}}(1-x)Top}. \quad (2)$$

Consider the case of the increase of the reconfiguration time share ($x = 0.1...0.9$), and the computational complexity of the functional tasks is much bigger than the computational complexity of the reconfiguration task. Then, the following graph is conducted, as is shown in Fig. 2. The time of the functional tasks solving is critical for the nodes reliability.

Then consider the case, when the overall computational complexity of the reconfigurations grows while the time of the reconfigurations is a constant (when we try to reconfigure the system in a short time period by means of the computational workload increase). So, it is seen that the best reliability function values are for the minimal reconfiguration time and minimal workload, generated by the reconfiguration.

The next graph (Fig. 4) demonstrates that the attempt to set the reconfiguration of the constant computational complexity to the small time period leads to the overall decrease of the reliability function value (Fig. 3).

So, analyzing the graphs, the following conclusions can be made:

- the reliability function of the node can be increased by means of the decrease of the reconfiguration time;
- yet, there are cases, when the attempt to minimize the time of reconfiguration is a cause of the reliability function degrading;
- at the edge and in the fog it is extremely hard to provide the reconfiguration plan, so, besides the theoretical possibility to model the optimal reconfiguration time, it is hardly possible in practice under conditions of the highly dynamic environment.

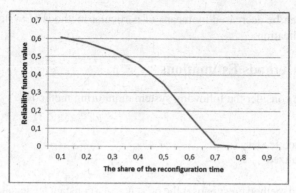

Fig. 2. The reliability function influenced by the reconfiguration time.

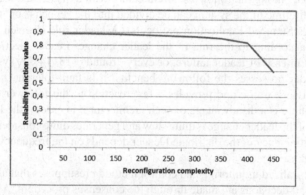

Fig. 3. The node reliability function influenced by the reconfiguration complexity.

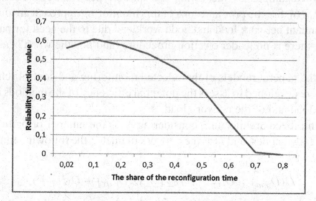

Fig. 4. The degrading of the reliability function affected by the reconfiguration time minimization.

The latter determines the general approach to the efficient reconfiguration procedure: under conditions of the uncertainty of the reconfigurations frequency and duration, the recovery time can be decreased by means of particular methods of system monitoring and control application.

4 Control Methods Estimations

In this paper we consider the following system monitoring methods:

- centralized;
- with distributed leader;
- fully decentralized.

A centralized method presupposes the presence of a constant leader and its followers. The leader stays itself through the lifetime of the system and handles all the changes, which take place among the followers. Architecture with a distributed leader differs in a way that the lifetime of the system can be divided into the "epochs" or "rounds" (e.g., RAFT and ViewStamped Replication protocols). A leader role is given to each node consequently, according to the rule of the leader change. Leader election procedure can be applied in case of leader failure, or every "round" [13, 14]. A system with the distributed leader possesses the following benefits: it is fault-tolerant, non-redundant in sense of network traffic and provides a fast reaction to the follower configuration changes. Yet, there is a disadvantage of such architecture: in case of the leader failure, the procedure of the leader change is quite slow and generates quite considerable network load. So, the proficiency of the distributed leader depends on the frequency of the leader election procedure.

Fully decentralized monitoring and control method presupposes that all participants are equal, and all decisions are made through the consensus procedure. As we consider the leaderless set of participants, a consensus should be leaderless as well, which can be provided, for example, by the voting consensus types (PBFT, Swirlds Hashgraph algorithm) [15, 16]. So, the pros and cons of this monitoring approach are quite obvious: there is a redundant network load and node workload due to the need for participants to communicate, there is no leader election procedure (and no "the worst" cases of leader election).

Based on the general models of the selected monitoring and control schemes, some estimations were developed to assess the potential efficiency of the methods in the angles of nodes workload and of the network load.

For the centralized architecture, considering N as the number of participants, F as the number of failed nodes, and D as the network diameter, the following time estimation is proposed:

$$O(D_{min}) + O(N - F) \leq t \leq O(D_{max}) + O(N-F). \tag{3}$$

Indeed, to detect failure the leader must to gather the messages from all followers, to check the list of active nodes and to make a conclusion about the absent nodes.

For the distributed leader the following estimation gas been made:

$$O(D_{min}) + O(N - F) \leq t \leq 2O(D_{max}) + 2(N - F)O((D_{max}) + O(N - F). \tag{4}$$

I.e., the detection of the follower failure includes:

– failure detection made by leader in case of the follower failure;
– leader failure detection and leader change procedure in case of the leader failure.

Fully decentralized monitoring approach presupposes the following estimation of the failure detection time:

$$2O(D_{max}) + O(NF) < t < K(2O(D_{max}) + O(NF)). \tag{5}$$

An operation of the failure detection includes the consensus on the failed nodes for all participants. Yet, there can be situations, where the consensus is impossible (split voting). Then, the operation has to be repeated (coefficient K in the equation).

Turning to the estimations of the computational complexity of the failure detection, the following estimations were developed.

For the centralized approach the computational complexity of the failure detection concludes the following and consists in the nodes list analysis:

$$A_{min} = k; \; A_{max} = k(N-F-1), \tag{6}$$

where F is the number of the failed nodes; N is the number of nodes before the failure; A_{min} is estimation of the minimal computational complexity; A_{max} is estimation of the maximum computational complexity; V_{data} is the context data value.

The computational complexities for the approaches with the distributed leader and for the fully distributed approach are as follows:

$$K < A < 2k(N-F-1) + 2b(N-F-1)V_{context}, \tag{7}$$

$$A = 2k(N-F-1) + 2b(N-F-1) + k(N-F). \tag{8}$$

And, finally, the computational complexity of the information exchange for approaches with the distributed leader and for the fully decentralized approach per node are as follows:

$$A_{leader} = O(2(N - 1)), \tag{9}$$

$$A_f = O(2), \tag{10}$$

$$A_d = O(2(N - 1)). \tag{11}$$

The following graphs (Fig. 5, 6 and 7) illustrate the results of simulation.

One can see that the approach with the distributed leader is quite efficient in case when the leader failures are rare, while the decentralized approach can be more proficient in cases of relatively small number of nodes and frequent reconfigurations.

Then, if we place the developed estimations into the node reliability function estimations, the following graph can be generated (Fig. 8).

These estimations show that with the operational functioning time increase (0.1–0.9) the efficiency of the decentralized method decreases (P_node) due to the redundant

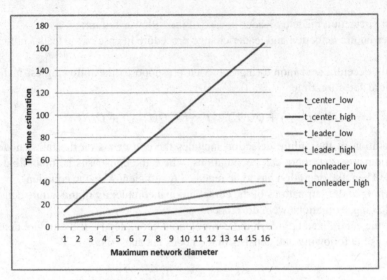

Fig. 5. Failure detection time dependent on the D_{max}.

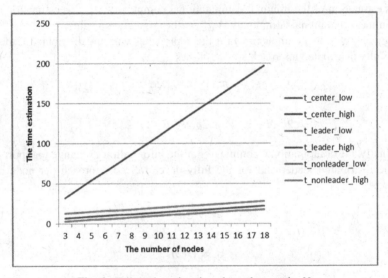

Fig. 6. Failure detection time dependent on the N.

monitoring information exchange. The distributed leader-based monitoring approach is efficient when only followers fails, or the failures of the leader is seldom because of the leader change procedure. So, the distributed leader-based monitoring method is efficient in the conditions of the relatively stable environment or if there is a possibility to set the leader to the stable nodes.

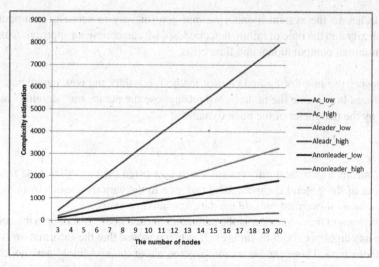

Fig. 7. Failure detection complexity dependent on the N.

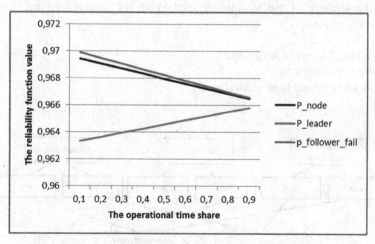

Fig. 8. Reliability function values affected by the operational time value.

5   A Technique to Provide an Efficient System Recovery

Considering the results generated in the previous sections, the following important conclusions must be made:

- decreasing the reconfiguration time, we can improve the efficiency of the system functioning. Yet, it is hardly possible to predict and to plan reconfigurations in the dynamic environments;

- approaches to the system monitoring and control vary in sense of computational complexity and the time of failure detection, so, we can choose an appropriate method with minimal computational and time costs.

Choosing the monitoring and control method, consider the new parameter, which characterizes how stable the node is. We presuppose the parameter "stability" as the 1 divided by the parameter of the node dynamics:

$$S = 1/d, \tag{12}$$

where d means a statistical information about how often the particular node failed the processing of the general computational task due to the various reasons from the node failures to node movement outside the data transmission range.

To implement the estimation of the parameter S, each node, initiating in the network, asks for its neighbors about its failures. It is presupposed that the information is saved in the nodes logs. There can be no information about the absolutely new node, so, it receives S of a biggest value: $S = 1$. Further, in case of failures (movements), these changes are written to the nodes logs changing the value of S.

So, the strategy of the monitoring method choice depends on the following parameters:

- the number of nodes in the group;
- "stability" parameter S;
- network velocity and bandwidth (Fig. 9).

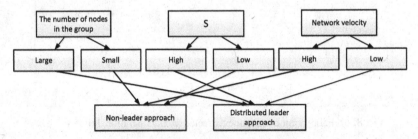

Fig. 9. The strategy choice based on the network and device features.

In general, the final strategy choice depends on the sum of factors, entering into each strategy block.

6 Conclusions

This paper is an effort to improve the efficiency of the system recovery procedure for the unstable and dynamic environments, such as fog and edge of the network applying to robotics. Under the conditions of uncertain reconfigurations and their number, it is almost impossible to model and estimate the workload plan to improve the nodes reliability. So, we propose the approach to its improvement by means of the appropriate monitoring and control method choice.

Summing up, the main contribution of this paper is: it has been shown that the relation between the time of the functional tasks processing and the total time of the reconfigurations affects the node reliability.

However, the estimations have shown the ambiguous results: the approach with the distributed leader can give brilliant results only if very few reconfigurations are produced by the leader failure. The non-leader monitoring is worse than the distributed leader-based method in the sense of network load and redundancy, but, due to the leader absence, there is no leader election procedure. So, the non-leader monitoring strategy can be preferably used when the network velocity is high and the environment is dynamic.

Acknowledgement. The reported study was funded by RFBR according to the research project №. 18-29-03229, №. 19-07-00907.

References

1. Aissioui, A., Ksentini, A., Gueroui, A., Taleb, T.: On enabling 5G automotive systems using follow me edge-cloud concept. IEEE Trans. Veh. Technol. 1 (2018). https://doi.org/10.1109/TVT.2018.2805369
2. Fan, Ch., Li, L.: Service migration in mobile edge computing based on reinforcement learning. J. Phys.: Conf. Ser. (2020). https://doi.org/10.1088/1742-6596/1584/1/012058
3. Wang, S., Xu, J., Zhang, N., Liu, Y.: A survey on service migration in mobile edge computing. IEEE Access **6**, 23511–23528 (2018). https://doi.org/10.1109/ACCESS.2018.2828102
4. Puliafito, C., Vallati, C., Mingozzi, E., Merlino, G., Longo, F., Puliafito, A.: Container migration in the fog: a performance evaluation. Sensors **19**, 1488 (2019). https://doi.org/10.3390/s19071488
5. Afanasyev, I., et al.: Towards the internet of robotic things: analysis, architecture, components and challenges. In: 2th International Conference on Developments in eSystems Engineering (DeSE), pp. 3–8 (2019). https://doi.org/10.1109/DeSE.2019.00011
6. Kehoe, B., Patil, S., Abbeel, P., Goldberg, K.: A survey of research on cloud robotics and automation. IEEE Trans. Autom. Sci. Eng. **12**(2), 398–409 (2015)
7. Romeo, L., Petitti, A., Marani, R., Milella, A.: Internet of robotic things in smart domains: applications and challenges. Sensors **20**(12), 3355 (2020). https://doi.org/10.3390/s20123355
8. Bajeh, A.O., et al.: Internet of robotic things: its domain, methodologies, and applications. In: Singh, K.K., Nayyar, A., Tanwar, S., Abouhawwash, M. (eds.) Emergence of Cyber Physical System and IoT in Smart Automation and Robotics. ASTI, pp. 135–146. Springer, Cham (2021). https://doi.org/10.1007/978-3-030-66222-6_9
9. Boschi, A., Francesco, S., Vittorio, M., Marcello, Ch.: A cost-effective person-following system for assistive unmanned vehicles with deep learning at the edge. Machines **8**(49) (2020). https://doi.org/10.3390/machines8030049
10. Tanwani, A.K., Mor, N., Kubiatowicz, J., Gonzalez, J.E., Goldberg, K.: A fog robotics approach to deep robot learning: application to object recognition and grasp planning in surface decluttering. In: 2019 International Conference on Robotics and Automation (ICRA), pp. 4559–4566 (2019). https://doi.org/10.1109/ICRA.2019.8793690

11. Galin, R., Meshcheryakov, R., Samoshina, A.: Mathematical modelling and simulation human-robot collaboration, pp. 1058–1062 (2020). https://doi.org/10.1109/RusAutoCon49 822.2020.9208040
12. Galin, R., Meshcheryakov, R., Kamesheva, S.: Distributing tasks in multi-agent robotic system for human-robot interaction applications. In: Ronzhin, A., Rigoll, G., Meshcheryakov, R. (eds.) ICR 2020. LNCS (LNAI), vol. 12336, pp. 99–106. Springer, Cham (2020). https://doi.org/10.1007/978-3-030-60337-3_10
13. Oki, B.M.: Viewstamped replication for highly available distributed systems. Technical report. Massachusetts Institute of Technology, USA (1988)
14. Howard, H., Mortier, R.: Paxos vs. Raft: have we reached consensus on distributed consensus? pp. 1–9 (2020). https://doi.org/10.1145/3380787.3393681
15. Akhtar, Z.: From blockchain to hashgraph: distributed ledger technologies in the wild, pp. 1–6 (2019). https://doi.org/10.1109/UPCON47278.2019.8980029
16. Castro, M., Liskov, B.: Practical byzantine fault tolerance. In: OSDI (1999)

Development of Matrix of Combined Force and Proximity Sensors for Use in Robotics

Konstantin Krestovnikov⬤, Aleksei Erashov(✉) ⬤, and Aleksandr Bykov⬤

St. Petersburg Federal Research Center of the Russian Academy of Sciences (SPC RAS), 39, 14th Line, 199178 St. Petersburg, Russia
{k.krestovnikov,erashov.a}@iias.spb.su

Abstract. The paper presents the development of a matrix of combined force and proximity sensors of a capacitive type for use in robotics. The sensor has a simple structure, and is structurally composed of three layers, which makes it possible to manufacture the sensor with a small thickness. To produce the sensor, readily available materials and technologies are used. The developed interface circuit for signal processing of primary capacitive converters allows them to be combined into matrices of various configurations, where each converter is a matrix cell. The dimensions of the cells of the prototype matrix sensor used in the experiments is 12 × 12 mm, and its total thickness is 4.2 mm. In the experiments, the characteristics of the sample of the matrix of combined sensors were obtained by the approach of objects made of various materials, as well as the dependence of the output signal of the matrix sensor on the applied pressure force. The highest sensitivity to the proximity of the manufactured sensor array is observed in the range from 0 to 1.8 mm for both types of objects, while the sensitivity of the prototype to the approach of metal objects is on average greater than the sensitivity to the approach of objects made of non-conductive materials. The prototype of the matrix of combined sensors has a high sensitivity to the applied force in the area up to 10 N, while the matrix of sensors allows to unambiguously determine the force applied to the matrix cells up to 25 N. The developed solution can be used to control the gait of walking robots, as well as in manipulation systems to improve the process gripping and manipulating objects.

Keywords: Combined matrix sensor · Robotic sensors · Proximity and force measurement

1 Introduction

In modern robotics, the force-torque sensing of robots can be used to grasp objects and manipulate them [1], organization of a human-machine interface in cyber-physical systems [2], as well as for the implementation of algorithms for stable gait of anthropomorphic robots [3]. For these purposes, single pressure sensors or sensor matrices made up of separate pressure sensors can be used, with the help of which it is possible to obtain data on the pressure distribution over the surface covered by these sensors [4]. The use of sensor matrices allows to improve the accuracy of gripping objects for manipulators

© Springer Nature Switzerland AG 2021
A. Ronzhin et al. (Eds.): ICR 2021, LNAI 12998, pp. 113–125, 2021.
https://doi.org/10.1007/978-3-030-87725-5_10

and the determination of the zero moment point for walking robots [5]. Existing sensors differ in their structure, principles of operation and manufacturing technologies [6].

Typically, array sensors have a multi-layer structure. Thus, in [7], a matrix of flexible pressure sensors of a capacitive type, produced by screen printing, is proposed. At the base of the sensor is a thin polyamide substrate 25 μm thick. A three-layer structure has a matrix of pressure sensors [8], which is supposed to be used to determine the pressure distribution over the surface of an object. The upper and lower layers of the sensor matrix are made of fabric in the form of parallel metal strip-electrodes separated by non-conductive polyethylene terephthalate. A pressure-sensitive carbon polymer foam middle layer is sandwiched between the two electrodes. When a force is applied to the sensor, the conductive layer contracts, causing a drop in resistance. A similar application of a pressure sensor array is discussed in [9]. The surface elements of the sensor array are fabricated using a pressure sensitive polymer sandwiched between the conductive paths on the Mylar sheets. An excellent solution is proposed in [10] for a pressure sensor array based on single electrode triboelectric generators. The sensor matrix is supported by a polyethylene glycol terephthalate (PET) film with a thickness of 250 μm. To cover the bottom of the sensor, a PET film with an ethylene vinyl acetate copolymer is used, and a polydimethylsiloxane film covers the top of the sensor, which serves as an electrification layer that generates triboelectric charges when touched.

The sensors discussed above in research papers work as part of a matrix and measure the applied pressure force. Most of the sensors are exceedingly difficult to manufacture, and some of them are not designed to be placed on the robot's body. To obtain the most complete information about the environment, the robot must receive data not only about pressure, but also about the distance to objects in the immediate vicinity. Therefore, the use of combined pressure and proximity sensors will allow the robot to get the most complete picture of the environment, avoid collisions with objects and better grip objects. Combined measurement of different physical parameters is possible by sensors based on the same physical principle: optical [11, 12], capacitive [13], however, different physical principles of sensor operation are more often used: optical principle for distance measurement and piezoresistive principle for pressure measurement [14], capacitive principle for measuring the proximity of an object with inductive [15] or a resistive method for determining the applied force [16].

Thin film sensor [11], consisting of polymer LEDs and photodiodes, is designed to determine the touch and distance to the object. The sensor is placed on a square glass substrate with a side of 2.54 mm and a thickness of 1.1 mm; LED and photodiode elements are applied to the substrate by photolithography and etching. The light emitted by polymer LEDs reflects off an approaching object and falls back onto the photodiodes, which changes the signal. The sensory matrix prototype consists of seven cells. The proposed solution allows to determine the proximity of an object up to 40 mm.

Combined capacitive pressure and proximity sensor [13] is designed as a multilayer structure. A sheet of polyethylene terephthalate with parallel electrode strips is used as a substrate. To measure pressure and distance to an object, this sensor uses two modes of operation and requires switching between them. Also, several operating modes for measuring pressure and proximity are used in capacitive-type sensor arrays [17, 18], but their size can make it difficult to install sensors in robotic equipment. In the presented circuit solutions, the sensors do not have their own reference signal, it is supplied separately.

The development of a matrix of infrared sensors is presented in [12]. The matrix is located on an aluminum foil substrate and measures the applied pressure and the proximity of the object. These matrices are made using organic thin-film transistors. The cells of the sensitive surface of the pressure sensor are arranged in the form of a 6 × 10 matrix, the size of each cell is 27.5 × 27.5 mm. The maximum permissible force that can be applied to the sensitive area of the sensor is 100 kN. The matrix of infrared sensors measuring the distance to the object has a dimension of 10 × 10, with a cell size of 1 × 1 cm. Microlenses over the infrared sensors concentrate light and increase sensitivity. The maximum distance at which the object was detected is 115 mm with the sensor's sensitive area of 3.1 cm^2.

Sensor based on eutectic indium-gallium alloy (EGaIn), developed by [16]. The sensor array consists of nine capacitive sensors arranged in two layers and a spiral pressure sensor. Capacity is measured using a CapSense controller. As the conductive object approaches the electrodes, capacitance is formed between the electrodes and the conductive object, when the conductive object touches the sensor panel, the mutual capacitance between the matrix cells decreases. The magnitude of the applied force is determined by the change in the resistance of the sensor. The sensor measures distances up to 8.7 cm and contact pressures up to 110 kPa.

As noted, there are composite sensor matrices based on different operating principles. For example, on a flexible matrix of combined pressure and proximity sensors [14] are VL53L0X optical rangefinders and piezoresistive pressure sensors. The presented solution includes two types of sensors that are part of the same matrix and work independently of each other. The optical sensors used are not suitable for installation on robots operating in aggressive environments due to the high probability of sensor contamination. The inductive-capacitive principle of operation is at the heart of the flexible sensor [15], with which it is possible to measure the magnitude of external pressure and distance to an object using inductive and capacitive modes, which are switched on separately. The sensor is made based on a 10 × 10 matrix and consists of carbon microcoils with a soft dielectric elastomer substrate. The sensor cell of the sensor consists of a dielectric layer and an electrode layer. The dielectric layer includes silicone elastomer and carbon coils, and the electrode layer contains a flexible printed circuit board with electrodes. The dimensions of the pressure-sensitive region are 32 × 23 mm, with a distance between the cells of 2 mm. With the help of the proposed solution, it is possible to measure pressure in the range up to 330 kPa and to determine the distance to metal objects in the range up to 150 mm.

There are also solutions with a combination of sensors that convert other physical parameters. For example, the HEX-O-SKIN combined module [19] is equipped with several discrete sensors for temperature, proximity, and accelerometers. The HEX-O-SKIN modules are located in an elastic material and are connected to each other through four ports, forming a matrix. In [20] a sensor has been developed that detects temperature, deformation, and external pressure.

Despite the advantage of the small size of the considered prototypes of the combined sensors, there is a problem of increased manufacturing complexity. The need to use nanotechnology, high temperatures and increased accuracy of equipment operation complicate the production process. Resistive and capacitive cells, laser and optical sensors are used. The combination of pressure and proximity sensors located in the matrix and working simultaneously is shown only in [12]. Sensors presented in [15] and [13], measure external pressure and distance to objects, however, they require switching the operating modes. Analysis [21] showed that combined solutions have certain advantages when applied in robotics, therefore, the development of such sensors is an urgent scientific task. The aim of this work is to develop a matrix combined sensor for measuring force and determining the proximity to an object, which does not require switching between operating modes and is manufactured using simple technologies and available materials. In our solution, we also want to implement the possibility of simple scaling of the matrix sensor, which will allow it to be adapted to the surfaces of the robot of various shapes.

2 Sensor Structure and Schematics

The developed matrix of primary capacitive transducers (PCT) for measuring the pressure force and distance to the object is a three-layer structure, the elements of which are shown in Fig. 1.

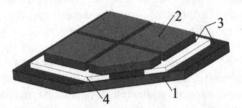

Fig. 1. Structural diagram of the PCT matrix.

The matrix consists of a base (1) and divided cells (2). The base and the cells have metallization layers (3), which form between themselves a capacitance C(P) (Fig. 2), by changing which the applied force is measured. The central layer (4) is a strip of elastically deformable material that runs along the perimeter of the electrodes. Elastically deformable material provides the PCT with the ability to linearly change the distance between the metallization layers when an external force is applied to the PCT. Thus, the sensitivity and the range of the measured pressure depend on the parameters of the deformable element. Figure 2 shows a block diagram of one cell of a combined matrix sensor.

When approaching, a capacitive coupling is formed between the object, the metallization layer of the matrix base and the inner metallization layer of the cell. A decrease in the distance between the object and the sensor leads to an increase in the values of the capacities C(A) and C(A'). When an external force is applied to the PCT due to a change in the thickness of the deformable spacer, the distance between the inner layers of metallization changes, which leads to an increase in the capacitance C(P).

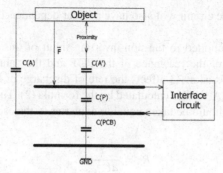

Fig. 2. Block diagram of each cell of the matrix.

An interface circuit was developed to process the output signal of the PCT. The schematic diagram consists of two parts: generator and amplifier. The interface circuit uses a high-frequency square-wave generator with an operating frequency of 270 kHz. The amplifying part of the interface circuit is represented by an operational amplifier operating in a non-inverting mode. The interface circuit shown in Fig. 3 is designed in such a way that the number of amplifying parts of the circuit can be different, thereby making it possible to combine force and proximity primary transducers into matrices of various configurations. Up to ~100 matrix cells can be connected to one generator.

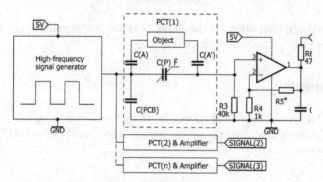

Fig. 3. Interface circuit.

The interface circuit converts the change in the capacitance of the PCT into a change in voltage, which allows further processing of the signal by means of the ADC of the microcontroller or other measuring instruments. The proposed circuit design is based on the measurement of an indirect parameter – the reactive resistance of the PCT (1):

$$X_C(P) = \frac{d}{2\pi F \varepsilon \varepsilon_0 S},\tag{1}$$

where d is the distance between the electrodes, F is the signal frequency, ε is the relative permittivity of the medium, ε_0 is the electrical constant, S is the area of the electrodes.

The reactive resistance of the PCT linearly depends on the distance between the electrodes C(P); when using a linearly deformable spacer material, the output voltage value from the interface circuit will also have a linear dependence on the force applied to the sensor.

The voltage U_{in} supplied to the non-inverting input of the operational amplifier depends on the value of the reactance of the PCT and the value of the resistor R3. The resistance of the resistor R3 affects the rate of discharge of capacitance C(P) and capacitors C(A) and C(A$'$) and is calculated by the formula (2). The time constant of the capacitor discharge τ should be taken equal to a quarter of the oscillation period of the HF pulse generator:

$$R_3 = \frac{\tau}{4C_{max}}, \tag{2}$$

where $C_{max} = \frac{\varepsilon\varepsilon_0 S}{d_{min}}$, and d_{min} is minimum distance between electrodes.

The gain of the operational amplifier depends on the resistance value of the voltage divider R4R5 and is calculated by the formula (3):

$$K = 1 + \frac{R_5}{R_4}. \tag{3}$$

The value of the output signal of the operational amplifier is U_{out}, calculated by the formula (4):

$$U_{out} = KU_{in}. \tag{4}$$

The operational amplifier output is the output from the sensor cell and is a DC voltage, the ripple of which is smoothed by capacitor C5.

3 Experiments

To obtain the values of the output signals from the experimental sample of the matrix of combined pressure force and proximity sensors, a test bench was used [22]. Figure 4 shows the test bench.

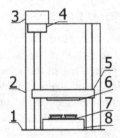

Fig. 4. The test bench design [22].

The test bench consists of a frame (2) fixed to a base (1). A stepper motor (3) moves the nut-screw transfer screw (4), driving the carriage (5) with a sample (6) attached to it. The test bench allows to change the pressure force on the test sample (7) smoothly and accurately, and the pressure force is monitored using a reference device (8). The microcontroller-based control system provides high repeatability of experiments and allows the object to be moved relative to the sensor with an accuracy of 1.64 μm. To ensure high measurement accuracy of the sensor output signal, the signal is processed by a 16-bit ADC, the subsequent experimental results are presented in the measured ADC values.

In accordance with the presented structure, a prototype of the matrix of combined force and proximity sensors was manufactured. The matrix consists of four cells of 12 × 12 dimensions. In the manufacture of FR4 fiberglass with a thickness of 1.6 mm and silicon sheet 1 mm thick, the total thickness of the matrix is 4.2 mm. Electrical calibration was not applied to the sensors before measurements.

A number of experiments were carried out to approach the sensor matrix of geometrically identical samples of various materials, as well as to communicate the external pressure force to the PCT matrix. These specimens were mounted on the test bench in two ways: without angular misalignment (Fig. 5a) and with an angular misalignment of 45° (Fig. 5b).

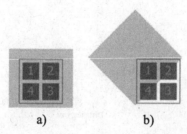

a)   b)

Fig. 5. Placement of samples above the sensor array: a) without angular displacement, b) with angular displacement.

Figure 6 shows the dependence of the output signals of the PCT when approaching an aluminum object. The sample is mounted on a stand without angular displacement relative to the sensor.

Figure 7 shows the dependence of the PCT output signals when an aluminum object is approached with an angular displacement of the sample by 45° in such a way that cell 3 is not overlapped by the sample, 2 and 4 are partially overlapped, and cell 1 is completely overlapped.

As can be seen from the Fig. 6, using the manufactured sensor array, it is possible to determine the distance to the object in the range of distances up to 4–8 mm. This range can be expanded by increasing the size of the PCT or changing the frequency of the interface circuit. The highest sensitivity of the fabricated sensor array is observed in the linear section from 0 to 1.8 mm, the sensitivity of matrix cells 1, 2, 3, and 4 is 1375, 1382, 1713, and 879 ADC value/mm, respectively. Differences in the readings between the matrix cells are due to the uneven thickness of the damping silicone layer of the PCT and the peculiarities of its manufacture.

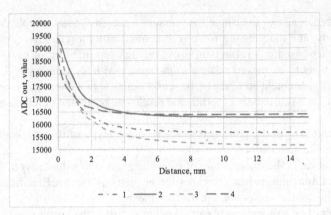

Fig. 6. Dependence of the sensor output signals on the approach of an aluminum object without angular displacement.

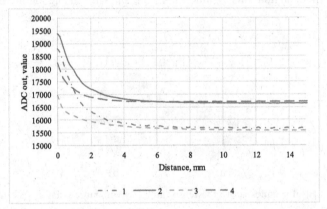

Fig. 7. Dependence of the sensor output signals on the approach of an aluminum object with angular displacement.

The output signals of completely and partially overlapped cells do not differ significantly from the values when the PCT is completely overlapped by the sample. The change in the signal of the matrix cell, which during the experiment the sample did not overlap, is much less than in the previous experiment. On average, the absolute deviation of the curves in Fig. 6 and 7 was 10, 339, 444 and 302 ADC value for cells 1–4 respectively. The non-overlapped cell had a larger deviation. The values with the overlapped cell differ the least. Experiments were also carried out with conductive samples of steel and copper. The received signal characteristics are similar to the results in Fig. 6 and 7.

Several experiments were carried out with samples from dielectric materials: from plywood and from plastic. Figures 8 and 9 show the dependences of the PCT output signals on the distance to the plastic sample without angular displacement and with angular displacement, respectively.

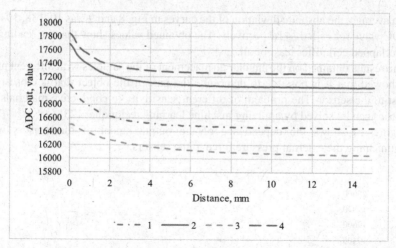

Fig. 8. Dependence of the sensor output signals on the approach of a plastic object without angular displacement.

The sensitivity of PCT to samples made of dielectric materials is lower than to samples from conductive materials. With the help of the developed sensor matrix, it is possible to determine the distance to dielectric materials in the range of up to 6 mm.

Figure 9 shows that the change in the signal of the cell not covered by the sample has noticeably changed in comparison with the proximity of objects made of conducting materials. The maximum sensitivity of the matrix cells is in the range from 0 to 1.8 mm and is 236, 237, 127, and 238 ADC value/mm for each matrix cell, respectively.

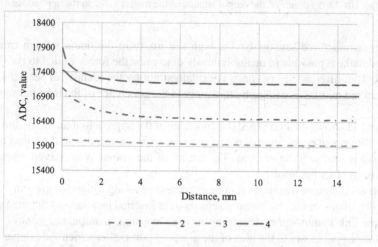

Fig. 9. Dependence of the sensor output signals on the approach of a plastic object with angular displacement.

On average, the absolute deviation of the curves in Fig. 8 and 9 was 10, 138, 193 and 96 ADC value for cells 1–4 respectively. The obtained values show that the readings of the overlapped cell differ least of all.

The results obtained on the angular displacement of the samples with different materials showed that it is possible to determine the part of the object that is closest and farthest to the sensor. The problem of different sensitivity to conductive materials and dielectrics can be solved by applying machine learning techniques [23].

Figure 10 shows the dependence of the output signal of the sensors when communicating the external pressure force to the sensors.

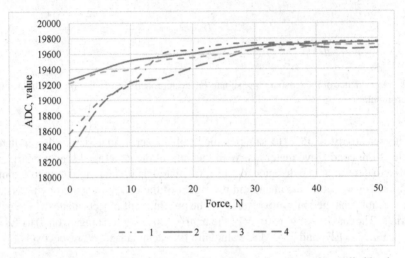

Fig. 10. Dependence of the output signals of the matrix cells on the applied load.

The manufactured sensors have a high sensitivity in the linear section from 0 to 10 N and make it possible to unambiguously determine the force applied to the PCT up to 25 N. The difference in readings is explained not by the identity of the cells of the manufactured matrix, as well as by the errors in the adherence of the material sample to the cells.

Figure 11 shows the combined dependences of the approach of an aluminum object and the subsequent application of the force to the sensor. The moment the object touches the sensor is uniquely determined. The nature of the graphs is preserved when using objects from other materials.

Proposed solution was applied in development of an algorithm for grasping various objects [1]. In this study, 2 × 2 matrix sensors were inserted into the two-fingered gripper of a three-link manipulator. According to the algorithm, manipulator control system brings the gripper closer to the area of the grasping point, after which the gripper aligns, approaches the grasping point and the object is gripped. The probability of successful grip was 97%.

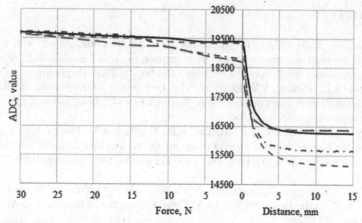

Fig. 11. Combined dependences of the approach of the object to the sensor and the subsequent application of an external force.

4 Conclusion

A distinctive feature of the proposed solution is the combined measurement of the pressure force and proximity and the interface scheme with common generator to all cells of the matrix. Determination of the force or distance to the object does not require switching the operating modes of the sensor array. Presented design scheme allows changing dimensions and amount of the matrix cells up to ~100 units. For the manufacturing of the sensor, a set of available materials can be used: foil-clad fiberglass and silicone, which, together with the structure used, makes it possible to simplify the process of manufacturing the sensor.

Single sensors of the same size as the matrix sensor are less compact and require more wires to be connected. The matrix structure of the sensors will make it possible to determine the distribution of forces over the area covered by the sensors more accurately, as compared to single sensors, which will allow implementing algorithms for stable gait of robots on uneven surfaces and algorithms for regulating the force of gripping objects [1]. The using of combined sensors for implementation of gait of walking robots will also allow one to align the foot relative to the surface [24–26].

Experiments on the objects made of different materials have shown that the sensitivity of the developed matrix of combined sensors to conducting objects approaching is, on average, greater than the sensitivity to objects made of non-conducting materials approaching. The prototype presented in the work with the size of each cell 12×12 mm can determine the approach of an object at a distance of 8 mm and measure the applied force in the range of up to 25 N.

Further research will be aimed at increasing the sensitivity of the proximity matrix cells, as well as at developing algorithms for processing signals from the matrix of combined sensors to obtain close readings of the cells.

References

1. Erashov, A., Krestovnikov, K.: Algorithm for controlling manipulator with combined array of pressure and proximity sensors in gripper. In: 16th International Conference on Electromechanics and Robotics "Zavalishin's Readings" (2021). (In press)
2. Ronzhin, A.L., Budkov, V.Y., Ronzhin, A.L.: User profile forming based on audiovisual situation analysis in smart meeting room. SPIIRAS Proc. **4**(23), 482–494 (2012). (In Rus.). https://doi.org/10.15622/sp.23.28
3. Gorobtsov, A.S., Andreev, A.E., Markov, A.E., Skorikov, A.V., Tarasov, P.S.: Features of solving the inverse dynamic method equations for the synthesis of stable walking robots controlled motion. SPIIRAS Proc. **18**(1), 85–122 (2019). https://doi.org/10.15622/sp.18.1.85-122
4. Ohmura, Y., Kuniyoshi, Y., Nagakubo, A.: Conformable and scalable tactile sensor skin for curved surfaces. In: Proceedings of International Conference on Robotics and Automation, pp. 1348–1353 (2006)
5. Kovalev, A., Pavliuk, N., Krestovnikov, K., Saveliev, A.: Generation of walking patterns for biped robots based on dynamics of 3D linear inverted pendulum. In: Ronzhin, A., Rigoll, G., Meshcheryakov, R. (eds.) ICR 2019. LNCS (LNAI), vol. 11659, pp. 170–181. Springer, Cham (2019). https://doi.org/10.1007/978-3-030-26118-4_17
6. Lumelsky, V.J., Shur, M.S., Wagner, S.: Sensitive skin. IEEE Sens. J. **1**(1), 41–51 (2001)
7. Khan, S., Lorenzelli, L., Dahiya, R.S.: Screen printed flexible pressure sensors skin. In: 25th Annual SEMI Advanced Semiconductor Manufacturing Conference (ASMC), pp. 219–224. IEEE (2014). https://doi.org/10.1109/ASMC.2014.6847002
8. Cheng, J., Sundholm, M., Zhou, B., Hirsch, M., Lukowicz, P.: Smart-surface: large scale textile pressure sensors arrays for activity recognition. Pervasive Mob. Comput. **30**, 97–112 (2016)
9. Srinivasan, P., Birchfield, D., Qian, G., Kidané, A.: A pressure sensing floor for interactive media applications. In: Proceedings of the 2005 ACM SIGCHI International Conference on Advances in Computer Entertainment Technology, pp. 278–281. ACM (2005)
10. Wang, X., et al.: Self-powered high-resolution and pressure-sensitive triboelectric sensor matrix for real-time tactile mapping. Adv. Mater. **28**(15), 2896–2903 (2016)
11. Bürgi, L., Pfeiffer, R., Mücklich, M., Metzler, P., Kiy, M., Winnewisser, C.: Optical proximity and touch sensors based on monolithically integrated polymer photodiodes and polymer LEDs. Org. Electron. **7**(2), 114–120 (2006). https://doi.org/10.1016/j.orgel.2005.12.002
12. Fattori, M., Cantatore, E., Pauer, G., Agostinelli, T., Stadlober, B., Joanneum, H.G.: Flexible pressure and proximity sensor surfaces manufactured with organic materials. In: 2017 7th IEEE International Workshop on Advances in Sensors and Interfaces (IWASI), pp. 53–58. IEEE (2017)
13. Zhang, B., et al.: Dual functional transparent film for proximity and pressure sensing. Nano Res. **7**(10), 1488–1496 (2014). https://doi.org/10.1007/s12274-014-0510-3
14. Liang, J., Wu, J., Huang, H., Xu, W., Li, B., Xi, F.: Soft sensitive skin for safety control of a nursing robot using proximity and tactile sensors. IEEE Sens. J. **1**(1), 3822–3830 (2019). https://doi.org/10.1109/JSEN.2019.2959311
15. Nguyen, T.D., et al.: Highly sensitive flexible proximity tactile array sensor by using carbon micro coils. Sens. Actuat. A **266**, 166–177 (2017)
16. Rocha, R., Lopes, P., de Almeida, A.T., Tavakoli, M., Majidi, C.: Soft- matter sensor for proximity, tactile and pressure detection. In: 2017 IEEE/RSJ International Conference on Intelligent Robots and Systems (IROS), pp. 3734–3738. IEEE (2017)
17. Goeger, D., Blankertz, M., Woern, H.: A tactile proximity sensor. In: SENSORS, pp. 589–594. IEEE (2010). https://doi.org/10.1109/ICSENS.2010.5690450

18. Alagi, H., Navarro, S.E., Mende, M., Hein, B.: A versatile and modular capacitive tactile proximity sensor. In: 2016 IEEE Haptics Symposium (HAPTICS), pp. 290–296. IEEE (2016). https://doi.org/10.1109/HAPTICS.2016.7463192
19. Mittendorfer, P., Cheng, G.: Humanoid multimodal tactile-sensing modules. IEEE Trans. Rob. **27**(3), 401–410 (2011)
20. Huang, Y., Fang, D., Wu, C., Wang, W., Guo, X., Liu, P.: A flexible touch-pressure sensor array with wireless transmission system for robotic skin. Rev. Sci. Instr. **87**(6), 065007 (2016). https://doi.org/10.1063/1.4954199
21. Krestovnikov, K., Cherskikh, E., Zimuldinov, E.: Combined capacitive pressure and proximity sensor for using in robotic systems. In: Ronzhin, A., Shishlakov, V. (eds.) Proceedings of 15th International Conference on Electromechanics and Robotics "Zavalishin's Readings". SIST, vol. 187, pp. 513–523. Springer, Singapore (2021). https://doi.org/10.1007/978-981-15-5580-0_42
22. Krestovnikov, K., Erashov, A., Bykov, A.: Development of circuit solution and design of capacitive pressure sensor array for applied robotics. Robot. Tech. Cybern. **8**(4), 296–307 (2020). https://doi.org/10.31776/RTCJ.8406
23. Kozyr, P., Saveliev, A., Kuznetsov, L.: Determining distance to an object and type of its material based on data of capacitive sensor signal and machine learning techniques. In: 2021 International Siberian Conference on Control and Communications (SIBCON), pp. 1–5. IEEE (2021). https://doi.org/10.1109/SIBCON50419.2021.9438932
24. Petrenko, V.I., Tebueva, F.B., Gurchinsky, M.M., Antonov, V.O., Pavlov, A.S.: Predictive assessment of operator's hand trajectory with the copying type of control for solution of the inverse dynamic problem. SPIIRAS Proc. **18**(1), 123–147 (2019). https://doi.org/10.15622/sp.18.1.123-147
25. Medvedev, M.Y., Kostjukov, V.A., Pshikhopov, V.K.: Optimization of mobile robot movement on a plane with finite number of repeller sources. SPIIRAS Proc. **19**(1), 43–78 (2020). https://doi.org/10.15622/sp.2020.19.1.2
26. Al Mashhadany, Y.I.: Design and analysis of 7-DOF human-link manipulator based on hybrid intelligent controller. SPIIRAS Proc. **19**(4), 774–802 (2020). https://doi.org/10.15622/sp.2020.19.4.3

The Efficiency Improvement of Robots Group Operation by Means of Workload Relocation

Eduard Melnik, Irina Safronenkova$^{(\boxtimes)}$, and Sergey Kapustyan

Federal Research Centre the Southern Scientific Center of the Russian Academy of Sciences, 41, Chekhov Street, 344006 Rostov-on-Don, Russian Federation

Abstract. The paper deals with a problem of workload relocation in a heterogeneous group of unmanned aerial vehicles (UAV) during the area monitoring under the changing environmental conditions. One of the stages of a monitoring problem solving, involving a UAVs distribution by the scan bands, is described. It was noted that, when this stage is being performed, there is not a possibility to take into account any factors of environment. However, it is important because of on-board energy resources limitations. This fact jeopardizes the fulfillment of the entire mission of the group. To avoid this situation, it was proposed to use a decision-making technique, based on ontological analysis, on the need to relocate the workload in a group of mobile robots. It is shown that with an increase in the number of environmental conditions changes, the time of using extra computing resources decreases, which leads to the need to engage more of them to perform the task. A comparative assessment of the amount of resources involved in the implementation of two analogous methods for solving the problem of workload relocation depending on the frequency of changes in environmental conditions is carried out. The results of experiments have shown that the effectiveness of using the ontology-based method in a dynamic environment is higher than the local device group (LDG) method. This allows to increase the time of joint mission execution by a group of robots.

Keywords: UAVs group · Scan · Ontology · Workload relocation · Fog computing · Cloud computing

1 Introduction

Currently, monitoring systems are widely used in many areas of human activity: in industrial production and at infrastructure facilities for assessing the state of complex technical facilities, in the socio-economic sphere for assessing and making managerial decisions, in healthcare, in the field of observation of natural phenomena and prevention of their dangerous consequences [1–3]. A great number of monitoring system's application areas as well as high requirements (speed, reliability, the ability to solve tasks in real time), actualizes the problem of such systems effective functioning in difficult conditions.

© Springer Nature Switzerland AG 2021
A. Ronzhin et al. (Eds.): ICR 2021, LNAI 12998, pp. 126–137, 2021.
https://doi.org/10.1007/978-3-030-87725-5_11

The most promising architecture of control subsystems of complex systems is a distributed architecture based on "cloud", "edge" and "fog" computing [4–6]. This architecture implies to solve common tasks (including control tasks) in the "cloud" layer, while data collection tasks and preprocessing tasks are solved, as a rule, by means of "edge" and "fog" devices. In [7] authors made the first review on fog computing within healthcare informatics. They concluded the following: (1) there is a significant number of computing tasks in healthcare that require or can benefit from fog computing principles, (2) processing on higher network tiers is required due to constraints in wireless devices and the need to aggregate data, (3) privacy concerns and dependability prevent computation tasks to be completely moved to the cloud. In [8] the combined method of monitoring of hazardous phenomena and predicting of hazardous processes and security of coastal infrastructure and providing of safety of human lives based on "fog computing", blockchain and Internet of Things was proposed.

One of the components of a monitoring system is often a group of mobile robots. For example, in [9] it was proposed to use a multi-robotic complex on the basis of heterogeneous UAVs group as a monitoring system component. Multi-robotic complexes usage allows to decrease some conflicting and difficult to achieve requirements, applied to individual multifunctional robots in group. Group-based usage of robots often does not suggest a presence of any significant on-board energy resources. This allows to make mobile robot's size miniature. However, this approach also has a number of lacks, such as a limited on-board energy resource and mobile robot radius of direct communication. To solve this problem robots retransmitters, which can be used as a group leader and a data store, are introduced into the group. It is important to notice that the environment, where MR performs assigned tasks, has a great impact on the amount of consumed onboard resources. In view of the fact that, MR has limited time for the problem solving, it is necessary to take into account environmental factors. Otherwise, a situation may arise when the MR is not able to complete the assigned task.

In this paper, we propose a technique that includes an ontological analysis procedure and makes it possible to make a decision on the need to relocate the workload in the MR group using the example of the area monitoring problem solving by a heterogeneous UAV group controlled by the UAV leader, taking into account changing environmental conditions.

2   UAV Distribution by Scan Bands

The formal statement of a monitoring problem carried out by a heterogeneous group of UAVs is given in [10] and involves the implementation of several stages, the last of which is to determine a specific scan band (trajectory) for each UAV of the subgroup.

After a UAV $R_{j_s} (j_s \in [1, N_s])$ of a group are distributed by subareas of scanning, it is necessary to determine a specific scan band for each UAV.

Let for subarea S_s scanning N_s UAV are given, i.e. a subarea S_s is divided into N_s bands with a width no more than L.

First, it is necessary to determine input-output UAV points for each band. For each band it can be determined by two points as can be seen from Fig. 1.

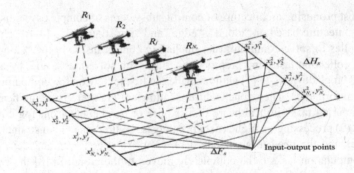

Fig. 1. Input-output points of bands scanning.

The coordinates of input-output points are $\langle \overline{x}_{js'}^1, \overline{y}_{js}^1 \rangle$, $\langle \overline{x}_{js'}^2, \overline{y}_{js}^2 \rangle$, $(j = \overline{1, N_s})$, defined by expressions:

$$
\begin{aligned}
\overline{x}_{js}^1 &= x_s^c - \frac{\Delta F_s}{2}, \\
\overline{y}_{js}^1 &= y_s^c - \frac{\Delta H_s}{2} + (j_s - 1) \cdot L + \frac{L}{2}, \\
x_{js}^1 &= x_s^c + (\overline{x}_{js}^1 - x_s^c) \cdot \cos\varphi_s - (\overline{y}_{js}^1 - y_s^c) \cdot \sin\varphi_s, \\
y_{js}^1 &= y_s^c + (\overline{x}_{js}^1 - x_s^c) \cdot \sin\varphi_s + (\overline{y}_{js}^1 - y_s^c) \cdot \cos\varphi_s,
\end{aligned}
\tag{1}
$$

and

$$
\begin{aligned}
\overline{x}_{js}^2 &= x_s^c - \frac{\Delta F_s}{2}, \\
\overline{y}_{js}^2 &= y_s^c - \frac{\Delta H_s}{2} + (j_s - 1) \cdot L + \frac{L}{2}, \\
x_{js}^2 &= x_s^c + (\overline{x}_{js}^2 - x_s^c) \cdot \cos\varphi_s - (\overline{y}_{js}^2 - y_s^c) \cdot \sin\varphi_s, \\
y_{js}^2 &= y_s^c + (\overline{x}_{js}^2 - x_s^c) \cdot \sin\varphi_s + (\overline{y}_{js}^2 - y_s^c) \cdot \cos\varphi_s,
\end{aligned}
\tag{2}
$$

where ΔF_s – length of a scanning area S_s;
ΔH_s – width of a scanning area S_s;
L – width of a UAV scanning band;
φ_s – orientation angle of a subarea S_s;
$\langle x_s^c, y_s^c \rangle$ – coordinates of a scanning subarea geometric centers;
$\langle \overline{x}_{js'}^1, \overline{y}_{js}^1 \rangle$, $\langle \overline{x}_{js'}^2, \overline{y}_{js}^2 \rangle$ – intermediate coordinate values of coordinates bands centers before turning through the angle φ_s.

At the previous step it was defined that a subgroup size corresponds to the number of scan bands, on which a specific subarea can be divided. Then, the UAV-leader RL_s assigned to a given subarea defines a scan band for each UAV $R_{j_s}(j_s \in [1, N_s])$. However, it is necessary to define input-output points for each scan band of each subarea $\langle \overline{x}_{js'}^1, \overline{y}_{js}^1 \rangle$, $\langle \overline{x}_{js'}^2, \overline{y}_{js}^2 \rangle$. To avoid emergency situations, it is necessary that UAVs move in one direction in adjacent subareas. The UAV-leader makes a decision about input-output points for its UAV subgroup. For example, according to the minimum of the total movements of the UAV $R_{j_s}(j_s \in [1, N_s])$, assigned to these subareas.

Each UAV-leader RL_s puts the obtained values of input-output point coordinates into a Distributed Ledger to make these values available for the rest of the UAV-leaders.

3 A Decision-Making Technique on the Need to Relocate the Workload in a UAV Group

In this paper we suppose that a UAV group has to scan some area. Moreover, the distributed architecture of a control subsystem of this process should be implemented on the basis of cloud, fog and edge computing (Fig. 2).

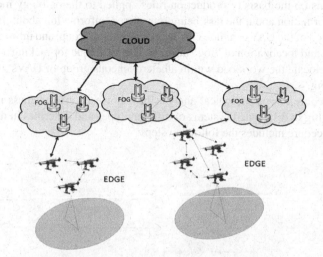

Fig. 2. The distributed architecture of a control subsystem.

Since the environmental conditions, in which the UAV group operates, are difficult to predict, changeable, and have a direct impact on the amount of consumed onboard resources, then after assigning scan bands for each UAV, a situation may arise when a certain UAV is not able to perform the assigned task because of the limited resources.

Multi-robotic interactions involve the collective solution of a common problem. It means that each MR has to act in the best interests of all of the group to successfully complete the mission. If the UAV onboard resources are insufficient to complete the task assigned to it, the following solutions to this problem are possible:

1. Workload relocation between the UAVs, included in a group, in such a way that the mission assigned to this subgroup is completed on time.
2. Extra resources involving through the devices of the "fog" layer to perform the assigned task.
3. Scan band redistribution.

We will assume that each UAV is aware of a resource status and localization in space of its neighbors, which are in the radius of direct communication. Every UAV of

130   E. Melnik et al.

a subgroup sends its data about resource status and its localization in space to the UAV leader.

Thus, each UAV is able to assess the state of its resources to solve the subtask allocated to it. If these resources are not enough, then the UAV, which has information about the neighboring UAVs, generates a proposal to the UAV leader about a possible choice for workload relocation to the computational resources of the neighboring UAV. The UAV leader, in turn, makes a decision on the expediency or inexpediency of this relocation. If the UAV does not find choices for workload relocation from among its neighbors, then it informs the leader about this, and he makes a decision either to attract extra resources from the "fog" layer, or to redistribute the scan bands. The UAV-leader makes these decisions on the basis of production rules applied to the ontology model, which describes information about the task being transferred, information about the resources and localization of the UAVs included in the considered subgroup, and information about the resources and localization of "fog" devices. The technique for making a decision on the need to relocate the workload within a heterogeneous group of UAVs with a leader is shown in Fig. 3.

The procedure of an ontological analysis has shown its effectiveness in workload problem solving in distributed systems of different types and describes in detail in [11, 12]. This procedure includes the following steps:

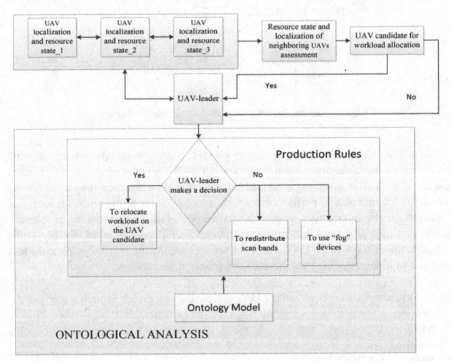

Fig. 3. The decision-making technique on the need to relocate the workload in a group of MR.

1. Initial data classification according with ontology classes, which describe a specified domain.
2. Application of production rules to ontology classes in order to restrict the set of computational nodes obtained as a result of collecting information about available resources.
3. Making a decision on the preferred set of nodes for workload relocation.

According with the proposed technique it is necessary to develop an ontology model, describing an area of workload relocation within a heterogeneous UAV group and taking into account the influence of environmental factors, and production rules, on the basis of which a decision is made on the need to relocate workload.

4   The Development of an Ontology Model of Workload Relocation in a Heterogeneous UAV Group Operating in the Changeable Environmental Conditions

Based on methodology described in [13], in the current paper an ontology of workload relocation in heterogeneous UAV group operating in the changeable environmental conditions was developed. To describe a specified domain in the form of ontology model sufficiently and correctly it is necessary to form a set of concepts, which are represented in ontology as a class hierarchy.

So, an ontology model includes the following concepts: environment (wind speed and wind direction, precipitation, obstacles); UAV (resources (productivity, energy

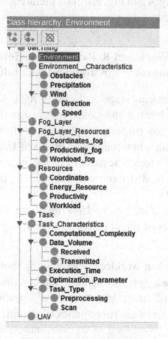

Fig. 4. A class hierarchy.

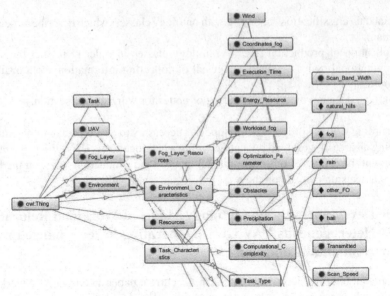

Fig. 5. The fragment of an ontology model.

resources, workload)), scan band width, scan speed, current coordinates in space); fog layer (productivity, workload, coordinates in space); task (type, computational complexity, time of execution, volumes of transmitted and received data); optimization parameter (scan area, patrol time). In Fig. 4 and Fig. 5, a class hierarchy and a fragment of developed ontology model are presented.

4.1 Production Rules of Workload Relocation in a Heterogeneous UAV Group Operating in the Changeable Environmental Conditions

At the heart of the decision-making stage on the preferred UAV, which is ready to allocate part of its resources to solve some sub-tasks, which was initially assigned to another UAV, is a system of production rules that links a class of ontology describing the area of workload relocation within a heterogeneous group of UAVs, taking into account the influence of environmental factors. The main basis for the production rules development was the main principles of the distribution of subtasks by processors in heterogeneous computing systems [14, 15].

We will assume the following: every UAV involving into the group has a limited on-board resource and radius of direct communication; fog devices are static and have some computing resources.

Case 1. Consider the case when workload relocation within the MR group is possible: **IF** task_characteristics {task_type = scan; computational complexity = Θ; optimization_parameter = patrol_time; data_volume = significant; execution_time = T} **AND** environment_ characteristics {precipitation = rain, wind = headwind, obstacles = no} **AND** *resources* {workload = ψ; coordinates = $\langle x_j, y_j \rangle$; scan_speed = V_j; scan_band_width = L_j} *satisfy* task_characteristics **THEN** *relocate on UAV* {$d_i = \min$}, where d_i - the distance between the UAV that was originally assigned the sub-task and the UAV that is able to complete it on time.

Case 2. If there is not a MR in a group, which is able to solve the sub-task on time, then it is necessary to use fog layer resources:
task_characteristics {task_type = scan; computational complexity = Θ; optimization_parameter = patrol_time; data_volume = significant; execution_time = T} **AND** environment_ characteristics {precipitation = rain, wind = headwind, obstacles = no} **AND** *resources* {workload = ψ; coordinates = $\langle x_j, y_j \rangle$; scan_speed = V_j; scan_band_width = L_j} do not *satisfy* task_characteristics **THEN** *relocate on fog node* {workload_fog = ψ_f; productivity_fog = ρ_f; coordinates_fog = $<x_f; y_f>$; d_i = min},

where d_i – the distance between the UAV that was originally assigned the sub-task and the fog node, which is able to solve it on time.

The efficiency of the proposed technique was tested using computational experiments.

5 Simulation and Discussion

Let's assume that the UAV's onboard energy resources are not enough to solve the task. In this case, it is necessary to reallocate the workload in such a way that the common mission is completed successfully, i.e. to solve the problem of workload relocation for a limited time, during which all the UAVs of the group are able to perform the tasks assigned to them. In accordance with the decision-making technique on the need to relocate the workload described above, there are two choices for solving the current problem: workload relocation within the group's UAVs and engaging resources from the "fog" layer. In both cases, we mean the use of extra resources. It is also worth noting that in these cases, there are changing environmental conditions (changing distances between the UAV-leader or between UAVs), which have a direct impact on the workload distribution. For example, if the UAV leader is sufficiently far away from the "fog" layer device during the scanning process, then it is not advisable to transfer data for processing to this device. The question of changing roles in the MR group is raised, which, with great faith, will lead to the need to solve the problem of workload relocation. Next, we will assume that the number of changes in the environment conditions is equal to the number of workload reallocations.

In turn, the amount of resources involved is directly proportional to the time of use of these resources:

$$W_{ext} = T_{epu} \cdot P_{epu}, \tag{3}$$

where W_{ext} – extra resources amount; T_{epu} – time of extra resources using; P_{epu} – extra productivity of engaged resources.

Under the conditions of devices productivity to perform more volume of work it is necessary to increase the time of using extra resources, taking into account changes in the environmental conditions:

$$T_{epu} = T_{scan} - N \cdot T_{wr}, \tag{4}$$

where T_{scan} – time of selected area scanning; N – workload relocations number per a time unit; T_{wr} – workload relocation time.

From formulas (3), (4), it can be seen that the amount of resources involved (W_{ext}) depends on the amount of reallocations N and the time required for reallocations.

We will give explanations in the context of the problem being solved. Suppose that after UAV distribution by scan bands, there is a situation that the available resources are not enough to complete the mission. In this case, it is necessary to redistribute the workload between the UAVs of the group or involve the devices of the "fog" layer and do this as quickly as possible. The issues related to parameter T_{wr} minimization and were discussed in detail in [16, 17].

The purpose of this experiment is to obtain comparative estimates of the amount of computing resources involved in the workload relocation problem solving using the method based on ontological analysis and the method based on local device groups (LDG) [18] under the different environmental conditions. The main characteristic of the environment will be its dynamics, i.e. the number of workload relocation per unit of time. It is worth noting that during the mission, the MR, spends on-board energy resources to solve a wide range of tasks, including optimization, related to the organization of the group's work. Currently, such problems are solved using various evolutionary algorithms, the solution quality of which increases with the increase in the number of iterations they perform. In this paper, we study the monkey algorithm and the annealing method from the point of view of possible extra performance, numerical estimates of which were obtained in [17]. Quantitative estimates of the time of using extra productivity in the implementation of the ontology-based method and the LDG-based method were also obtained earlier in [16]. The results of the experiment are presented in Figs. 6, 7, 8, 9.

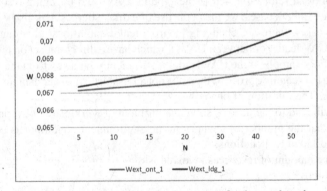

Fig. 6. The dependence of the amount of involved resources for the ontology-based ($W_{ext\_ont\_1}$) and the LDG-based ($W_{ext\_ldg\_1}$) methods on N with $T_{wr} = 1/1000T_{scan}$.

Based on the given graphs (Figs. 6, 7, 8, 9), the following conclusions can be drawn:

1. With an increase in the number of workload relocations, the volume of engaged resources increases.
2. The effectiveness of using the ontology-based method in a dynamic environment is higher than the local device group (LDG) method.

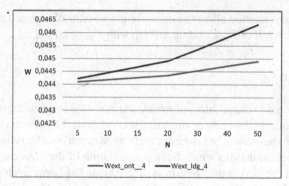

Fig. 7. The dependence of the amount of involved resources for the ontology-based ($W_{ext\_ont\_4}$) and the LDG-based ($W_{ext\_ldg\_4}$) methods on N with $T_{wr} = 1/1000T_{scan}$ for the annealing method.

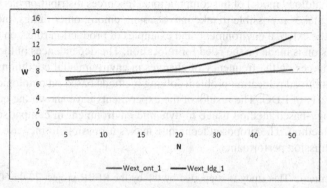

Fig. 8. The dependence of the amount of involved resources for the ontology-based ($W_{ext\_ont\_1}$) and the LDG-based ($W_{ext\_ldg\_1}$) methods on N with $T_{wr} = 1/100T_{scan}$ for the monkey algorithm.

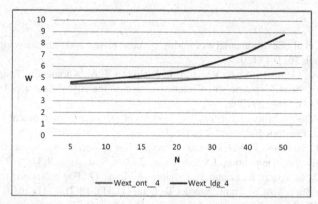

Fig. 9. The dependence of the amount of involved resources for the ontology-based ($W_{ext\_ont\_4}$) and the LDG-based ($W_{ext\_ldg\_4}$) methods on N with $T_{wr} = 1/100T_{scan}$ for the monkey algorithm.

3. Ontology-based method allows to decrease the amount of engaged resources up to 3% with $T_{wr} = 1/1000T_{scan}$ and up to 44% with $T_{wr} = 1/100T_{scan}$.

6   Conclusion

This work is devoted to the problem of workload relocation in a heterogeneous group of UAVs that scan area in changing environmental conditions. Environmental factors have a direct impact on the amount of resources spent by MR, which affects the success of the mission. To prevent situations when the implementation of the mission is under threat, due to the lack of the UAV's own resources, a technique has been developed that makes it possible to make a decision on the need to relocate the workload. This technique is based on the procedure of ontological analysis, which allows limiting the set of choices for relocating the workload in each specific case and speeding up the decision-making process. An ontology model of the computational resources distribution has been developed, which makes it possible to take into account, among other things, the factors of influence of the external environment, and examples of production rules, on the basis of which a decision is made on the need for relocation. The dependences of the volume of engaged resources on the frequency of changes in environmental conditions are investigated for workload relocation problem solving methods based on ontological analysis and on the basis of LDG. The results of the experiments have shown the effectiveness of the ontology-based method usage in dynamic environment in comparison with the LDG-based method. The proposed technique makes it possible to increase the time of cooperative mission performance.

Acknowledgement. This study is supported by the by the RFBR project 20-04-60485 and the GZ SSC RAS N GR project AAAA-A19-119011190173-6.

References

1. Secerov, I., et al.: Environmental monitoring systems: review and future development. Wirel. Eng. Technol. **10**, 1–18 (2019)
2. Sigora, G.A., Gutnik, S.A., Azarenko, E.I., Nichkova, L.A., Khomenko, T.: Increasing the efficiency of the atmospheric air monitoring system in the city of Sevastopol. Monit. Syst. Environ. 1(43), 118–128 (2021)
3. Gaisky, V.A.: Reliability and accuracy of systems of the natural environment control Part 3. Monit. Syst. Environ. 4(42), 111–118 (2020)
4. Goethals, T., Turckand, F., Volckaert, B.: Nearreal-time optimization of fog service placement for responsive edge computing. J. Cloud Comput. Adv. Syst. Appl. **9**(34), 1–17 (2020)
5. Puliafito, C., Mingozzi, E., Longo, F., Puliafito, A., Rana, O.: Fog computing for the internet of things: a Survey. ACM Trans. Internet Technol. (TOIT). **18**(2), 1–41 (2019)
6. Naeem, R.Z., Bashir, S., Amjad, M.F., Abbas, H., Afzal, H.: Fog computing in internet of things: practical applications and future directions. Peer-to-Peer Netw. Appl. **12**(5), 1236–1262 (2019). https://doi.org/10.1007/s12083-019-00728-0
7. Kraemer, F.A., Braten, A.E., Tamkittikhun, N., Palma, D.: Fog computing in healthcare – a review and discussion. IEEE Access **5**, 9206–9222 (2017)

8. Orda-Zhigulina, M.V., Melnik, E.V., Ivanov, D.Y., Rodina A.A., Orda-Zhigulina, D.: Combined method of monitoring and predicting of hazardous phenomena. Adv. Intell. Syst. Comput. **984**, 55–61 (2019)

9. Kapustyan, S.G., Gayduk, A.R.: Information support of UAV group actions in solving monitoring tasks of large areas. In: Proceedings of the II International Scientific Conference in memory of Corresponding Member RAS D.G. Matishov, pp. 332–335. SSC RAS Publishers, Rostov-on-Don (2020)

10. Kalyaev, I.A., Kapustyan, S.G., Usachev, L.Z.: The method of solving the problem of the distribution of goals in the group of UAVs by network-centric control system. Izvestiya SFedU Eng. Sci. **12**, 55–70 (2016)

11. Klimenko, A.B., Safronenkova, I.B.: A technique of workload distribution based on parallel algorithm structure ontology. In: Silhavy, R., Silhavy, P., Prokopova, Z. (eds.) CoMeSySo 2019 2019. AISC, vol. 1046, pp. 37–48. Springer, Cham (2019). https://doi.org/10.1007/978-3-030-30329-7_4

12. Klimenko, A.B., Safronenkova, I.B.: An ontology-based approach to the workload distribution problem solving in fog-computing environment. Adv. Intell. Syst. Comput. **985**, 62–72 (2019)

13. Ontology Development 101: A Guide to Creating Your First Ontology, ontology101.pdf (stanford.edu). Accessed 11 June 2021

14. Gergel', V.P., Strongin, R.G.: Fundamentals of Parallel Computing for Multiprocessor Computing Systems. Izdatel'stvo NNGU im. N.I. Lobachevskogo, Nizhny Novgorod (2003)

15. Voevodin, V.V., Voevodin, Vl.V.: Parallel computing. BHV-Peterburg, Saint Petersburg (2002)

16. Klimenko, A.B., Safronenkova, I.B.: The comparative estimation of workload relocation approaches in the fog- and edge-computing environments. J. Phys. Conf. Ser. **1399**(3), 033036 (2019)

17. Melnik, E.V., Safronenkova, I.B., Klimenko, A.B.: The restrictions forming in the workload relocation problem in DCAD systems as a condition for design quality increasing. Izvestiya TulGU Eng. Sci. **2**, 357–364 (2021)

18. Kalyaev, I., Melnik, E., Klimenko, A.: A technique of adaptation of the workload distribution problem model for the Fog-computing environment. In: Silhavy, R. (ed.) CSOC 2019. AISC, vol. 986, pp. 87–96. Springer, Cham (2019). https://doi.org/10.1007/978-3-030-19813-8_10

Visual Data Processing Framework for a Skin-Based Human Detection

Valery Myrzin[1], Tatyana Tsoy[1], Yang Bai[2], Mikhail Svinin[2],
and Evgeni Magid[1]

[1] Laboratory of Intelligent Robotics Systems (LIRS), Intelligent Robotics
Department, Institute of Information Technology and Intelligent Systems,
Kazan Federal University, Kazan, Russia
{tt,magid}@it.kfu.ru
[2] Information Science and Engineering Department, College of Information Science
and Engineering, Ritsumeikan University, 1-1-1 Noji-higashi, Kusatsu, Shiga
525-8577, Japan
{yangbai,svinin}@fc.ritsumei.ac.jp
https://kpfu.ru/eng/itis/research/laboratory-of-intelligent-robotic-systems,
http://en.ritsumei.ac.jp/academics/college-of-information-science-and-engineering/

Abstract. For a large variety of tasks autonomous robots require a robust visual data processing system. This paper presents a new human detection framework that combines rotation-invariant histogram of oriented gradients (RIHOG) features and binarized normed gradients (BING) pre-processing and skin segmentation. For experimental evaluation a new *Human body dataset* of over 60000 images was constructed using the Human-Parts dataset, the Simulated disaster victim dataset, and the Servosila Engineer robot dataset. Random, Liner SVM, Quadratic SVM, AdaBoost, and Random Forest approaches were compared using the Human body dataset. Experimental evaluation demonstrated an average precision of 90.4% for the Quadratic SVM model and showed the efficiency of RIHOG features as a descriptor for human detection tasks.

Keywords: Visual data processing · Skin segmentation · Feature extraction · Image classification · Mobile robot

1 Introduction

In the recent decades a consistent growth of interest to a human-robot interaction (HRI) field is being indicated. Such interactions have many application areas along with challenges to overcome, and a significant number of issues is tied to a natural difference in human and robot perception of an environment [9]. There are several areas where robust perception of human beings is crucial for a robot in order to effectively perform its tasks [26]. Industrial robots that work in a tight collaboration with a human need a human visual perception system to decrease a potential risk of harming people, which work within the same workspace [13].

© Springer Nature Switzerland AG 2021
A. Ronzhin et al. (Eds.): ICR 2021, LNAI 12998, pp. 138–149, 2021.
https://doi.org/10.1007/978-3-030-87725-5_12

Social robots heavily rely on visual and voice recognition to act according to their corresponding roles such as a teacher [38], a nurse [2], a personal assistant [6] etc. Autonomous surgical robots require a strong and precise visual perception of a human body in order to perform complicated operations successfully [20].

Another field that heavily rely on robot perception capabilities is Urban search and rescue (USAR) [25]. UAVs and UGVs can be used in cooperation with USAR teams to detect victims allowing to reduce safety risk for the teams at a disaster site [24,34]. SLAM-based navigational algorithms [31] and properly implemented communication protocols [28] allow rescue robots to explore the disaster site without endangering the rescuers life. Victims identification system with a built-in robot sensor as an integral part of such rescue robots is crucial for increasing a number of survivors. Detecting disaster victims is a challenging task due to articulated nature of human body, cluttered background environment, large area covered by dust layer [1]. Considering such obstacles only a part of human body may be seen from the robot camera which makes victim detection even more challenging.

This paper takes a closer look at various image processing methods and aggregate them into a single framework suitable for a human body detection by a Servosila Engineer rescue robot camera [30,36]. For each frame we used binarized normed gradients (BING, [7]) approach for a windows generation proposal. Next, extracted RIHOG [23] features were classified and combined with a skin segmentation method in order to achieve a robust human body identification system.

The rest of the paper is structured in the following way. An overview of related work is introduced in Sect. 2. Section 3 describes image processing algorithms typically used for a human detection. Experimental results are presented in Sect. 4. Finally, we conclude in Sect. 5.

2   Related Work

A large number of research works are devoted to a selection of a so-called visual saliency - an area of an image that visually stands out from its surroundings. Itti et al. [18] were the first to introduce the visual saliency approach, which had been inspired by a visual system of early primates. The authors used a color, an intensity, and an orientation of an image to create saliency maps, which are then used for a region of interest identification. Harsen et al. [14] proposed another approach of finding saliency based on a graph calculation. The Graph-Based Visual Saliency (GBVS) approach was modified using Local Entropy Feature specially for a disaster victim detection in [16]. Fast, accurate, and size-aware salient object detection (FASA) algorithm [40] used a combination of saliency probability and global contrast maps to calculate a final saliency map. Cheng et al. [7] developed a new method for finding saliency using a normalized gradient magnitude of low-resolution images to create a fast algorithm for image pre-processing. Bharath et al. [5] used saliency calculation as an integral part of a framework for classification and scene understanding in an image.

Pre-processing algorithms only reduce a region of interest (ROI) for an estimated object and are unable to recognize an object itself. To recognize the object it is required to distinguish it using classification, i.e., to determine if the object corresponds to a certain class. Classification can be done by various machine learning techniques, which use feature descriptors extracted from an image. The descriptors are vectors with a high enough discriminative power allowing to distinguish one object from another. A number of research works were devoted to an effective descriptor development, e.g., Dalal and Triggs [11] proposed a method of human recognition based on a feature descriptor - a histogram of orientated gradients (HOG), which successfully described a local shape of an object and kept invariance to various conditions of illumination, shadowing, noise, etc.

A significant number of scientists adopted HOG for various classification tasks including disaster victims detection [4,32]. Soni and Sowmya [35] developed a framework for a HRI in search and rescue operations and proposed methods for human body parts recognition. Davis and Sahin [12] combined HOG with RGB, Thermal, and Depth images to create a robust multi-layer classifier. Huang and Chu [17] used HOG with Support Vector Machines (SVM) learning to detect a person and developed a specific system to determine if a victim was immobilized by a heavy object. Liu et al. [23] proposed a modification of HOG adding invariance to an object orientation with a help of Fourier analysis and data translation to a polar system. Other researchers used a rotation invariant histogram of oriented gradients (RIHOG) to supplement a Bag of Visual Words classification method for the task of disaster victims identification [22].

Other works related to determination of a victim presence in an image included various skin segmentation techniques [10,19], e.g., Hoshino and Niimura used Optical Flow combined with Convolution Neural Network to achieve a real-time human detection[15]. Perera et al. [29] applied a video stream stabilization and signal processing to track human chest movements in order to detect a process of the human breathing, and then localized the human in an image based on the breathing region.

3   Image Data Processing

The proposed algorithm workflow is presented in Fig. 1. It consists of several steps including pre-processing, skin segmentation, and feature extraction. For the pre-processing step we adopted BING method, which generates a reliable window proposal. Next, the skin segmentation is used to rearrange the window proposal in order to use the windows with skin entries first. The feature extraction is performed in the final window proposal, which is then classified to accomplish the detection process.

3.1   Pre-processing

In the classic approach of determining a desired object location within an image the entire image is scanned with a fixed size window and a predefined step.

Afterwards a region of the image in all windows is classified for a presence of an object of interest. Such process is called a sliding window paradigm. The problem of this method is a consumption of a significant amount of computational resources, which reduces the efficiency of the detector and makes it unsuitable for real-time detection tasks due to slow computations. Many works were devoted to various image pre-processing algorithms that attempted to solve the sliding window problem and reduce the problem by reducing a search area of the object thus increasing a speed of the image processing.

According to Cheng et al. [7], Binarized Normed Gradients were designed to speed up the sliding window paradigm. The authors discovered that generic objects with a well-defined closed boundary could be discriminated by looking at a norm of gradients magnitude with a suitable resizing of their corresponding image windows into a small fixed size. Taking this feature as a basis in their algorithm, the size of all windows in the image was changed to 8×8 pixels. Thus, processing of the entire image resulted in a 64-dimensional gradient magnitude vector. The support vector machine method was used for training the 64-dimensional descriptors to differentiate generic objects on the image and evaluate objectness. With a help of SVM model, the 64-dimensional vector was translated to its binary analog, thus reducing the time of image processing to $0.003\,\text{s}$ (300 FPS) and providing a windows that cover an area with the required object with a high probability of 96%.

This method fits well for the original idea of a human detector, which requires to quickly determine an expected location of an object and perform a fast classification based on data from a mobile robot camera. The use of BING significantly reduced a computational cost of image processing, as it allowed to use generated probability regions as a classification zone and thus not to use a sliding window on the entire image. For our method we used BING on 1280×720 input images from the robot camera to generate a set of bounding boxes. Next, the bounding boxes were ordered according to objectness scores [37] and then used together with the skin segmentation step to rearrange them based on the skin presence inside the bounding box.

3.2 Skin Segmentation

According to [10], for skin segmentation we used a pregenerated transformation matrix, which is referred as Color Attention Vectors (CAVs):

$$CAV = \begin{pmatrix} 0.5902 & -0.7543 & -0.1467 \\ -0.7543 & 1.2729 & -0.4443 \\ 0.1467 & -0.4443 & 0.2783 \end{pmatrix}. \tag{1}$$

Skin attention map (SAM) for an image was obtained by:

$$SAM(x,y) = CAV \cdot I(x,y), \tag{2}$$

where I denotes the image reshaped in $3 \times (I_{width} \cdot I_{height})$ dimension. SAM showed the affinity of a pixel to the skin region. We manually thresholded SAM to obtain skin segmentation map.

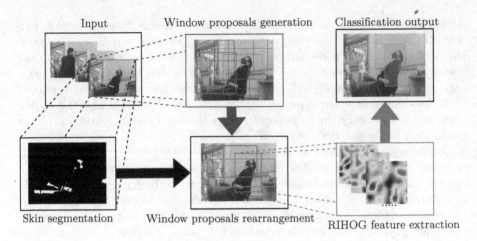

Input   Window proposals generation   Classification output

Skin segmentation   Window proposals rearrangement   RIHOG feature extraction

Fig. 1. Framework of the proposed image processing algorithm.

BING bounding boxes rearrangement with the help of SAM was performed in the following way: the bounding boxes that contain skin pixels did not change their order inside a queue, while other bounding boxes were transferred to a bottom of the queue. When the queue construction was completed, the bounding boxes were sent for the feature extraction algorithm.

3.3 Feature Extraction

We used square shape centroids of the rearranged bounding boxes and resized them into 64×64 cell blocks, which were then used as an input for RIHOG feature extraction process. RIHOG features encoded gradient information in rotation-invariant manner. Taking a gradient of a pixel as g, we defined an orientation distribution function at each pixel as a delta function:

$$P(\varphi) = ||g|| \delta(\varphi - \psi(g)), \tag{3}$$

where $||g||$ was a gradient magnitude and $\psi(g)$ represented the gradient orientation. This function was projected into Fourier space. Afterwards Fourier coefficients for a pixel were defined as follows:

$$f_m = \frac{1}{2\pi} P(\varphi) e^{-im\varphi} d\varphi = ||g|| e^{-im\psi(g)}, \tag{4}$$

where m denotes Fourier basis degree. From Eq. 4 above the gradient information could be represented by a sequence of Fourier coefficients. f_m applied to each point of the image generated a Fourier field F_m, which already described the entire image as a matrix with Fourier coefficient:

$$F_m = \frac{1}{2\pi} ||G|| e^{-im\psi(G))}, \tag{5}$$

where G denotes the gradient of the image patch.

For the next step we computed basis functions for regional descriptors using an angular part of a circular ring as Fourier basis. Thus functions for computing regional descriptors were defined as follows:

$$U_{j,k}(r,\varphi) = \wedge(r - r_j, \sigma)e^{-ik\varphi}, \tag{6}$$

where $\wedge$ is a triangular function with a width of 2σ and defined as $\wedge(x,\sigma) = max(\frac{\sigma-|x|}{\sigma}, 0)$, k is a degree of Fourier basis, r_j is a radius of j circular ring from a point (r,φ).

As it was shown in the above Eq. 6, each pixel can be described by a particular number of rings that contained regional information and varied function parameters; this way an image of any size could be described at the cost of a computational loss.

Using the $U_{j,k} * F_m$ convolution operation, we created the rotation-invariant regional descriptor that described HOG values in the region covered by $U_{j,k}$. Then, to obtain vectors with values invariant to rotations, we performed the following computation:

$$\overline{(U_{j_1,k_1} * F_{m_1})}(U_{j_2,k_2} * F_{m_2}), \forall k_1 - m_1 = k_2 - m_2. \tag{7}$$

The regional descriptors created using the multiplication from the above Eq. 7 is an effective way to create many invariant features applying different parameters instead of only taking the magnitude of expansion coefficients; this allowed to increase the final feature vector. Thus, using different combinations of k and m we received a final RIHOG descriptor that was rotation-invariant and at the same time had all the HOG based descriptors advantages.

4   Experiments

4.1   Datasets

In our experiments for human detection task we used the following datasets:

1. Human-Parts dataset [39] includes 14,962 images and 106,879 annotations, which includes human body, head and hands as annotated classes.
2. MPII Human Pose dataset [3] includes around 25000 images containing over 40000 people with annotated body joints.
3. Simulated disaster victim dataset [10] consists of two parts SDV1 and SDV2. SDV1 contains 128 images and ground truth binary images with skin segmentation. SDV2 contains 15 video clips, a total of 6315 frames and 557 ground truth skin segmentation for particular frames.
4. Servosila Engineer robot dataset. The constructed by LIRS[1] dataset contains frames recorded from Servosila Engineer camera as shown on Fig. 2.

---

[1] Laboratory of Intelligent Robotic Systems, https://kpfu.ru/eng/itis/research/laboratory-of-intelligent-robotic-systems.

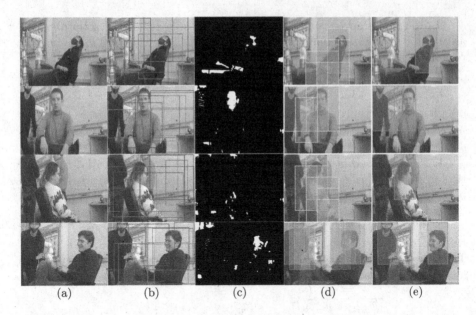

(a) (b) (c) (d) (e)

Fig. 2. Detection algorithm results with Linear SVM classifier using Servosila Engineer camera images: (a) input image, (b) BING window proposals, (c) Dadwhal et al. skin segmentation [10], (d) Positive classified bounding boxes, (e) Non-maximum suppression bounding boxes.

The datasets were used to create a new *Human body dataset*, which consist of over 60000 64 × 64 resolution images for machine learning algorithms. The positive part of the dataset mainly contained an upper part of a human body. The negative part focused on cluttered background segments of the images surrounding a human body.

4.2 Experiment Setup

The RIHOG extraction algorithm implementation was adapted to 64 × 64 size images and human detection task, some parameters were adjusted in order to meet new requirements. First five degrees of Fourier features were used F_m : $m \in [0;4]$, for $U_{j,k}(r,\varphi)$ the following parameters used: $k \in [-4;4]$, $\sigma = 9$, $r_j \in \{0, 9, 18, 27\}$. By combining m and k parameters in Eq. 7 on each individual ring j and coupling the values between the rings j_a and $j_b, \forall a \neq b$, we obtained a 233-dimensional final real vector that described a circular area around a single pixel.

For description of the above mentioned 64 × 64 images from The Human body dataset, we decided to take only 9 central pixels of those images in order to reduce the training time of various machine learning algorithms, which finally provided 233 × 9 = 2097 - dimensional feature vector, and since a diameter of the largest local ring was 54 pixels, which was enough for the classification purposes.

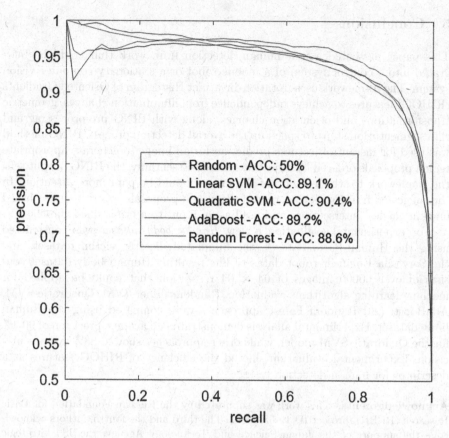

Fig. 3. PR curves and average accuracy values for the proposed algorithm.

4.3   Classification Evaluation

We trained Linear and Quadratic SVM [8], Random Forest [21] and AdaBoost [33] classifiers for performance evaluation of RIHOG features on the new data. For training we used 2097-dimensional feature vectors extracted from the Human body dataset. Those features, based on description of a human body or a background, were divided into a positive set and a negative set respectively. We used 5-fold cross-validation to evaluate detection performance of our framework, precision-recall curves and average accuracy that are shown in Fig. 3. Qualitative image examples for each step of our detection framework were captured with Servosila Engineer robot [27] camera; they are demonstrated in Fig. 2.

Validation performance showed around 88% average precision for Liner SVM, Random Forest and AdaBoost models, and reached 90.4% for the Quadratic SVM model. The results demonstrated a strong discriminative power of RIHOG features and their effectiveness particularly for a human classification with an articulated body position.

5   Conclusions

This paper presented a new human detection framework that could be integrated into a control system of a mobile robot or a stationary computer vision system. The framework uses Rotation-Invariant Histogram of Oriented Gradients (RIHOG) features to achieve independence from illumination changes, geometric transformations and orientation changes, along with BING pre-processing and skin segmentation steps to speed up the overall detection process. BING method was used for instant objectness prediction for an image to generate appropriate region proposals ordered by objectness scores. Essentially, the BING output tells the framework to which region of the image should be paid more attention. In the suggested framework the order of the region proposals was rearranged based on skin entries' intersections and used as an input to a pre-trained classifier.

For experimental evaluation a new *Human body dataset* was constructed using the Human-Parts dataset, the Simulated disaster victim dataset, and the Servosila Engineer robot dataset. The resulting Human body dataset consists of over 60000 images of 64 × 64 resolution that could be applied for machine learning algorithms evaluation. Random, Liner SVM, Quadratic SVM, AdaBoost, and Random Forest approaches were compared using the Human body dataset. Experimental analysis demonstrated an average precision of 90.4% for the Quadratic SVM model, while other approaches showed 88% average precision. Experimental evaluation showed the efficiency of RIHOG features as a descriptor for human detection tasks.

Acknowledgments. This work was supported by the Russian Foundation for Basic Research (RFBR), project ID 19-58-70002. The third and the fourth authors acknowledge the support of the Japan Science and Technology Agency, the JST Strategic International Collaborative Research Program, Project No. 18065977. This work is part of Kazan Federal University Strategic Academic Leadership Program.

References

1. Abbyasov, B., Lavrenov, R., Zakiev, A., Yakovlev, K., Svinin, M., Magid, E.: Automatic tool for gazebo world construction: from a grayscale image to a 3d solid model. In: 2020 IEEE International Conference on Robotics and Automation (ICRA), pp. 7226–7232. IEEE (2020)
2. Alvarez, J., Campos, G., Enríquez, V., Miranda, A., Rodriguez, F., Ponce, H.: Nurse-bot: a robot system applied to medical assistance. In: 2018 International Conference on Mechatronics, Electronics and Automotive Engineering (ICMEAE), pp. 56–59. IEEE (2018)
3. Andriluka, M., Pishchulin, L., Gehler, P., Schiele, B.: 2D human pose estimation: new benchmark and state of the art analysis. In: IEEE Conference on Computer Vision and Pattern Recognition (CVPR) (June 2014)
4. Andriluka, M., et al.: Vision based victim detection from unmanned aerial vehicles. In: 2010 IEEE/RSJ International Conference on Intelligent Robots and Systems, pp. 1740–1747. IEEE (2010)

5. Bharath, R., Nicholas, L.Z.J., Cheng, X.: Scalable scene understanding using saliency-guided object localization. In: 2013 10th IEEE International Conference on Control and Automation (ICCA), pp. 1503–1508. IEEE (2013)
6. Chebotareva, E., Safin, R., Hsia, K.-H., Carballo, A., Magid, E.: Person-following algorithm based on laser range finder and monocular camera data fusion for a wheeled autonomous mobile robot. In: Ronzhin, A., Rigoll, G., Meshcheryakov, R. (eds.) ICR 2020. LNCS (LNAI), vol. 12336, pp. 21–33. Springer, Cham (2020). https://doi.org/10.1007/978-3-030-60337-3_3
7. Cheng, M.M., Zhang, Z., Lin, W.Y., Torr, P.: Bing: binarized normed gradients for objectness estimation at 300fps. In: Proceedings of the IEEE Conference on Computer Vision and Pattern Recognition, pp. 3286–3293 (2014)
8. Cortes, C., Vapnik, V.: Support-vector networks. Mach. Learn. **20**(3), 273–297 (1995)
9. Crick, C., Osentoski, S., Jay, G., Jenkins, O.C.: Human and robot perception in large-scale learning from demonstration. In: Proceedings of the 6th International Conference on Human-robot Interaction, pp. 339–346 (2011)
10. Dadwhal, Y.S., Kumar, S., Sardana, H.: Data-driven skin detection in cluttered search and rescue environments. IEEE Sens. J. **20**(7), 3697–3708 (2019)
11. Dalal, N., Triggs, B.: Histograms of oriented gradients for human detection. In: 2005 IEEE Computer Society Conference on Computer Vision and Pattern Recognition (CVPR 2005), vol. 1, pp. 886–893. IEEE (2005)
12. Davis, M., Sahin, F.: Hog feature human detection system. In: 2016 IEEE International Conference on Systems, Man, and Cybernetics (SMC), pp. 002878–002883. IEEE (2016)
13. Galin, R., Meshcheryakov, R.: Automation and robotics in the context of industry 4.0: the shift to collaborative robots. In: IOP Conference Series: Materials Science and Engineering, vol. 537, p. 032073. IOP Publishing (2019)
14. Harel, J., Koch, C., Perona, P.: Graph-based visual saliency. In: Advances in Neural Information Processing Systems, pp. 545–552 (2007)
15. Hoshino, S., Niimura, K.: Robot vision system for real-time human detection and action recognition. In: Strand, M., Dillmann, R., Menegatti, E., Ghidoni, S. (eds.) IAS 2018. AISC, vol. 867, pp. 507–519. Springer, Cham (2019). https://doi.org/10.1007/978-3-030-01370-7_40
16. Htwe, K.Y., Thein, T.L.L.: Region of interest detection based on local entropy feature for disaster victim detection system. In: 2018 IEEE 7th Global Conference on Consumer Electronics (GCCE), pp. 390–391. IEEE (2018)
17. Huang, P.R., Chu, E.T.H.: Indoor trapped-victim detection system. In: 2017 IEEE SmartWorld, Ubiquitous Intelligence & Computing, Advanced & Trusted Computed, Scalable Computing & Communications, Cloud & Big Data Computing, Internet of People and Smart City Innovation (SmartWorld/SCALCOM/UIC/ATC/CBDCom/IOP/SCI), pp. 1–6. IEEE (2017)
18. Itti, L., Koch, C., Niebur, E.: A model of saliency-based visual attention for rapid scene analysis. IEEE Trans. Pattern Anal. Mach. Intell. **20**(11), 1254–1259 (1998)
19. Kawulok, M., Kawulok, J., Nalepa, J., Smolka, B.: Self-adaptive algorithm for segmenting skin regions. EURASIP J. Adv. Signal Process. **2014**(1), 1–22 (2014). https://doi.org/10.1186/1687-6180-2014-170
20. Li, Y., et al.: Super: a surgical perception framework for endoscopic tissue manipulation with surgical robotics. IEEE Robot. Autom. Lett. **5**(2), 2294–2301 (2020)
21. Liaw, A., Wiener, M., et al.: Classification and regression by randomforest. R News **2**(3), 18–22 (2002)

22. Liu, B., Wu, H., Zhang, Y., Xu, W., Mu, K., Yao, Y.: Rihog-bovws for rotation-invariant human detection. In: IOP Conference, vol. 428, p. 10 (2018)
23. Liu, K., et al.: Rotation-invariant hog descriptors using fourier analysis in polar and spherical coordinates. Int. J. Comput. Vis. **106**(3), 342–364 (2014)
24. Magid, E., et al.: Artificial intelligence based framework for robotic search and rescue operations conducted jointly by international teams. In: Ronzhin A., Shishlakov V. (eds) Proceedings of 14th International Conference on Electromechanics and Robotics "Zavalishin's Readings". Smart Innovation, Systems and Technologies, vol. 154, pp. 15–26. Springer, Singapore (2020). https://doi.org/10.1007/978-981-13-9267-2_2
25. Magid, E., Tsubouchi, T.: Static balance for rescue robot navigation: discretizing rotational motion within random step environment. In: Ando, N., Balakirsky, S., Hemker, T., Reggiani, M., von Stryk, O. (eds.) SIMPAR 2010. LNCS (LNAI), vol. 6472, pp. 423–435. Springer, Heidelberg (2010). https://doi.org/10.1007/978-3-642-17319-6_39
26. Magid, E., Zakiev, A., Tsoy, T., Lavrenov, R., Rizvanov, A.: Automating pandemic mitigation. Adv. Robot. **35**(9), 572–589 (2021)
27. Moskvin, I., Lavrenov, R.: Modeling tracks and controller for Servosila engineer robot. In: Ronzhin, A., Shishlakov, V. (eds.) Proceedings of 14th International Conference on Electromechanics and Robotics "Zavalishin's Readings". SIST, vol. 154, pp. 411–422. Springer, Singapore (2020). https://doi.org/10.1007/978-981-13-9267-2_33
28. Pashkin, A., Lavrenov, R., Zakiev, A., Svinin, M.: Pilot communication protocols for group of mobile robots in USAR scenarios. In: 2019 12th International Conference on Developments in eSystems Engineering (DeSE), pp. 37–41. IEEE (2019)
29. Perera, A.G., Khanam, F.T.Z., Al-Naji, A., Chahl, J., et al.: Detection and localisation of life signs from the air using image registration and spatio-temporal filtering. Remote Sens. **12**(3), 577 (2020)
30. Ramil, S., Lavrenov, R., Tsoy, T., Svinin, M., Magid, E.: Real-time video server implementation for a mobile robot. In: 2018 11th International Conference on Developments in eSystems Engineering (DeSE), pp. 180–185. IEEE (2018)
31. Safin, R., Lavrenov, R., Martínez-García, E.A.: Evaluation of visual SLAM methods in USAR applications using ROS/Gazebo simulation. In: Ronzhin, A., Shishlakov, V. (eds.) Proceedings of 15th International Conference on Electromechanics and Robotics "Zavalishin's Readings". SIST, vol. 187, pp. 371–382. Springer, Singapore (2021). https://doi.org/10.1007/978-981-15-5580-0_30
32. Salfikar, I., Sulistijono, I.A., Basuki, A.: Automatic samples selection using histogram of oriented gradients (hog) feature distance. EMITTER Int. J. Eng. Technol. **5**(2), 234–254 (2017)
33. Schapire, R.E.: Explaining adaboost. In: Schölkopf, B., Luo, Z., Vovk, V. (eds.) Empirical Inference, pp. 37–52. Springer, Heidelberg (2013). https://doi.org/10.1007/978-3-642-41136-6_5
34. Simakov, N., Lavrenov, R., Zakiev, A., Safin, R., Martínez-García, E.A.: Modeling USAR maps for the collection of information on the state of the environment. In: 2019 12th International Conference on Developments in eSystems Engineering (DeSE), pp. 918–923. IEEE (2019)
35. Soni, B., Sowmya, A.: Victim detection and localisation in an urban disaster site. In: 2013 IEEE international conference on robotics and biomimetics (ROBIO), pp. 2142–2147. IEEE (2013)

36. Tsoy, T., Zakiev, A., Shabalina, K., Safin, R., Magid, E., Saha, S.K.: Validation of fiducial marker systems performance with rescue robot servosila engineer onboard camera in laboratory environment. In: 2019 12th International Conference on Developments in eSystems Engineering (DeSE), pp. 495–499. IEEE (2019)

37. Valdenegro-Toro, M.: Objectness scoring and detection proposals in forward-looking sonar images with convolutional neural networks. In: Schwenker, F., Abbas, H.M., El Gayar, N., Trentin, E. (eds.) ANNPR 2016. LNCS (LNAI), vol. 9896, pp. 209–219. Springer, Cham (2016). https://doi.org/10.1007/978-3-319-46182-3_18

38. Verner, I.M., Polishuk, A., Krayner, N.: Science class with robothespian: using a robot teacher to make science fun and engage students. IEEE Robot. Autom. Mag. **23**(2), 74–80 (2016)

39. Xiaojie Li, L.y., Qing Song, F.Z.: Detector-in-detector: multi-level analysis for human-parts. arXiv preprint arXiv:**** (2019)

40. Yildirim, G., Süsstrunk, S.: FASA: fast, accurate, and size-aware salient object detection. In: Cremers, D., Reid, I., Saito, H., Yang, M.-H. (eds.) ACCV 2014. LNCS, vol. 9005, pp. 514–528. Springer, Cham (2015). https://doi.org/10.1007/978-3-319-16811-1_34

Classification of Aerial Manipulation Systems and Algorithms for Controlling the Movement of Onboard Manipulator

Vinh Nguyen[1] , Tien Ngo[2] , Quyen Vu[1] , and Andrey Ronzhin[1]([⊠])

[1] St. Petersburg Federal Research Center of the Russian Academy of Sciences (SPC RAS),
14-th line of V.I. 39, 199178 St. Petersburg, Russia
ronzhin@iias.spb.su

[2] Le Quy Don Technical University, 236 Hoang Quoc Viet, 10000 Hanoi, Vietnam

Abstract. Instrumentation of an unmanned aerial vehicle (UAV) with devices for physical interaction with ground-based objects is a popular scientific branch in the domain of robotics. Physical interaction of an onboard aerial manipulation system with objects complicates the UAV stabilization process, what, in turn, impairs the positioning of UAV and reduces navigational accuracy of the moving end of the mechanism. In this paper, the problem of the manipulator motion control for an unmanned aerial vehicle is considered. We also propose algorithms for the calculation of the angles of joints of the manipulator, based on the solutions of the direct and inverse kinematics problems. The developed algorithms ensure retaining of the center of mass of an aerial manipulator system on the vertical axis and minimum displacement of the center of mass horizontally when moving the end mechanism along the reference trajectory.

Keywords: Unmanned aerial vehicle · UAV · Aerial manipulation system · Stability of aerial manipulator system

1 Introduction

Manipulator-aided interaction with objects, where the manipulator is mounted on an UAV, is a relevant problem, because UAVs can reach many locations, which, in certain instances, are inaccessible for alternative ground-based robotic platforms [1–3]. Though, extending an aerial robotic vehicle with an onboard manipulator system poses serious issues, because any physical interactions of an UAV with ground-based objects influence the overall stability of the aerial manipulator system. In flight of the UAV, equipped with a mobile manipulator system, the mass distribution within the vehicle changes and additional dynamic reaction forces arise [4]. The design of the mechanism for object gripping and manipulation influences the acceptable payload mass, inertial and dynamic characteristics of the whole UAV. It is important to ensure, that the mass of this object would be low, and its center of mass would be positioned to the bottom part of the UAV. In this case, the reaction forces and torque, arising when the UAV is in motion, would not seriously impact its stability. Influence of the contact forces, permeating

© Springer Nature Switzerland AG 2021
A. Ronzhin et al. (Eds.): ICR 2021, LNAI 12998, pp. 150–161, 2021.
https://doi.org/10.1007/978-3-030-87725-5_13

from the end gripper to the UAV, can be minimized, joining the aerial manipulator with the bottom of the UAV [5]. Such aspects are often neglected in the common platform stabilization algorithms, so a novel algorithm is required, that would be suitable to solve such problems. It is also important to consider, that the manipulators perform various kinds of motion: translation, rotation, with payload and without it, what influences the UAV diversely and impairs its stability [4].

In this paper, some problems are considered, related to the manipulator control, and respecting the instability of its base and interactions with ground-based objects. One of the main objectives is to ensure stability of the aerial manipulator system in gripping the ground-based objects, which should be achieved through the development of algorithms for stabilization of the UAV manipulator in motion.

The paper is organized as follows. In Sect. 2 the developed classification of the aerial manipulator system, based on the regulatory documents is provided. The results of modeling of the manipulator of an unmanned aerial vehicle are provided in Sect. 3. Conclusions are provided in Sect. 4.

2 Classification of Aerial Manipulation Systems

When creating UAVs classifications, the goal is not only to differentiate existing systems, but also to fix their parameters and areas of application in normative legal acts. This is due to the fact that it is quite difficult to create general rules for all types of UAVs, so different categories of UAVs may have different requirements depending on their characteristics. Most of these requirements relate exclusively to the security characteristics of the system, and they are also important from operational, commercial, legal, and other points of view.

Recently, UAVs have been used in a wide range of applications, including power line inspection; pipeline inspection; ship inspection; mine inspection; dam inspection; anomaly detection/prevention; early fire detection and forest protection; hazard monitoring; traffic monitoring; environmental monitoring; search and rescue operations; emergency response; border patrol; harbor patrol; police surveillance; aerial photography; SWAT support; imaging and mapping; intelligence, surveillance, and reconnaissance; chemical spraying; crop dusting; night vision; and entertainment industry and filming [6]. UAVs may operate autonomously or with remote control. The UAV is an integral part of the unmanned aerial system, which includes the UAV, communications system, and ground control station. The UAV overcomes the limitations of ground transport systems in terms of availability and speed.

There are a large number of criteria that can be used to classify UAVS, including the principle of flight, type of take-off and landing, take-off weight, maximum range and altitude, other characteristics such as overall dimensions, wingspan, operating conditions, functionality, and combinations of criteria. Figure 1 shows the classification of UAVs based on the key characteristics that are most widely used in design and operation.

Ground-based control systems are also involved in the operation of UAVs, which are responsible for exchanging information with UAVs and/or between several UAVs. With the development of technologies, a transition is being made from controlling the movement of UAVs for solving surveillance tasks to interacting with ground objects. Of particular interest is the grasping and retrieval of objects during UAV hovering;

this requires a combination of approaches implemented for manipulating ground robots with control methods and the capabilities of aircraft in the range of speeds and vertical working space. Regarding the terminology, it is worth commenting that, in contrast to the classic formed notations in the aviation field, in the field of multirotor UAVs, the terminology is not yet fully settled and for hover mode, different scientific schools use the synonyms hovering, suspending, and others.

The creation of aerial manipulation systems opens prospects for new UAV applications, such as the search and delivery of objects in hard-to-reach areas, and in general, the creation of network logistics supply chains over large territories [7].

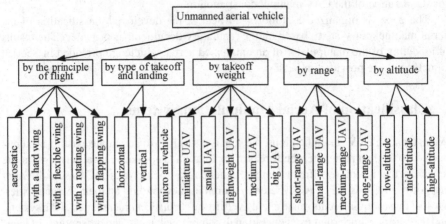

Fig. 1. Classification of UAV.

Placing the payload on the suspension allows the vehicle to safely deliver it to the ground without having to land the aerial system itself. In [8], physical interaction with objects on the ground was performed using an unmanned helicopter for cargo transportation on a suspension. When transporting suspended cargo, the force of the cable causes a torque on the fuselage of the helicopter, which depends on the orientation of the helicopter and its forward movement. Therefore, there are difficulties associated with control due to the wind, the downward flow of the rotor and the dynamics of the payload swing relative to the helicopter. The weight of the cargo is crucial because the cost of an unmanned aerial system increases exponentially with this load. To avoid this limitation, the possibility of joint transportation of one cargo by several unmanned helicopters is also being investigated [9]. Compared to manned helicopter transport the use of multiple unmanned helicopters has the following advantages: 1) the cost of two small helicopters is often less than that of a single manned transport helicopter with a dual payload capacity, and 2) when the weight of the cargo exceeds the capabilities of a manned helicopter, it is impossible to ensure coordination between the helicopters to perform the transport, while the use of multiple unmanned helicopters is fully automated. However, there are drawbacks when multiple unmanned helicopters are connected to the load, the translational and rotational movement of one particular helicopter directly affects the rotation dynamics of all other helicopters, so the development of control algorithms is a very important and complex task.

In recent years, multirotors have been investigated for the task of transporting suspended small and light loads. For example, the anti-rocking maneuver controller for a quadrotor with an attached suspended load is considered in [10], and in [11] a simplified guidance law is proposed to solve the problem of autonomous landing with a suspended payload. The problems of using several multirotors together to transport suspended loads, such as a liquid-filled container suspended on rigid light links to quadrotors, are also being studied [12]. The development of a controller for the safe transportation of loads to the desired location with minimal fluctuations and without collisions is presented in the work [13]. Development of robot configurations that ensure static balance of the payload in the desired position while respecting cable tension restrictions and provide stability analysis of the payload [11].

The next step in the development of methods of physical interaction with ground objects is aerial manipulations performed by UAVs [14]. For this purpose, UAVs must be able to hover to position the end mechanism or gripper attached to the manipulator of the multirotor and transport the ground object. Aerial manipulation systems consist of two subsystems, namely an aerial platform and an interaction/manipulation mechanism (such as a robot manipulator or instrument) used for physical interaction with the environment or with objects in it. Attaching one or more manipulators or grippers/instruments to the aerial platform opens up unlimited potential for using UAVs in a wide variety of areas, such as: checking and servicing high-rise pipes in chemical plants [15], cutting high-voltage cables [16], rotating the valve [17], inspecting bridges [18], monitoring aggressive environments [19], canopy sampling [20], rock climbing [21], object transportation [22], landing and charging, object assembly, etc.

Among aerial platforms with autonomous flight capabilities, such as multirotors, unmanned helicopters, and fixed-wing UAVs, only multirotors are suitable for aerial manipulation due to their ability to hover.

Therefore, multirotors are the most frequently discussed aerial platforms for manipulating ground objects. Multirotors come in various configurations depending on the number of power nodes (rotor arms), the way the propellers are attached, the configuration of the power nodes, the orientation of the power nodes, the number of propellers on the blades, and the configuration of the propellers. As for the number of propellers, the most popular are tricopters [23], quadrotors [24, 25], hexacopters [26] and octocopters [27]. Among these multirotors, quadrotors are the most widely used aerial manipulation platforms due to their simple mechanical design and ability to hover, as well as low cost, maneuverability, and affordable precision control. The configuration of power nodes can be either with one propeller on the node, or a coaxial configuration, which means two propellers on the node [28]. A single-propeller configuration on a node provides higher efficiency than a coaxial configuration, but these platforms are less compact. Based on the orientation of the power node, the most popular configuration is the transverse configuration compared to the "plus" configuration. Multirotors with coplanar rotors have internal movement restrictions that can be compensated by using the degrees of freedom of the manipulators when performing aerial manipulation tasks, but this leads to a decrease in the permissible payload mass. Multirotors with non-coplanar rotors can overcome the above-mentioned restrictions on the movement of the aerial platform, so that the number of degrees of freedom of the manipulators can be reduced [29]. Most multirotors use two-blade propellers, and the results of [30] show that the three-blade version of the propellers gives a lower efficiency but can be useful for reducing noise and risk due to lower required revolutions.

Unmanned helicopters are also widely used in aerial manipulations after multirotors [31, 32]. They also have the ability to hover, like multirotors, but have a better load capacity compared to multirotors. Unmanned helicopters for aerial manipulation have two types of configurations: classic and Flutter design. The first configuration consists of a single large main rotor that is responsible for the overall lift of the system, while a smaller tail rotor or ducted fan balances the helicopter against unwanted main rotor torque. The Flutter design is a helicopter concept with two mutually engaged rotors of opposite rotation at the top, which avoids the use of a tail rotor. These platforms can lift a payload equal to the empty helicopter's own weight. Also, the absence of a tail rotor avoids the associated energy costs for torque compensation mentioned in the classical configuration [33]. Figure 2 shows the classification of aerial unmanned platforms suitable for physical interaction with ground objects.

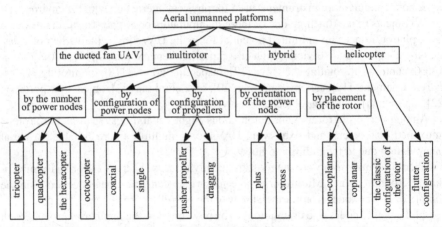

Fig. 2. Classification of aerial unmanned platforms for physical interaction with ground objects.

Compared to a multirotor, helicopters have greater lateral drag due to a larger side area, so wind disturbances cause more positioning errors. The inability to attach the manipulator to the top of the helicopter limits their use for checking ceiling surfaces, such as bridges. Helicopters also tend to be less maneuverable, especially in confined spaces [34].

The next category of aerial platforms is UAVS with channel propellers with a tail support [35, 36]. It consists of two subsystems and a torque generating mechanism: a fixed-pitch rotor driven by an electric motor, and a set of control blades located under the main propeller. The ducted fan configuration has features that make aerial vehicle flexible and suitable for operation in many contexts, some of which are unusual for aerial vehicle. In addition to the typical operating mode of an aerial vehicle in free flight, the fact that all moving and engaged parts are protected by an air duct makes the UAV suitable for physical interaction with the environment.

And finally, the recent emergence of the hybrid aerial platform for aerial manipulation. For example, airships can be used as UAVS when working together with a quadrotor [37] equipped with 3 identical manipulators for performing capture tasks. An innovative concept is the use of a transformable suspended platform where the entire platform can act as a gripper. In this case, the aerial platform consists of rotor power nodes, which can change their configuration in comparison with multi-motor blades with fixed rotors [38], etc.

Taking into account the options analyzed above, we will further consider a new classification of air handling systems that include three main functional elements: 1) aerial platform; 2) manipulator; 3) end mechanism. Figure 3 shows the main types of aerial manipulation systems and their components in the developed classification.

Aerial manipulation systems can consist of several manipulators attached to an aerial platform. The grips have the main advantages of 1) easy to build, 2) easy to model and manage, and 3) relatively inexpensive cost; but have the following disadvantages: 1) limited working space and 2) limited gripping capacity in terms of mass and volume. The manipulator consists mainly of two parts: one or more arms with several degrees of freedom attached to the aerial platform, and grips with various types of sensors. The manipulator significantly expands the working space compared to the gripper device and can use the redundancy of the manipulator to compensate for position errors when moving the aerial platform, so it is used in tasks that require complex movements.

Manipulators have the following disadvantages: 1) complex mechatronic system, 2) heavy weight; 3) complex control and 4) UAV destabilization. In addition to the parameters presented in the developed classification, when evaluating the capabilities of the UAV, the flight range, wingspan, mass of the permissible payload, range of the manipulator and other characteristics are also evaluated. In addition to the above-mentioned types of aerial manipulation systems, there are many other studies on soft grips and manipulators in practice, but there are not many successful practical implementations yet.

3 Modeling of UAV Manipulator

In this study, disturbances of the internal environment are not considered, we assume that the aerial manipulation system is ideally suited for interaction with ground objects. The external environment always contains disturbances and obstacles. These factors cause the aerial manipulation system to become unstable when interacting with ground objects. The aerial manipulation system itself is unstable, so the impact of the disturbance causes a strong vibration of the working end mechanism. Therefore, in this study, we will conduct an analysis to give the most stable model of the manipulator and design a controller for stabilizing the aerial manipulation system. Interaction of the aerial manipulation system with ground objects will be easier, even if the system is affected by disturbances.

The aerial manipulation system works stably when the center of mass of the manipulator is on the vertical y axis of the system. In order to analyze the ability of the manipulator to keep its center of mass always on the vertical axis during its operation,

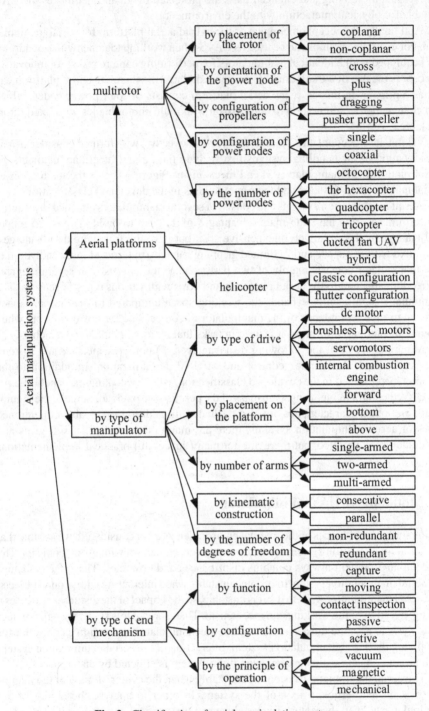

Fig. 3. Classification of aerial manipulation systems.

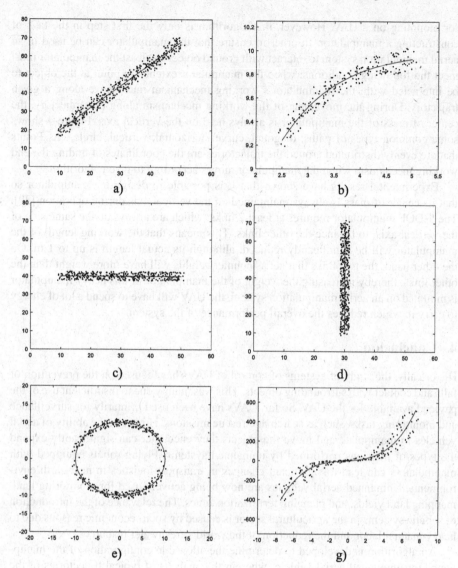

Fig. 4. Distribution of coordinates of the working mechanism around the motion trajectory.

a manipulator consisting of n links was considered. The Denavit-Hartenberg algorithm for assigning coordinate frames was used in this study.

An algorithm was developed for finding sets of angles between joints that satisfy the condition that the center of mass of the manipulator is on the vertical axis. The algorithm for calculating the coordinates of the key points of all links of the manipulator while keeping its center of mass on the vertical axis. The algorithm allows to determine all the positions of the manipulator, ensuring that the center of mass of the manipulator is on the vertical axis. This algorithm is the basis for designing a manipulator designed for mounting on a UAV. However, this algorithm is only the first step in the task of constructing a manipulator. In order to ensure that the manipulator can be used in an aerial manipulation system to interact with ground objects, at least the manipulator must meet the following conditions: when the manipulator extends to point at the object to be interacted with, the manipulator's working mechanism must move along a given trajectory. During the movement of the working mechanism along this trajectory, the center of mass of the manipulator is always held on the vertical axis. Figure 4 shows some common types of paths: diagonal, curve, horizontal, vertical, circle, etc. Points that are evenly distributed around the trajectories are the coordinates of finding the end working mechanism when the manipulator moves according to given algorithm.

Experimental results have shown that it is possible to design the manipulator so that its center of mass is always maintained on the vertical axis during operation [39]. The 5-DOF manipulator requires at least 2 links, which are always on the same side of the vertical axis, to balance the other links. This means that the working length of the manipulator will be significantly reduced, although its actual length is up to 1 m. On the other hand, the two links that act as counterweights will have more weight than the other links, thereby increasing the weight of the manipulator. If this heavy manipulator is mounted on an aerial manipulation system, the UAV will have to spend a lot of energy to carry it, which reduces the overall performance of the system.

4 Conclusion

Historically, the study of systems of control of UAVs has focused on the prevention of falls and contact with surrounding objects. This was mainly due to insufficient use of the payload available for the UAV. So far, UAVs have been used primarily for surveillance and monitoring tasks, such as search and rescue missions. However, the ability of aerial vehicles to manipulate and move the objects they encounter can significantly expand the types of missions performed by unmanned systems. Flying robots equipped with manipulators can lead to significant changes in transport logistics in near-earth environments. Unmanned aerial vehicles are now being actively used for monitoring land, mapping land yields, and planning fertilization zones. The relevance of the introduction of robotic systems in the agricultural sector is caused by socio-economic reasons due to heavy manual labor and the reduction of the world's freshwater resources.

An algorithm is developed to determine the allowable configuration of the manipulator for unmanned aerial vehicle, wherein the analysis of typical trajectories of the end working mechanism and the calculation of sets of angle ranges between the manipulator links that provide movement along specified trajectories while maintaining the center of mass of the manipulator on the vertical axis of the aerial manipulation system. The developed algorithm of calculation of coordinates of key points of all links of the manipulator, depending on the angles of joints on the basis of the decision of tasks of direct and inverse kinematics, wherein limiting the displacement of the centers of mass of the manipulator with its links and the end working mechanism for horizontal and vertical axes and thereby providing the movement mechanism of the limit trajectory is the minimum shift of the coordinates of the center of mass of the manipulator horizontally.

Currently, the use of UAVs for direct interaction with the environment is still limited due to its instability [40, 41]. A number of studies have been conducted on this topic, but most of them are performed at the modeling level. Certainly, working with objects using a manipulator mounted on a UAV and studying the features of controlling multirotor platforms equipped with a manipulator grip are promising areas for further research.

References

1. Danko, T.W., Oh, P.Y.: Design and control of a hyper-redundant manipulator for mobile manipulating unmanned aerial vehicles. J. Intell. Robot. Syst. **73**, 709–723 (2014)
2. Kochetkov, M.P., Korolkov, D.N., Petrov, V.F., Petrov, O.V., Terentev, A.I., Simonov, S.B.: Application of cluster analysis with fuzzy logic elements for ground environment assessment of robotic group. SPIIRAS Proc. **19**(4), 746–773 (2020). https://doi.org/10.15622/sp.2020. 19.4.2
3. Medvedev, M.Y., Kostjukov, V.A., Pshikhopov V.X.: Method for optimizing of mobile robot trajectory in repeller sources field. Inform. Autom. **20**(3), 690–726 (2021). https://doi.org/10. 15622/ia.2021.3.7
4. Gardecki, S., Kasiński, A., Bondyra, A., Gąsior, P.: Multirotor aerial platform with manipulation system - static disturbances. In: Szewczyk, R., Zieliński, C., Kaliczyńska, M. (eds.) ICA 2017. AISC, vol. 550, pp. 357–366. Springer, Cham (2017). https://doi.org/10.1007/978-3-319-54042-9_33
5. Suarez, A., Heredia, G., Ollero, A.: Compliant and lightweight anthropomorphic finger module for aerial manipulation and grasping. In: Robot 2015: Second Iberian Robotics Conference, vol. 417, pp. 543–555 (2015)
6. Valavanis, K., Vachtsevanos, J.: Handbook of Unmanned Aerial Vehicles. Springer, Netherlands (2015)
7. Pound, P., Bersak, D.R., Dollar, A.M.: Grasping from the air: hovering capture and load stability. In: IEEE International conference on robotics and automation, pp. 2491–2498 (2011)
8. Bernard, M., Kondak, K.: Generic slung load transportation system using small size helicopters. In: 2009 IEEE International Conference on Robotics and Automation, pp. 3258–3264 (2009)
9. Bernard, M., Kondak, K., Maza, I., Ollero, A.: Autonomous transportation and deployment with aerial robots for search and rescue missions. J. Field Robot. **28**, 914–931 (2011)
10. Graham, K.: Development of a quadrotor slung payload system. University of Toronto, Toronto. Master Thesis, no. 27541348 (2019)
11. Vargas, A., Ireland, M., Anderson D.: Swing free manoeuvre controller for RUAS slung-load system using ESN. In: 1 World Congress on Unmanned Systems Engineering. Oxford. (2014)
12. Sayyadi, H., Soltani, A.: Modeling and control for cooperative transport of a slung fluid container using quadrotors. Chin. J. Aeronaut. **31**(2), 262–272 (2018)
13. Shirania, B., Najafib, M., Izadia, I.: Cooperative load transportation using multiple UAVs. Aerosp. Sci. Technol. **84**, 158–169 (2019)
14. Michael, N., Fink, J., Kumar, V.: Cooperative manipulation and transportation with aerial robots. Auton Robot. **30**, 73–86 (2011)
15. Aeroarms URL: www.aeroarms-project.eu
16. Lin, T., Li, Y., Qi, J., Meng, X.: Modeling and controller design of hydraulic rotorcraft aerial manipulator. In: 27th Chinese Control and Decision Conference (2015)
17. Shimahara, S., Leewiwatwong, S., Ladig, R., Shimonomura, K.: Aerial torsional manipulation employing multi-rotor flying robot. In: 2016 IEEE/RSJ International Conference on Intelligent Robots and Systems (IROS), pp. 1595–1600 (2016)
18. Sanchez-Cuevas, P.J., Heredia, G., Ollero, A.: Multirotor UAS for bridge inspection by contact using the ceiling effect. In: 2017 International Conference on Unmanned Aircraft Systems (ICUAS), pp. 767–774 (2017).

19. Cacace, J., Finzi, A., Lippiello, V., Loianno, G., Sanzone, D.: Aerial service vehicles for industrial inspection: task decomposition and plan execution. Appl. Intell. **42**(1), 49–62 (2014). https://doi.org/10.1007/s10489-014-0542-0

20. Kutia, J., Stol, K., Xu, W.: Aerial manipulator interactions with trees for canopy sampling. IEEE/ASME Trans. Mechatron. **23**(4), 1740–1749 (2018)

21. Pope, M.T., Kimes, W.C., Jiang, H., Hawkes, E.W.: A multimodal robot for perching and climbing on vertical outdoor surfaces. IEEE Trans. Robot. **33**(1), 38–48 (2017)

22. Kim, S., Choi, S., Kim, H.J.: Aerial manipulation using a quadrotor with a two DOF robotic arm. In: 2013 IEEE/RSJ International Conference on Intelligent Robots and Systems, pp. 4990–4995 (2013)

23. Papachristos, P., Alexis, K., Tzes, A.: Efficient force exertion for aerial robotic manipulation: exploiting the thrust-vectoring authority of a tri-tiltrotor UAV. In: 2014 IEEE International Conference on Robotics and Automation (ICRA), pp. 4500–4505 (2014)

24. Arleo, G., Caccavale, F., Muscio, G., Pierri, F.: Control of quadrotor aerial vehicles equipped with a robotic arm. In: 21st Mediterranean Conference on Control and Automation, pp. 1174–1180 (2013)

25. Yang, H., Lee, D.: Dynamics and control of quadrotor with robotic manipulator. In: 2014 IEEE International Conference on Robotics and Automation (ICRA), pp. 5544–5549 (2014)

26. Jiang, G., Voyles, R.M.: Hexrotor UAV platform enabling dextrous aerial mobile manipulation. In: 2013 IEEE International Symposium on Safety, Security, and Rescue Robotics (SSRR) (2014)

27. Heredia, G., Jimenez-Cano, A.E., Sanchez, I., Llorente, D.: Control of a multirotor outdoor aerial manipulator. In: IEEE/RSJ International Conference on Intelligent Robots and Systems, pp. 3417–3422 (2014)

28. Suarez, A., Soria, P.R, Heredia, G., Arrue, B.C.: Anthropomorphic, compliant and lightweight dual arm system for aerial manipulation. In: 2017 IEEE/RSJ International Conference on Intelligent Robots and Systems (IROS), pp. 992–997 (2017)

29. Ryll, M., Bicego, D., Franchi, A.: Modeling and control of fast-hex: a fully–actuated by synchronized–tilting hexarotor. In: 2016 IEEE/RSJ International Conference on Intelligent Robots and Systems (IROS), pp. 1689–1694 (2016)

30. Theys, B., Dimitriadis, G., Hendrick, P., De Schutter, J.: Influence of propeller configuration on propulsion system efficiency of multi-rotor unmanned aerial vehicles. In: 2016 International Conference on Unmanned Aircraft Systems (ICUAS), pp. 195–201 (2016)

31. Kuciński, T., et al.: Deployable manipulator technology with application for UAVs. In: Sąsiadek, J. (eds.) Aerospace Robotics II. GeoPlanet: Earth and Planetary Sciences, pp. 93–103. Springer, Cham (2015). https://doi.org/10.1007/978-3-319-13853-4_9

32. Kondak, K., Krieger, K., Albu-Schäeffer, A., Schwarzbach, M.: Closed-loop behavior of an autonomous helicopter equipped with a robotic arm. Int. J. Adv. Robot. Syst. **10**(2), 145 (2013)

33. Bejar, M., Ollero, A., Kondak, K.: Helicopter based aerial manipulators. In: Ollero, A., Siciliano, B. (eds.) Aerial Robotic Manipulation. STAR, vol. 129, pp. 35–52. Springer, Cham (2019). https://doi.org/10.1007/978-3-030-12945-3_3

34. Huber, F., Kondak, K., Krieger, K., Sommer, D.: First analysis and experiments in aerial manipulation using fully actuated redundant robot arm. In: IEEE/RSJ International Conference on Intelligent Robots and Systems, pp. 3452–3457 (2013)

35. Gentili, L., Naldi, R., Marconi, L.: Modeling and control of VTOL UAVs interacting with the environment. In: 2008 47th IEEE Conference on Decision and Control, pp. 1231–1236 (2008)

36. Marconi, L., Naldi, R.: Control of aerial robots: hybrid force and position feedback for a ducted fan. IEEE Control Syst. Mag. **32**(4), 43–65 (2012)

37. Korpela, M., Danko, T.W., Oh P.Y.: Designing a system for mobile manipulation from an unmanned aerial vehicle. In: 2011 IEEE Conference on Technologies for Practical Robot Applications (2011)
38. Zhao, M., Kawasaki, K., Chen, X., Noda, S., Okada, K., Inaba, M.: Whole-body aerial manipulation by transformable multirotor with two-dimensional multilinks. In: 2017 IEEE International Conference on Robotics and Automation (ICRA), pp. 5175–5182 (2017)
39. Nguyen, V., Saveliev, A., Ronzhin, A.: Mathematical modelling of control and simultaneous stabilization of 3-DOF aerial manipulation system. In: International Conference on Interactive Collaborative Robotics, pp. 253–264 (2020)
40. Lavrenov, L.O., Magid, E.A., Matsuno, F., Svinin, M.M., Suthakorn, J.: Development and implementation of spline-based path planning algorithm in ROS/Gazebo environment. SPIIRAS Proc. **18**(1), 57–84 (2019). https://doi.org/10.15622/sp.18.1.57-84
41. Medvedev, M.Y., Kostjukov, V.A., Pshikhopov, V.X.: Method for optimizing of mobile robot trajectory in repeller sources field. Inform. Autom. **20**(3), 690–726 (2021). https://doi.org/10.15622/ia.2021.3.7

'MEOW' – A Social Robot Platform for School

Egor Polyntsev[✉], Vladimir Zhelonkin, and Evgeny Shandarov

Laboratory of Robotics and Artificial Intelligence, Tomsk State University of Control, Systems and Radioelectronics (TUSUR University), 40, Prospect Lenina, 634050 Tomsk, Russian Federation

Abstract. New social robot platform for using at educational purposes presented. The robot proposed looks like a cat with paws, ears and moustache. Robot could speak, process speech, process video. Main concept of robot was simple and robust construction, low prime cost and visual appeal for children. First prototype of robot was based on Raspberry Pi and commercially available peripheral components: camera, servos, microphones and LEDs. Basic design principles, hardware and software requirements were described. Numerical parameters were presented, such as speech generation time, sign detection time, etc. Four emotional states of the robot were developed, such as 'happiness', 'sadness', 'confusion' and 'smirk'. With use of developed speech and video processing modules and emotional states five child-robot interaction scenarios were implemented and then presented to kids on exhibitions. Robot attracted kids' attention. Kids had positive reactions to the robot and described it as friendly and nice.

Keywords: Social robotics · Robot teacher · Educational robotics

1 Introduction

A concept of using social robot as a teacher was firstly proposed in 1984 by Papert [1]. Since then, many works were done to investigate benefits [1–3] and limitations [4] of using robots in educational process. Recent research prove that using robot could be helpful when learning foreign language [5], learning new words [6], on speech therapy [7] and for inclusive learning [8, 9].

In work [4] a complex review on social robots in education was performed. Article combines the results on more than 80 studies and compiles them. The assessment of the use of robots in the learning process was carried out according to three main criteria: effectiveness for the educational process, implementation and role. As a result of the research, it was revealed that the presence of a robot in physical embodiment at a lesson is more effective than using its virtual counterparts. The robot can be used as a teacher-tutor, peer and novice. A robot in the role of a teacher can be used to learn a second language [10], to practice and automate sounds in speech therapist lessons [11], to provide moral support to a child [12]. The research carried out indicates the effectiveness of using the robot in the educational process. It is of great interest that practically half of research were carried out with robot NAO from SoftBank/Aldeberan Robotics. NAO is a 25 DOF bipedal humanoid robot with software framework NAOqi. NAOqi offers a wide

A. Ronzhin et al. (Eds.): ICR 2021, LNAI 12998, pp. 162–171, 2021.
https://doi.org/10.1007/978-3-030-87725-5_14

set of functions for developers allowing them use voice and visual interfaces, creating animations, network interactions. The dominance of NAO for human-robot interaction can be attributed to its wide availability, appealing appearance, accessible price point, technical robustness, and ease of programming [2]. Hence, NAO has become an almost de facto platform for many studies in robots for learning [2, 3]. Long awaiting social robot platform for education is Kebbi Air from NUWA Robotics. Kebbi was introduced in 2018 and expected for sale in late June 2021. Kebbi's main futures includes 12 DOF; AI Voice System & Object Recognition; Movement, Touch and Facial Recognition; 7″ Multi-touch Display, SDK for Android and Unity IDE developers. The estimated retail price for Kebbi Air will be around 700 USD.

LRAI from TUSUR have great experience in this direction [9–15] too, applies for development NAO robot platform using other leading research results [16–26]. Recent research shown presence of severe restrictions for the massive appearance of robots in schools of Russia. The main restriction is very high price per one robot. To date, NAO could be bought in Russia for about 1 million rubles, which is quite expensive for local schools. That is why developer team from LRAI TUSUR decided to design new accessible, simple and reliable robot platform especially for educational use.

2 Problem Statement

Our personal experience on working with NAO robot helped to identify some disadvantages of a platform: high price, complicated construction, low reliability and maintainability. After 6 years of use our NAO lost ability to move his legs and arms, it heats very fast and turns off after head movement. The main purpose of this work was the development of social robot to be used in educational process. Experience and research [8–11] done by LRAI from TUSUR University in this field of knowledge helped to define basic requirements to new robot platform:

- Robot should have attractive and friendly appearance.
- The cost of the robot must be low to promote the robot to the educational institutions of the Russian Federation (no more than 50k rubles).
- The robot must be reliable and maintainable, which means it must have a simple design and a minimum of degrees of freedom.

Basin on requirements above special requirements to hardware and software could formulated:

- Hardware requirements:

  - The robot should be stationary.
  - The robot must be equipped with a microcontroller with Linux operating system.
  - The robot must have a screen for displaying emotions and E-content.
  - The robot must have a microphone to implement speech recognition.
  - The robot must have a camera to implement the vision system.
  - The robot must be equipped with speaker and power amplifier.

- The robot must have structural elements that provide interactivity and do not allow the robot to associate with the PC at the mental level.

- Software requirements:

  - The robot must have access to the network to receive educational content from the cloud storage.
  - Robot should have machine vision module.
  - Robot should have a software for peripheral control (LEDs, servos).
  - Robot should have software for the implementation of speech recognition.
  - Robot should have a speech synthesis software.
  - Robot should have control software.
  - Robot should have software for integration with a web application.

3   Implementation

Based on the formulated requirements for the robot, a cat-robot named "MEOW" was developed. The cat is pet, well known to children, since many families in Russia keep cats as pets. Kittens are cute, everyone loves them. Robot MEOW is shown in Fig. 1.

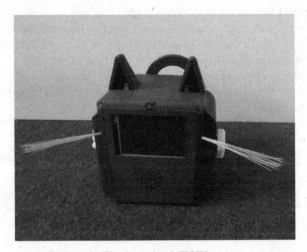

Fig. 1. Robot MEOW.

3.1   Hardware

Robot MEOW in current embodiment is based on Raspberry Pi 4B Raspberry Pi on ARM processor, with 2 GB of RAM, 2.4 and 5 GHz WiFi module, Bluetooth module, embedded DAC and USB3.0 interface running under Linux OS. Compact size of the board (85.6 mm × 56.5 mm × 17 mm) allow building portable, miniature devices on its basis. The cost of the Raspberry Pi 4B is 4–8 thousand rubles. A miniature touchscreen HDMI 3.5-in. display with a resolution of 480×320 pixels is connected to the board. The display shows operating system interface. A miniature camera with a resolution of 2592×1944 pixels and a viewing angle of $72°$ is connected to the microcomputer for implementing machine vision. A capsule microphone with a built-in ADC is connected to the USB connector to implement voice recognition. RGB LEDs are located in the ears and whiskers of the robot, are connected to the PWM pins through limiting resistors. Three stepper motors are connected to PWM pins, which allow the robot to move its hands and tail. Both LEDs and stepper motors allow robot to express emotions and reactions to user actions. A speaker and a miniature power amplifier connected to a Raspberry Pi in order to implement speech. Figure 2 shows robot's hardware scheme.

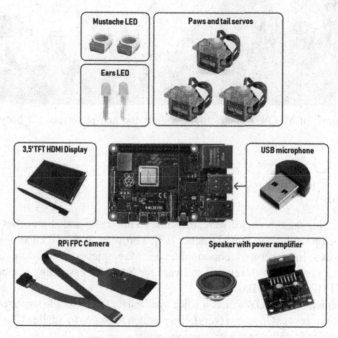

Fig. 2. Robot's hardware scheme.

The first body of MEOW was made of plywood and putty. After that sample, we decided to fabricate robot's body from a plastic. There was complete evolution of bodies presented in Fig. 3. In current embodiment, robot's body is made of PLA-plastic on a 3D printer. The body consists of two parts: a massive back, which houses most of all the elements and a front cover. Fastening of body parts is realized with screw connections. The case has seats inside for a microcomputer, servos, speaker, LEDs and a camera. The tail and feet are also made of PLA and are attached to the servos' shafts. The latest version of the robot has an impressive size: approximately $14 \times 17 \times 18$ cm (L × W × H). It is possible to manufacture body that is more compact.

5 V DC powers all electronic components. For normal operation of the Raspberry Pi, 2.5-3 A of current is required, for the display to work – 0.2 A, for the amplifier

- about 1 A, for the operation of servos about 0.3 A. All this of this impose serious requirement to the power supply and power wiring. We used a powerful desktop power supply with five USB ports for 2–3 A each. The power supply is external, not integrated into the case. Thick twenty-centimeter USB-USB C and USB-microUSB cables with an allowable current of up to 3 A were used as power wiring.

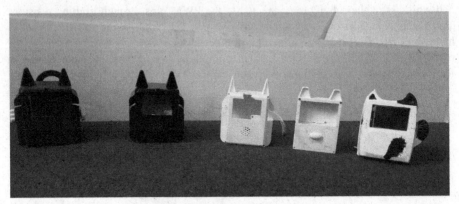

Fig. 3. Evolution of MEOW's bodies: right body is the first prototype, left body is to date embodiment.

3.2 Software

When developing the robot's software, the same technologies and approaches were used as when developing the NAO robot teacher [13]: a browser, WWW technologies, AJAX, cloud databases, local network communication. Many pieces of software are directly integrated with previously developed software for NAO. Programming languages used: Python, JS, PHP, MySQL, Bash.

To implement the MEOW voice, a voice synthesizer from Google was used (it works only if there is access to Google servers). It is planned to switch to Yandex Cloud Services or to a self-trained synthesizer with a unique voice.

Automatic speech recognition was implemented with Yandex API. The robot records the speech for 1–3 s and sends the.mp3 record to Yandex servers via TCP/IP POST method. Speech recognition works only if robot has access to Yandex servers. It is also possible implement streaming voice processing if necessary.

The machine vision module was based on OpenCV library. An algorithm for traffic signs recognizing has been implemented. The algorithm works as follows: initial image filtering by a threshold value to extract a red and blue mask; combining red and blue masks; contours search; filtering outlines by aspect ratio; cropping a suspicious outline; search for special points and comparison with reference marks (recognition). As a result, the developed algorithm made it possible to stably recognize 10 traffic signs. The average processing time of one 640×480-pixel frame with sign was 1.4 s, and frame without sign – 0.26 s.

LEDs and servo drives are controlled by pulse width modulation. The standard RPi.GPIO libraries for Python were used. On their basis, a small library was written for controlling LEDs and servos, which allows you to implement full-fledged sets of movements. For example, in order to display that the child answered the question correctly, the ears of the light up green, he wags his tail and raises up his paws.

All modules above are combined in control block, called RobotApp, which would be described below. RobotApp is python script, running in robot's OS, launched by launcher daemon. User interacts with robot throw web browser, running in full-screen mode on robot. All emotions, menus and control are implemented throw webpage. Content change and RobotApps control is implemented on JS. The software interaction scheme is shown in Fig. 4.

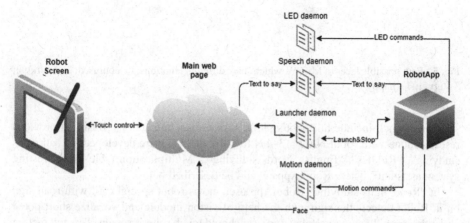

Fig. 4. Software interaction scheme

3.3 Robot Emotions

To make robot more attractive and alive a set of basic emotional reactions was developed. Emotional reaction consisted of facial expression (Fig. 5), sequence of movements of the paws and tail, color of ears and mustache LEDs. For example, to represent "Upset" emotion an upset face appears, paws and tail are moved down, ears and mustache colored red. To represent "Happy" emotion, which is for example the reaction to correct answer during test, happy face appears, eats and mustache turn green and MEOW wags the tail.

Developed control system, consisting of several daemon scripts running in MEOW's OS allow to implement quick emotional changes and in time give an emotional response to user's actions.

3.4 Human-Robot Interaction Scenario

Robot control system combine all modules described above in common applications, called RobotApps. RobotApps implement machine-human interaction scenario. RobotApp is designed to archive some educational purpose and consist of hard methodological

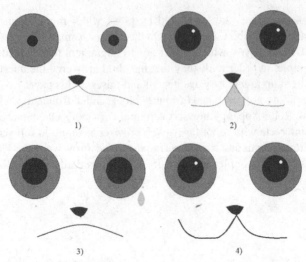

Fig. 5. Four possible faces of MEOW, which share different emotions: 1 – confused; 2 – smirking; 3 – upset; 4 – happy.

structure, which include all robot's phrases, reactions, and actions. Basin on previous research done with robot NAO [13–17] five RobotApps were developed: "Road signs studying", "Riddles", "English words studying", "Multiplication table" and "Testing system assistant". These RobotApps would be described below.

In "Road signs studying" RobotApp user shows robot special card with road sign on it. Robot detects the sign with the help of vision module and vocalize short poem about this sign. To stop the RobotApp user should touch robot's screen. This interaction scenario was previously implemented on NAO robot and presented in [13–17].

In "English words studying" RobotApp user interacts with robot orally. Robot voices interaction rules and then ask if user knows English words. Then user should answer positively or negatively. If the answer is "Yes", then robot gives short poem in Russian, which ends with English word. Poems are arranged in such a way that they contain a hint on the correct answer, and the rhyme hints at a consonant English word. After five wrong answers robot skips the poem and ask another one. To make process more attractive the robot counts the number of correct answers and voices them at the end. If the answer is "No" then robot start pronouncing the same poems, ending them with correct answer. After that robot offers to start knowledge test. User can stop RobotApp anytime orally with a stop-word or kinesthetically by touching MEOW's face.

In "Riddles" RobotApp robot gives a choice of riddles topic (animals, cities, letters etc.) and user select it orally. After that robot selects random riddles from its database and voices them. If user says that he/she doesn't know the answer or after five wrong answer robot skips the riddle. MEOW counts correct answers and gives the result at the end in the same way as in other RobotApps.

In "Multiplication table" robot handles the knowledge test of multiplication table. Robot generates random equation and voice it. User should give oral answer. After five wrong answers next equation is generated. RobotApp could be stopped orally or kinesthetically.

Another application was created for integration with virtual testing system. Special e-learning platform designed for automated testing of kids at different topics represented a web page connected to test database. When new question appeared on a screen web application send a command to robot to pronounce the question. If kid gave wrong answer, then robot showed "Upset" reaction, consisting of Sad face, red blinking ears and moustache. If the answer was correct, then robot showed smiling face, green blinking ears and moustache, which associated with reaction to correct answer. This RobotApp could be useful for kids with physical disabilities. Integration of social robot and interactive web-application was earlier described in [17]. In this work the same methods, approaches and programming languages were used as previously with NAO.

4 Designed Platform Evaluation

Developed platform was tested in laboratory conditions to verify whether it could be used in educational process or not. Obtained results are presented in Table 1.

Table 1. Robot MEOW numerical parameters.

Parameter	Value
Average speed of speech synthesis using Google API	100 ms
Average time of road sign recognition	1,4 s
Traffic sign recognition accuracy	88%
Average delay on web page when changing face	0,7 s

Obtained numerical parameters allow using robot as an assistant of teacher at preschool and elementary school: relatively high speed of speech generation and high accuracy of machine vision module allow RobotApps to work fast and stably and keep kid's attention attracted for about 5–7 min.

5 Conclusion

We developed a social robot platform for school use. MEOW robot has great potential for customization and for use in preschool and junior school. The platform developed was shown at the exhibition held as part of RoboCup Russia Open 2021 in Tomsk. During the exhibition MEOW worked in demo mode. A huge amount of feedback and suggestions were received. Developed RobotApps were verified by its possible users: to kids of age 6 to 16. Kids described robot as 'cute' and 'nice' and gave some comments about possible modifications. In most situations kids positively reacted a robot, probably because of its friendly appearance. It means that initial goals were achieved.

Acknowledgements. This work was financially supported by "Nauchnyy Tsentr "Polyus" LLC.

References

1. Papert, S.: New theories for new learnings. Sch. Psychol. Rev. **13**(4), 422–428 (1984). https://doi.org/10.1080/02796015.1984.12085122
2. Malik, N.A., Hanafiah, Y., Fazah, A.H.: Development of imitation learning through physical therapy using a humanoid robot. Procedia Comput. Sci. **42**, 191–197 (2014). https://doi.org/10.1016/j.procs.2014.11.051
3. Merkle, M.: Humanoid Service Robots: Customer Expectations and Customer Responses. Springer, Heidelberg (2021). https://doi.org/10.1007/978-3-658-34440-5
4. Belpaeme, T., et al.: Social robots for education: a review. Sci. Robot. **3**(21) (2018). https://doi.org/10.1126/scirobotics.aat5954
5. Serholt, S.: Breakdowns in children's interactions with a robotic tutor: a longitudinal study. Comput. Hum. Behav. **81**, 250–264 (2018). https://doi.org/10.1016/j.chb.2017.12.030
6. Belpaeme, T., et al.: Guidelines for designing social robots as second language tutors. Int. J. Soc. Robot. **10**(3), 325–341 (2018). https://doi.org/10.1007/s12369-018-0467-6
7. Westlund, J., Kory, M., et al.: Children use non-verbal cues to learn new words from robots as well as people. Int. J. Child-Comput. Interact. **13**, 1–9 (2017). https://doi.org/10.1016/j.ijcci.2017.04.001
8. Estévez, D., et al.: A case study of a robot-assisted speech therapy for children with language disorders. Sustainability **13**(5), 2771 (2021). https://doi.org/10.3390/su13052771
9. Daniela, L., Lytras, M.D.: Educational robotics for inclusive education. Technol. Knowl. Learn. **24**(2), 219–225 (2018). https://doi.org/10.1007/s10758-018-9397-5
10. Lowe, R., Andreasson, R., Alenljung, B., Lund, A., Billing, E.: Designing for a wearable affective interface for the NAO Robot: a study of emotion conveyance by touch. Multimodal Technol. Interact. **2**(1), 2 (2018). https://doi.org/10.3390/mti2010002
11. Andreasson, R., Alenljung, B., Billing, E., Lowe, R.: Affective touch in human–robot interaction: conveying emotion to the Nao robot. Int. J. Soc. Robot. **10**(4), 473–491 (2017). https://doi.org/10.1007/s12369-017-0446-3
12. Baxter, P., Ashurst, E., Read, R., Kennedy, J., Belpaeme, T.: Robot education peers in a situated primary school study: personalisation promotes child learning. PloS One, **12**(5) (2017). https://doi.org/10.1371/journal.pone.0178126
13. Prokazina, I.Y., et al.: Razrabotca scenariev vzaimodeystviya robot-rebenok dlya socialnogo robota. Collection of selected articles of the "Scientific session of TUSUR" **1**, 301–304 (2019). (in Russian)
14. Shandarov, E.S., Zimina, A.N., Ermakova, P.S.: Analiz povedeniya robota-assistenta v ramkakh razrabotki stsenariyev vzaimodeystviya robot-rebenok **8** (2014). (in Russian)
15. Zimina, A., Zolotukhina, P., Shandarov, E.: Robot-assistant behaviour analysis for robot-child interactions. In: Ronzhin, A., Rigoll, G., Meshcheryakov, R. (eds.) ICR 2017. LNCS (LNAI), vol. 10459, pp. 219–228. Springer, Cham (2017). https://doi.org/10.1007/978-3-319-66471-2_24
16. Zimina, A.N., Rimer, D.I., Sokolova, E.V., Shandarov, E.S., Shandarova, O.E.: Antropomorfnyi robot-pomoschnic utchitelya. Electron. Means Control Syst. **1–2**, 108–113 (2015). (in Russian)
17. Polyntsev, E.S., Klimov, A.A., Kodorov, A.E., Prokazina, I.Yu., Shandarov, E.S.: Systema integrtcii socialnogo robota i interactivnogo web prilojenya. Collection of Selected Articles of the Scientific Session of TUSUR **1**(1–1), 299–301 (2019). (in Russian)
18. Zimina, A., Rimer, D., Sokolova, E., Shandarova, O., Shandarov, E.: The humanoid robot assistant for a preschool children. In: Ronzhin, A., Rigoll, G., Meshcheryakov, R. (eds.) ICR 2016. LNCS (LNAI), vol. 9812, pp. 219–224. Springer, Cham (2016). https://doi.org/10.1007/978-3-319-43955-6_26

19. Gomilko, S., Zimina, A., Shandarov, E.: Attention training game with aldebaran robotics NAO and brain-computer interface. In: Ronzhin, A., Rigoll, G., Meshcheryakov, R. (eds.) ICR 2016. LNCS (LNAI), vol. 9812, pp. 27–31. Springer, Cham (2016). https://doi.org/10.1007/978-3-319-43955-6_4

20. Nalin, M., Bergamini, L., Giusti, A., Baroni, I., Sanna, A.: Children's perception of a robotic companion in a mildly constrained setting: how children within age 8–11 perceive a robotic companion. In: Proceedings of the Children and Robots Workshop at the IEEE/ACM International Conference on Human-Robot Interaction (HRI 2011), Lausanne, Switzerland. IEEE (2011)

21. Ros Espinosa, R., et al.: Child-robot interaction in the wild: advice to the aspiring experimenter. In: Proceedings of the ACM International Conference on Multi-modal Interaction, Valencia, Spain, pp. 335–342. ACM (2011)

22. Tanaka, F., Matsuzoe, S.: Children teach a care-receiving robot to promote their learning: field experiments in a classroom for vocabulary learning. J. Hum.-Robot Interact. 1, 78–95 (2012)

23. Medvedev, M.Y., Kostjukov, V.A., Pshikhopov, V.K.: Optimization of mobile robot movement on a plane with finite number of repeller sources. SPIIRAS Proc. 19(1), 43–78 (2020). https://doi.org/10.15622/sp.2020.19.1:2

24. Lavrenov, L.O., Magid, E.A., Matsuno, F., Svinin, M.M., Suthakorn, J.: Development and implementation of spline-based path planning algorithm in ROS/Gazebo environment. SPIIRAS Proc. 18(1), 57–84 (2019). https://doi.org/10.15622/sp.18.1.57-84

25. Medvedev, M.Y., Kostjukov, V.A., Pshikhopov, V.X.: Method for optimizing of mobile robot trajectory in repeller sources field. Inform. Autom. 20(3), 690–726 (2021). https://doi.org/10.15622/ia.2021.3.7

26. Kochetkov, M.P., Korolkov, D.N., Petrov, V.F., Petrov, O.V., Terentev, A.I., Simonov, S.B.: Application of cluster analysis with fuzzy logic elements for ground environment assessment of robotic group. SPIIRAS Proc. 19(4), 746–773 (2020). https://doi.org/10.15622/sp.2020.19.4.2

A Framework to Process Natural Speech in Service Robots Using a Combination of a Speech Recognition System, Universal Dependencies Extracted by Means of the Stanford Parser and an Expert System

Alessandro Presacco[✉][iD], Jesus Savage[iD], Julio Cruz[iD],
and Stephany Ortuño[iD]

Department of Electrical Engineering, Universidad Nacional Autónoma de México,
04510 Mexico City, Mexico

Abstract. One of the most challenging tasks in a service robot is the implementation of a framework to digitally process natural speech and to translate it into meaningful commands that the robot can understand and execute. Here we present an architecture aimed to process natural speech in our service robot Justina. It comprises of 3 parts: 1) A module to detect and analyze natural speech, 2) A module to parse the decoded speech and to extract universal dependencies and 3) A module based on an expert system to translate the universal dependencies into a set of instructions that the robot can execute.

Keywords: Natural speech recognition · Universal dependencies · Stanford parser · Service robots

1 Introduction

One of the hardest tasks in service robots built to interact with humans is the design of algorithms allowing robots to understand speech and to effectively convert it into a set of instructions that can be executed. The challenge of this task mainly comes from the complicated structure of natural speech, which has high variability and is rich in ambiguities and expectations. Importantly, humans use context to communicate their intentions and to infer the meaning of a conversation, making the decoding of spoken language an even more complex task to accomplish. Several approaches have been used to convert human speech into a set of instructions that are meaningful to robots, including mapping [2,8], long short-term memory networks [7], lexical unparsing [9], Human-Robot dialog [20] and semantic reasoning [1,3]. An additional layer of difficulty arises from the fact that even the most advanced Automatic Speech Recognition (ASR) systems, such as Google Cloud Speech-to-Text API, CMU Sphinx or Julius, still have an estimated word error rate (WER) of approximately ~20%. The WER tends to be

© Springer Nature Switzerland AG 2021
A. Ronzhin et al. (Eds.): ICR 2021, LNAI 12998, pp. 172–181, 2021.
https://doi.org/10.1007/978-3-030-87725-5_15

even worse in environments where service robots are typically employed, due to the presence of a significant amount of background noise. This high WER is likely to cause a significant decrease in the efficiency of the speech-to-commands analysis, as the wrong recognition of a word has the potential to dramatically change the meaning and the grammatical structure of a phrase. A recent study [18] tried to address this problem by adopting the use of encoder-decoder neural networks (e.g. sequence to sequence) with injection of noise. Promising results from this work suggested that the addition of noise injection into a neural network can increase the performance of semantic parsing by decreasing the negative effects of speech recognition errors. In a recent paper published by our lab [14], the semantic-reasoning module of our virtual and robot system (VIRBOT) was presented. In this module, the speech-to-command translation was based on a system that could generate conceptual dependencies (CDs) to represent the meaning of the command uttered by the user and processed by the ASR made available by the Microsoft Speech SDK engine [11]. The system was tested with commands typically used in the RoboCup and the results suggested that this framework has the potential to outperform the systems currently used in service robots. Following these promising results, here we present a development of our framework. Specifically, in order to parse the commands, we opted to utilize the Stanford Parser [10], which is known for its ability to extract Universal Dependencies (UDs). UDs were used to easily and flexibly find links between pair of words, which were then fed into an expert system (CLIPS, [13]), whose goal was to convert them into high level reasoning by applying facts and rules with the highest priority. Our framework tested in some of the commands most widely utilized in the RoboCup showed promising results. However, given the current limitations to access our lab due to the covid-19 pandemic, it is important to point out that testing was only executed from home using a simulator that replicated the software installed in our robot Justina.

2 Methods

2.1 Simulator

Our framework was tested employing a simulator previously implemented in our lab in the ROS environment by using a gazebo simulation world. A snapshot of our simulator is displayed in Fig. 1.

2.2 Speech Recognition System

The first layer of our framework is represented by the speech recognition system. Given the promising results obtained with the previous experiment [14], we opted to keep using the Microsoft Speech SDK engine [11]. As previously reported by our lab [14], some of the main benefits of using this system include the option to accept continuous speech without the need of a training phase and the free availability of its source code, thus making possible for us to modify it based

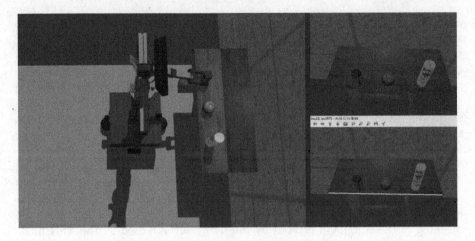

Fig. 1. Snapshot of the simulator used to test our framework.

on our needs. Additionally, Microsoft Speech SDK engine also allows for the use of grammars, that are specified using XML notation, thus constraining the sentences that can be uttered and reducing the number of recognition errors. A Hidden Markov Model was also added in order to estimate the probability of the model based on words sequence of the grammar.

2.3   Parsing the Command: The Stanford Syntatic Parser

The first step in parsing the text generated by the speech analyzer is to identify the grammatical structure of the sentences, that is to identify the key elements of the command(s) being uttered by the user, such as the verb, the subject, the object etc. The final goal is to create a set of UDs, which is "a framework for consistent annotation of grammar (parts of speech, morphological features, and syntactic dependencies) across different human languages" [21]. The annotation strategy lays its foundation on previously devised Stanford dependencies [4–6], Google universal part-of-speech tags [12], and the Interset interlingua for morphosyntactic features used in the HamleDT treebank collection [22]. This effort resulted in several key annotations used to define the relationship among different tokens of the selected text. One of the most successful and widely adopted probabilistic parser currently available is the Stanford Parser [10], which provides some of the most used core natural language processing (NLP) steps, such as tokenization and coreference resolution. The software was originally developed in Java, but subsequently was translated into other languages, such as python and C#. We opted to use the 3.9.2 version developed by Sergey Tihon in C# [19]. The following are some of the most frequently used UDs [21]:

1) **amod:** an adjectival modifier of a noun (or pronoun) (e.g. John has a big car. *amod* → ***big-car***)

2) **conj:** relation between two elements connected by a coordinating conjunction, such as and, or, etc.

3) **dobj:** noun phrase which is the (accusative) object of the verb (e.g. Bring me the book. *dobj* → *bring-book*)

4) **iobj:** the noun phrase which is the (dative) object of the verb (e.g. Give me the pen. *iobj* → *give-me*)

5) **nmod:** nominal modifiers of nouns or clausal predicates (e.g. Meet John at the table. *nmod* → *John-table*)

6) **root:** root of the sentence (e.g. Robot, give me the book. *root* → *Robot*)

Below is an example of UDs generated in response to a typical command sent to a service robot: **"Robot, meet John at the bookcase and follow him"**:

>   root(ROOT-0,Robot-1),
>   conj:and(Robot-1,meet-3),
>   dobj(meet-3,John-4),
>   case(bookcase-7,at-5),
>   det(bookcase-7,the-6),
>   nmod:at(John-4,bookcase-7),
>   cc(Robot-1,and-8),
>   conj:and(Robot-1,follow-9),
>   dobj(follow-9,him-10)

The numbers right next to each word in the UDs representation indicate the word position in the sentence.

2.4 Semantic Networks and Conceptual Dependencies (CDs)

Introduced by Sowa [16,17], semantic networks are a declarative and graphic notation intended to "represent knowledge and support automated systems for reasoning about the knowledge" [16,17]. The basic idea behind this theory is that knowledge can be stored in the form of graphs, with nodes representing objects in the world, and arcs representing relationships between those objects. Semantic networks are extensively used in artificial intelligence, because they represent knowledge or support reasoning. Conceptual dependencies (CDs), which were first introduced by Schank in 1972 [15], can be viewed as a special case of semantic network, where the use of concepts and of different types of arrow is emphasized. CDs are based on the idea that an action is the basis of any propositions that describe events and are made up of conceptualizations, which are formed by an action, an actor and a set of roles that depend on the action. According to Shank, an action can be defined as something that an actor can apply to an object. Schank proposes a finite set of primitive actions that are the basic units of meaning which a complex idea can be constructed with. These primitive actions are different from the grammatical categories, as they are independent elements that can be combined to express the idea underlying a statement. One of the main advantages of CDs is that they allow the creation of a rule base system, which is capable of making inferences from a natural language system in the same way that people do. CDs facilitate the use of inference rules, because many inferences are already contained in the representation itself. The CD representation uses conceptual primitives and not the actual words contained in the sentence. These primitives represent thoughts, actions, and their relationships. The following are some of the most common CD primitives:

1) **ATRANS:** Transfer of ownership, possession, or control of an object. It requires an actor, an object and a container. Typical verbs that can be used are *to give, to bring*, etc.
2) **PTRANS:** Transfer of the physical location of an object. It requires an actor, an object and a destination. Typical verbs that can be used are *to navigate, to go*, etc.
3) **ATTEND:** The focus is mainly on verbs requiring some degree of attention, such as *to meet, to see*, etc.
4) **MOVE:** Movement of a body part by owner, like *to throw, to kick*, etc.
5) **GRASP:** Actor grasping an object, like *to get, to pick*, etc.
6) **SPEAK:** Actor asking or answering a question, like *to ask, to tell*, etc.

The following is a typical CDs structure generated in response to a command commonly used with service robots: **"Robot, bring me a book"**.

(Type of CD primitive: **ATRANS**)

(ACTOR: **Robot**)   (VERB: **bring**)

(OBJECT: **book**)   (IOBJECT: **me**)

2.5   Translating Universal Dependencies to High Level Reasoning: CLIPS

As seen in the examples reported in the subsection 2.4 *"Semantic networks and Conceptual Dependencies (CDs)"*, the command sent to our robot is first parsed and UDs are extracted. Then the CDs are identified and finally keywords(*bring*, *book* and *me*) are isolated and labels (e.g. **VERB**, **OBJECT**, etc.) are applied to each of them. The next step is to transform this information into a high level reasoning in order to instruct Justina to carry out the correct set of actions. This goal is achieved by using a speech expert system, that by means of specific rules and facts generate the set of instructions that best fit the command(s) uttered by the user. We opted to use CLIPS, a language developed by NASA [13], to develop them, as described in details in the previous paper published by our lab [14].

2.6   Experiment

Due to the restrictions imposed by the pandemic, we did not have access to the lab and therefore we were not allowed install and test our updated framework directly in Justina. We could only carry out tests at home in a quiet environment using a simulator. The user simply uttered the commands in front of the computer where our software and simulators were installed and the output of each of our modules was checked to evaluate the accuracy of the analysis.

3   Results

Here we report the results from six typical commands used in the RoboCup and that could also be applicable to real-life situations. The commands are assumed to be interpreted correctly by the speech analyzer, therefore only the outputs of the steps related to the Stanford Parser and the CLIPS are presented. The part of the output of the Stanford Parser referring to the actor (ACTOR: **Robot**) is omitted due to its redundancy.

Example 1

Command: **Robot, navigate to the kitchen**

Output of the Stanford Parser:

(PTRANS)navigate**(PREP)**to**(LOCATION)**kitchen

This command only implies a transfer of location, which means that all the CLIPS needs to do is to send to Justina a simple instruction indicating the new location. This is achieved with the following string:

CLIPS: **user_speech update_object_location location kitchen 1**

Example 2

Command: **Robot, take the coke and place it on the kitchen table**

Output of the Stanford Parser:

(GRASP)take**(OBJECT)**coke

(ATRANS)place**(PREP)**on**(LOCATION)**kitchen_table**(OBJECT)**it

This command implies two actions that Justina needs to execute in order to bring the coke to the kitchen table. The first one is the act to check the position where the coke is currently located, so Justina knows where to find it. Since no location is specified in the command, the coordinate of the **default_location** previously stored in the system will be used:

CLIPS: **user_speech get_object coke default_location 1**

The second action is to deliver the coke to the final destination, which is the kitchen table:

CLIPS: **user_speech deliver_in_position coke kitchen_table 2**

The numbers placed at the end of each the strings sent to CLIPS (e.g. 1, 2, etc.) indicate the order with which the actions need to be executed.

Example 3

Command: **Robot, put the coke on the kitchen table**

Output of the Stanford Parser:

(ATRANS)put**(PREP)**on**(LOCATION)**kitchen_table**(OBJECT)**coke

This command is very similar to the one presented in Example 2, with the important difference that only one CD is used. However, Justina still needs to perform two actions as in Example 2. The first one is implied and is the act to check the location where the coke is currently located. Since no location is specified in the command, the coordinate of the **default_location** previously stored in the system will be used:

CLIPS: **user_speech get_object coke default_location 1**

The second action is to deliver the coke to the final destination, which is the kitchen table:

CLIPS: **user_speech deliver_in_position coke kitchen_table 2**

Example 4

Command: **Robot, bring me the coke**

Output of the Stanford Parser:

(ATRANS)bring**(IOBJECT)**me**(OBJECT)**coke

This example is very important to show the complexity of converting a seemly simple command into an executable set of actions that Justina can carry out in order to deliver the coke. Even though only one CD is present, three different actions need to be performed. The first one is the act to check the location where the coke is currently located. Similarly to what seen in the Examples 2 and 3, CLIPS needs to execute the following string:

CLIPS: **user_speech get_object coke default_location 1**

The second action refers to specifying the location of the user whom Justina needs to hand the coke to:

CLIPS: **user_speech update_object_location location current_loc 2**

The last action is to physically deliver the coke to the user:

CLIPS: **user_speech handover_object coke 3**

Example 5

Command: **Robot, deliver the coke to the person waving in the kitchen**

Output of the Stanford Parser:

(ATRANS)deliver**(PREP)**to**(IOBJECT)**person**(OBJECT)**coke
(GERUND)waving**(PREP)**in**(LOCATION)**kitchen

This example poses a high level of difficulty due to presence of multiple actions that need to be carried out. In fact, despite the fact that only one CD is present, four different commands need to be performed. The first one is the act to check the location where the coke is currently located. Similarly to what seen in the Examples 2, 3 and 4, CLIPS needs to execute the following string:

CLIPS: **user_speech get_object coke default_location 1**

The second action refers to specifying the location of the individual whom Justina needs to hand the coke to. In this case the coke needs to be delivered to a *"person"* in the kitchen:

CLIPS: **user_speech update_object_location location kitchen 2**

The third action refers to finding the person in the kitchen:

CLIPS: **user_speech find_pgg_person waving kitchen 3**

The last action is to physically deliver the coke to the *"person"*:

CLIPS: **user_speech handover_object coke 4**

Example 6

Command: **Robot, navigate to the kitchen, find the coke, and deliver it to Jack at the bed**

Output of the Stanford Parser:

(PTRANS)navigate**(PREP)**to**(LOCATION)**kitchen

(GRASP)find**(OBJECT)**coke

(ATRANS)deliver**(PREP)**to**(IOBJECT)**Jack
(LOCATION)bed**(OBJECT)**it

This example has three CDs that can be executed with four different commands. The first one implies a transfer of location, which is identical to what shown in the first example. This is achieved with the following string:

CLIPS: **user_speech update_object_location location kitchen 1**

The second one is the act to check the location where the coke is currently located. Similarly to what seen in the Examples 2, 3, 4 and 5, CLIPS needs to execute the following string:

CLIPS: **user_speech get_object coke kitchen 2**

The third action refers to finding the person (*Jack* in this example) located nearby the bed:

CLIPS: **user_speech find_person_in_room Jack bed 3**

The last action is to physically deliver the coke to Jack:

CLIPS: **user_speech handover_object coke 4**

4 Discussion

In this paper we have presented a framework to process natural speech in service robots. The current work builds up over a similar framework that was developed in this lab in 2019 [14]. An important key component that we decided to change was the parser, in order to explore the feasibility of using a more powerful tool that could work in more complicated scenarios. Among the different options freely available, we have opted to utilize the Stanford Parser, because of its known ability to find the correct UDs in complex sentences. We tested our updated system with commands typically employed in the RoboCup and that could also be relevant in a real-world setting. Our promising results suggest that the Stanford Parser offers a solid alternative to the parser previously employed in our lab. Specifically, the Stanford Parser proved to be able to create reliable UDs that could be easily used by the expert system designed in CLIPS to create the final set of instructions to be sent to Justina. While these results are encouraging, several challenges still exist: 1) Due to the restrictions imposed by the pandemic, our updated framework was tested with a simulator and at home in a quiet environment. We obviously expect our service robot to operate in noisy environments, where the speech analyzer would be more prone to mistakes; 2) The Stanford Parser needs to be tested with more complex commands that would have the potential to introduce incorrect or unexpected assignments of UDs that would require manipulation of the input string. In other words, with more sophisticated commands, it is possible that we will need to reorganize the structure of the input string sent to the Stanford Parser, without however changing its meaning, in order to generate a predictable set of UDs that could be used with CLIPS; 3) Currently CLIPS can process a limited number of instructions that are restricted by the environment (e.g. our lab) where tests were executed. We will need to further develop our code to be able to execute a wider range of commands. Future work will be focused on addressing the above mentioned weaknesses of our system.

Acknowledgements. This work was supported by a graduate fellowship awarded by the Consejo Nacional de Ciencia y Tecnología (CONACYT), by a post-doctoral fellowship awarded by DGAPA UNAM and by PAPIIT-DGAPA UNAM, Mexico under Grant IG-101721.

References

1. Bastianelli, E., Castellucci, G., Croce, D., Basili, R., Nardi, D.: Effective and robust natural language understanding for human-robot interaction. In: ECAI, pp. 57–62 (2014)
2. Bisk, Y., Yuret, D., Marcu, D.: Natural language communication with robots. In: Proceedings of the 2016 Conference of the North American Chapter of the Association for Computational Linguistics: Human Language Technologies, pp. 751–761 (2016)
3. Cui, G., Wei, S., Chen, X.: Semantic task planning for service robots in open worlds. Future Internet **13**(2), 49 (2021)

4. de Marneffe, M.C., MacCartney, B., Manning, C.D.: Generating typed dependency parses from phrase structure parses. In: Proceedings of the 5th International Conference on Language Resources and Evaluation, LREC, pp. 449–454 (2006)
5. de Marneffe, M.C., Manning, C.D.: The Stanford typed dependencies representation. In: Proceedings of the COLING 2008 Workshop on Cross-Framework and Cross-Domain Parser Evaluation, pp. 1–8 (2008)
6. de Marneffe, M.C., et al.: Universal Stanford dependencies: a cross-linguistic typology. In: Proceedings of the 9th International Conference on Language Resources and Evaluation, LREC, pp. 4585–4592 (2014)
7. Fried, D., Andreas, J., Klein, D.: Unified pragmatic models for generating and following instructions. In: Proceedings of the North American Chapter of the Association for Computational Linguistics: Human Language Technologies, NAACL HLT, pp. 1951–1963 (2018)
8. Iocchi, L., Holz, D., Ruiz-del-Solar, J., Sugiura, K., Van Der Zant, T.: Robocup@home: analysis and results of evolving competitions for domestic and service robots. Artif. Intell. **229**, 258–281 (2015)
9. Klein, D., Manning, C.D.: Accurate unlexicalized parsing. In: Proceedings of the 41st Annual Meeting on Association for Computational Linguistics, ACL, pp. 423–430 (2003)
10. Manning, C.D., Surdeanu, M., Bauer, J., Finkel, J., Bethard, J.S., McClosky, D.: The Stanford CoreNLP natural language processing toolkit. The Association for Computer Linguistics (ACL), pp. 55–60 (2014)
11. Microsoft speech SDK (2006). http://www.microsoft.com/
12. Petrov, S., Das, D., Ryan McDonald, R.: A universal part-of-speech tagset. In: Proceedings of the Eight International Conference on Language Resources and Evaluation, LREC 2012, pp. 2089–2096 (2012)
13. Riley, G.: CLIPS reference manual version 60 technical report number JSC-25012 Software Technology Branch, Lyndon B Johnson Space Center, Houston, TX, USA (1994)
14. Savage, J., et al.: Semantic reasoning in service robots using expert systems. Robot. Auton. Syst. **114**, 77–92 (2019)
15. Schank, R.C.: Conceptual dependence: a theory of natural language understanding. Cogn. Psychol. **3**(4), 552–631 (1972)
16. Sowa, J.F.: Semantic Networks. Encyclopedia of Artificial Intelligence, vol. 2, pp. 1493–1511. Wiley, New York (1992)
17. Sowa, J.F.: Semantic Networks. Encyclopedia of Cognitive Science. Wiley Online Library (2006)
18. Tada, Y., Hagiwara, Y., Tanaka, H., Taniguchi, T.: Robust understanding of robot-directed speech commands using sequence to sequence with noise injection. Front Robot AI **3**(4) (2020)
19. Tihon, S.: (2019). https://www.nuget.org/packages/Stanford.NLP.CoreNLP/3.9.2
20. Thomason, J., Zhang, S., Mooney, R.J., Stone, P.: Learning to interpret natural language commands through human-robot dialog. In: IJCAI, pp. 1923–1929 (2015)
21. Universal Dependencies. https://universaldependencies.org/
22. Zeman, D.: Reusable tagset conversion using tagset drivers. In: Proceedings of the 6th International Conference on Language Resources and Evaluation, LREC 2008, pp. 213–218 (2018)

Prioritizing Tasks Within a Robotic Transportation System for a Smart Hospital Environment

Ruslan Safin[1], Roman Lavrenov[1](✉), Tatyana Tsoy[1], Evgeni Magid[1], Mikhail Svinin[2], Sumantra Dutta Roy[3], and Subir Kumar Saha[4]

[1] Laboratory of Intelligent Robotics Systems (LIRS),
Intelligent Robotics Department, Institute of Information Technology
and Intelligent Systems, Kazan Federal University, Kazan, Russia
{lavrenov,tt,magid}@it.kfu.ru

[2] Information Science and Engineering Department, College of Information Science
and Engineering, Ritsumeikan University, 1-1-1 Noji-higashi, Kusatsu,
Shiga 525-8577, Japan
svinin@fc.ritsumei.ac.jp

[3] Department of Electrical Engineering, Indian Institute of Technology Delhi,
IIT Campus, Hauz Khas, New Delhi, Delhi 110016, India

[4] Department of Mechanical Engineering, Indian Institute of Technology Delhi, IIT
Campus, Hauz Khas, New Delhi, Delhi 110016, India
sumantra@ee.iitd.ac.in, saha@mech.iitd.ac.in
https://kpfu.ru/eng/itis/research/laboratory-of-intelligent-robotic-systems,
http://en.ritsumei.ac.jp/academics/college-of-information-science-and-engineering/,
http://ee.iitd.ac.in/, http://mech.iitd.ac.in/

Abstract. This paper describes a design and an implementation of a small-scale robotic transportation system, which operates in a smart hospital environment. Within a proposed framework unmanned ground vehicles (UGV) perform transportation tasks between multiple stations that are located in different rooms. The UGVs navigate in the environment with moving objects in accordance with basic traffic rules, which consider priorities of particular tasks of each UGV. UGVs' behavior is defined by a state machine and transitions between these states, which allows to make the robots' behavior more predictable and controllable. Virtual experiments were carried out in a simulation of an entire floor of a small-size hospital building using the Gazebo simulator. The experiments confirmed that using various task priorities shorten a path length of robots with high priorities and thus reduce their task execution time.

Keywords: Smart hospital · UGV · Robot navigation · Path planning · Task-based robotic system · Service robots · Leading edge healthcare

© Springer Nature Switzerland AG 2021
A. Ronzhin et al. (Eds.): ICR 2021, LNAI 12998, pp. 182–193, 2021.
https://doi.org/10.1007/978-3-030-87725-5_16

1   Introduction

Along with industrial robots, service robots need to maintain accuracy and speed while performing various operations. In contrast to industrial robots, service robots operate in the same space with humans and other robots. This requires robots to operate according to some predefined rules to ensure predictability of the behavior and thus a more productive joint work with a human staff [11,23].

In the context of hospital environments, a transportation of objects is one of daily routines that could be delegated to service robots [16]. Currently, most transportation related tasks are performed manually and thus are human resource consuming, e.g., a patients' caring process involves delivering and collecting various objects several times a day. In turn, an automated transportation system (based on mobile service robots) allows to liberate hospital staff from transportation tasks [26] and benefits from a larger transport capacity, a possibility to optimize delivery routes, centrally assign priorities in task performance, and thus schedule a delivery order [8,9].

The paper is organized as follows. Section 2 summarizes related research including review of task based architecture, task manager and its GUI. In Sect. 3 a state machine structure and its implementation using the SMACH library is described [5]. Section 4 outlines robot movement rules, the corresponding states and transition conditions. Sections 5 and 6 describe a virtual environment setup for the system testing and experimental results. We conclude in the last Section.

2   Related Work

The main task of service robots, which are increasingly used in hospitals, is an automation of items delivery, which frees up staff time and increases an overall efficiency of such organizations [18]. One approach suggested using a mobile robot designed to automate delivery of medical items from one ward to another in a hospital [10]. The mobile platform Nomadic XR4000 used fluorescent lights of ceilings in order to determine its position and orientation. In [13] authors proposed a solution to improve the logistics of delivering items by robots by reducing a path traveled by the robots and task scheduling schemes, named deep Hungarian (d-Hungarian) and deep Voronoi (d-Voronoi). Paper [24] presented a task management problem for a mobile robot operating in an environment with humans and receiving new tasks from them. In our paper, we focus on an excessive autonomy of service robots, which implies a typical lack of a mechanism to interrupt (and control) ongoing tasks that are currently executed by the robots.

BačÍK et al. [3] described an approach, which included development of both hardware and software for a robot that performs delivery tasks in hospitals. It included a development of a powerlink interface to transfer data between a robot and a powerlink-compatible hardware, and improved a local path using Pure Pursuit Path Tracking Algorithm, which made initial path smoother and created a more continuous movement of the robot [4,7].

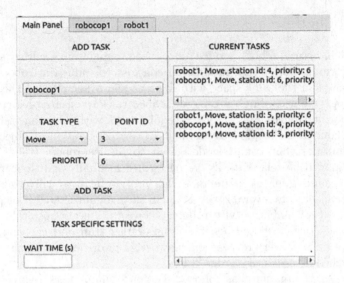

Fig. 1. Main menu of the task manager GUI.

3   Tasks with Priorities Scheduler Implementation

We designed a system that assumes robots being engaged in transportation tasks in accordance with a list of tasks assigned to a robot and priorities of these tasks. Tasks are assigned via a graphical user interface (GUI). The GUI allows to assign a station (position) identifier to a task and to select an identifier of a robot that will perform the task. Each station corresponds to a particular position on a hospital map. Optionally, it is possible to set a waiting time after arriving to a station. When leaving "wait time" field blank, the robot's state changes to WAIT_FOR_GOAL immediately upon a successful arrival to the task station. The task manager stores existing active tasks as queues (separately for each robot) and transfers started and completed tasks into appropriate states. Robots notify the manager when they start or finish a task.

The GUI main menu is shown in Fig. 1. A top panel is a list of tabs consists of a main menu tab and tabs for each robot. To display a status of tasks for an individual robot, tabs are provided for each launched robot. An example of a tab for a particular robot is shown in Fig. 2. The left side of the main menu contains functions for assigning tasks. The selection of all parameters (except the optional "wait time" parameter) is implemented as a drop-down list. A drop-down list of available robots is filled according to a list of names of robots to be launched. A station list is a set of station identifiers with station coordinates associated with each identifier. A priority list is a simple set of numbers from 0 to 9 that determines a position of a task in a robot's task queue. A priority of a task executed by a robot also determines the priority of a robot in the movement rules that the robots follow when navigating in a hospital.

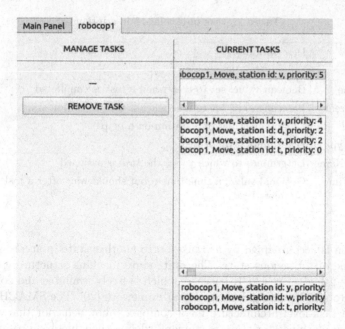

Fig. 2. Robot panel of the task manager GUI.

A task workflow works as follows. After a user assigns a task, the task is stored in the task manager's list of all tasks and is sent to a robot (to which the task is assigned). Each robot has its own task queue, which is updated each time a new task is assigned. When the robot receives a new task, the task is stored in the robot's queue and the queue tasks are reordered according to their priorities. The robot always executes the highest priority task from its queue. The task manager keeps track of all task states by receiving updates when the robot changes its task state to another. All assigned tasks are displayed in the GUI having either ongoing, pending (queued) or completed status. A task is considered completed when the robot has successfully arrived to its designated station and, depending on a presence of the wait_time parameter, has waited there for a specified time. After these conditions are met, the robot starts executing a next task from the queue, having previously informed the manager of a completion of a current task and a start of a new one. The tasks are stored as objects. A structure and a description of task fields are shown in Table 1.

4   Movement Rules Model

4.1   State Machine Implementation with SMACH

An overall behavior of a robot is defined by a finite state machine with various transitions from one state to another. The transitions depend on outcomes of a current state. Each state has its own set of outcomes, so that each state

Table 1. Task object fields description.

Field	Description
id	Unique identifier
isDone	Boolean value, set to true when a task is completed
isCurrent	Boolean value, set to true when a task execution starts
goalId	Unique identifier of a station on a map
taskType	Determines a robot task
robotName	Determines to which robot the task is assigned
waitTime	Optional value, a time that robot should wait after a task is completed

termination is accompanied by a transition to another state in accordance with an outcome of a previous state. The finite state machine structure was implemented by using the SMACH package, which is freely available and compatible with the Robot Operating System (ROS) framework [20]. The SMACH package provides a task-level architecture for a complex robot behavior that allows to create state machines (or state containers), define their hierarchy using nested finite state machines, introspect states, state transitions and data flow between them at runtime, etc. This approach facilitates a task of controlling a robot behavior by decomposing its intended behavior into corresponding states, and allows the robot's states to be handled using data transitions between the states and conditions under which the robot changes its behavior. Table 2 lists the implemented robot states and their descriptions. The structure of the implemented state machine is shown in Fig. 3 as a visualization provided by the package smach_viewer [6]. WAIT_FOR_GOAL and NAVIGATE_TO_GOAL as active states are shown on the left and right sides, respectively.

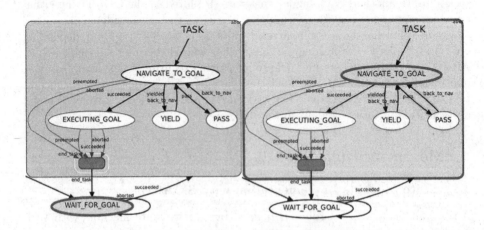

Fig. 3. SMACH active states smach_viewer package visualization.

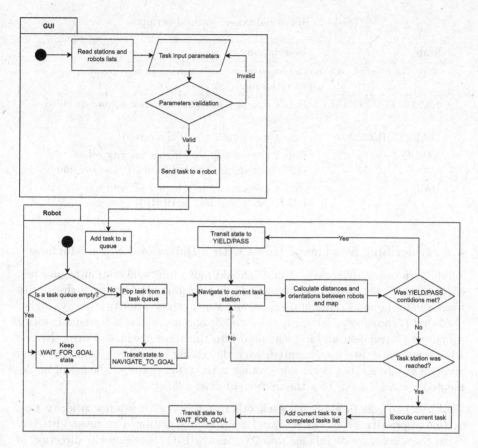

Fig. 4. System block diagram.

Figure 4 shows a block diagram of the developed application. On launch, the task manager module reads the lists of stations and robots. They can be selected through the GUI. When the task options are selected and a task is sent, it is being passed and saved by a robot that is responsible for completing the task. The robot, initially in WAIT_FOR_GOAL state, transits to NAVIGATE_TO_GOAL state as soon as the new task appears in the list of its tasks. While navigating, conditions for transition to PASS and YIELD states are checked. In the case of transition to one of these states, a navigation to the task station is suspended until the robot returns to NAVIGATE_TO_GOAL state. As soon as robot reaches the station, its state changes to EXECUTING_GOAL state, which simulates a process of completing the task. A transition from this state implies a completion of the task, and the robot's state changes to the initial WAIT_FOR_GOAL state.

Table 2. Robot behaviour states description.

State	Description
NAVIGATE_TO_GOAL	Robot autonomously navigates to a point specified in a task
EXECUTING_GOAL	Robot executes goal, i.e. waits for a time specified by a user
WAIT_FOR_GOAL	Robot waits until a goal is received
YIELD	Robot gives a way to a higher priority robot (HPR): drive off to a side from HPR's direction
PASS	Robot gives a way to a higher priority robot (HPR): stop and wait until HPR passes

4.2 Describing Movement Rules with a Behavioral State Machine

While performing their tasks, robots should move from one station to another, ensuring the freest possible movement both for robots performing high-priority tasks and for humans (patients, guests, and staff), whose priority is always higher than that of the robots. To satisfy these conditions, a model of movement rules for robots was developed and implemented into the state machine. Currently, two additional states are implemented, each describing the robot's behavior when giving a way to a robot performing a task with higher priority. The list of implemented and tested rules for the movement is as follows:

1. When two robots approach each other, a robot with a lower priority task (lower priority robot, LPR), after approaching within 4 m, must give way to the second robot (higher priority robot, HPR), changing the direction of motion by 90 degrees relative to an HPR motion direction and moving 70 cm in that direction. The robots are considered to be moving toward each other when a difference between a rotation angle (yaw) of one robot relative to a map coordinate system and a rotation angle of the second robot relative to the same system is less than or equal to 0.27 rad and a position of one robot relative to the other along the X-axis (relative to the robot coordinate system) is positive, i.e., the robots are directed toward each other. After the HPR overtakes the yielding LPR (i.e., it is behind the point where the yielding LPR left its original route), the LPR continues moving towards its task. This rule corresponds to the state YIELD.

2. If two robots are moving in such a way that a LPR crosses the path of a HPR (e.g., a LPR exits a room into a corridor where another robot is traveling along, bypassing an exit from the room), the LPR must stop and wait for the HPR to move away. It is assumed that the robot routes intersect when vectors formed by two points (where the first point corresponds to coordinates of the robot's current position and the second is located at a distance of 2 m in the direction of the robot's movement) intersect and an absolute value of an intersection angle is in the range of 1.47 to 2.87. The LPR continues to move once the intersection condition is no longer satisfied. This rule corresponds to the state PASS.

The state YIELD is intended for the case when two robots move towards each other and one of them (a LPR) should give a way to a HPR. The robot state machine transitions to YIELD state when the conditions for the first movement rule are satisfied. As the robots continue to approach each other, their local planners begin to create a local path that considers another robot as an obstacle. Without appropriate movement rules this may fore the robots to move in parallel paths in the same direction (while trying to avoid each other) and deviate from their global paths. Since the conditions for entering this state imply that a robot is on the path of another robot, the behavior of the robot in the YIELD state is implemented to move sideways far enough in a way that the local planner of the HPR's path does not (or only insignificantly) change its local path plan, and thus does not significantly affect the execution time of the HPR's task.

The state PASS also characterizes avoidance behavior, but involves a full stop of a LPR under conditions where its continued motion will cross a local path of a HPR. The state machine transitions to YIELD state when the second movement rule conditions are satisfied. The LPR behavior in the PASS state is a full stop and wait until the HPR passes in front of the LPR or until the condition to transition to this state is no longer met.

In cases where multiple robots are in such situations at the same time, the same rules are followed, and LPRs begin to perform the actions of the YIELD or PASS states relative to the first HPR they encounter. When robots with equal priorities fall under these conditions, a robot with a smallest remaining path length to its station starts executing the YIELD/PASS behavior. If we assume that a robot with a larger distance to its station should yield, a scenario could be possible in which a robot located at a larger distance from its station would eventually be forced to significantly increase its estimated path since it gives a way to other robots with the same priority more frequently.

To work with the robot navigation, the navigation stack of the ROS framework was used, along with move_base, amcl [25], mapping [17], and other ROS navigation core packages [14,15]. TEB local planner was used as a path planner due to robustness and flexibility of it's tuning provided by it's parameters [21,22].

5   Virtual Environment Setup

Experiments were conducted in a Gazebo [1] simulated hospital provided by an aws_robomaker_hospital_world package [2]. The AWS hospital world depicts one floor of a building, which consists of a lobby with reception and a waiting area, staircases, various rooms including storage rooms, several patient wards and a staff break room. A top view of the hospital environment is shown in Fig. 5.

Station signs were placed in the rooms to represent locations of some objects that robots should interact with, or locations where they typically need to deliver items. Experiments were conducted with two TIAGo Base and one Clearpath Ridgeback robots. TIAGo Base is equipped with the Hokuyo URG-04LX-UG1 LIDAR sensor and Ridgeback is equipped with the Hokuyo UST-10LX LIDAR sensor, which is essential for performing localization and navigation.

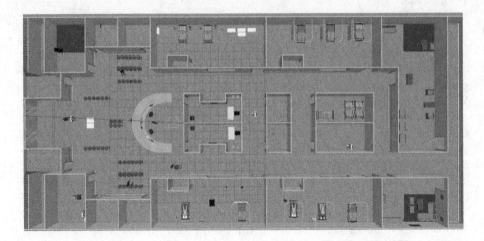

Fig. 5. Top down view of the Hospital World.

6   Virtual Experiments

At the beginning of the test runs, two TIAGo Base and one Clearpath Ridgeback robots were placed in different rooms of the virtual hospital; all state machines of the robots were in the state WAIT_FOR_GOAL. Next, the robots were assigned task sequences through the task manager GUI. The tasks had different priorities in a such way that the robots encounter each other while navigating to their stations and some robots would be forced to give way to others, i.e., at least once a transition from state NAVIGATE_TO_GOAL to states YIELD or PASS occurs. After the robots received the tasks, their state changed to NAVIGATE_TO_GOAL of the nested TASK state machine and they started navigating to the stations associated with tasks.

During the navigation, a LPR (with a lower priority task) encountered a HPR. An example visualized with the rviz [12] package is shown in Fig. 6. The paths built by the path planners are shown with curves: the yellow curve belongs to the Ridgeback and the red ones correspond to the TIAGo Base paths. Depending on the encounter conditions, the LPR (the TIAGo Base on the right), either transitioned to the YIELD state and made a way for the HPR (the Ridgeback on the left), or it transitioned to the PASS state and stopped to wait for the HRP to move further along its path.

Figure 7 shows two TIAGo Base robots freeing a way for the Ridgeback. The TIAGo Base approaching the higher priority Ridgeback entered the YIELD state, since the conditions for the first rule were met, and swerved aside to let it pass so that the local plan of the Ridgeback (yellow line) does not change. The local path of the TIAGo Base (red line above TIAGo Base on the right side of Fig. 7) changed accordingly to the rule YIELD. After the HPR traveled a sufficient distance, the yielding robot's state returned to NAVIGATE_TO_GOAL, and the robot continued towards its station. The experiment continued until

Fig. 6. The Clearpath Ridgeback (left) and TIAGo Base (right) robots are moving towards each other.

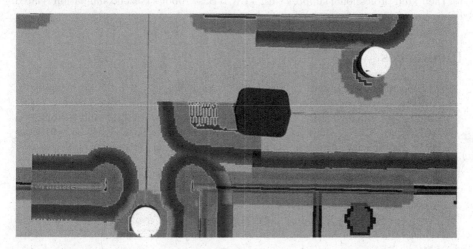

Fig. 7. The TIAGo Base robot in the active state YIELD gives way to the Ridgeback robot. (Color figure online)

all robots completed their tasks and returned to their initial state NAVI-GATE_TO_GOAL.

7   Conclusion and Future Work

This paper presented the framework and the implementation of a small-scale robotic transportation system, which operates in a smart hospital environment. The unmanned ground vehicles (UGV) performed transportation tasks between multiple stations that were located in different rooms. The UGVs navigated in the environment with moving objects in accordance with basic traffic rules, which consider priorities of particular tasks of each UGV. UGVs' behavior was defined by a state machine and transitions between these states, which made the robots' behavior more predictable and controllable. Virtual experiments were carried out in the Gazebo simulation of an entire floor of a small-size hospital building. The experiments confirmed that using various task priorities shorten a path length of robots with high priorities and thus reduce their task execution time.

While the original system was designed for a dynamic hospital environment, it could be extended for other environments where the problem of labor shortage or performance arises. As a part of the future work we plan to expand UGV movement rules model with a human detection [19] and avoidance.

Acknowledgements. This work was supported by the Russian Foundation for Basic Research (RFBR), project ID 19-58-70002. The fifth author acknowledges the support of the Japan Science and Technology Agency, the JST Strategic International Collaborative Research Program, Project No. 18065977. This work is part of Kazan Federal University Strategic Academic Leadership Program. Special thanks to PAL Robotics for their kind professional support with TIAGo Base robot's Gazebo simulation related issues.

References

1. Abbyasov, B., Lavrenov, R., Zakiev, A., Yakovlev, K., Svinin, M., Magid, E.: Automatic tool for gazebo world construction: from a grayscale image to a 3D solid model. In: 2020 IEEE International Conference on Robotics and Automation (ICRA), pp. 7226–7232 (2020). https://doi.org/10.1109/ICRA40945.2020.9196621
2. AWS robomaker: Amazon cloud robotics platform. https://github.com/aws-robotics/aws-robomaker-hospital-world
3. Bačík, J., Durovskỳ, F., Biroš, M., Kyslan, K., Perdukova, D., Padmanaban, S.: Pathfinder-development of automated guided vehicle for hospital logistics. IEEE Access **5**, 26892–26900 (2017)
4. Berntorp, K.: Path planning and integrated collision avoidance for autonomous vehicles. In: 2017 American Control Conference (ACC), pp. 4023–4028. IEEE (2017)
5. Bohren, J., Cousins, S.: The SMACH high-level executive [ROS news]. IEEE Robot. Autom. Mag. **17**(4), 18–20 (2010). https://doi.org/10.1109/MRA.2010.938836
6. Bohren, J.: SMACH smach_viewer package wiki page. http://wiki.ros.org/smach_viewer
7. Coulter, R.C.: Implementation of the pure pursuit path tracking algorithm. Technical report, Carnegie Mellon University (1992)
8. Fragapane, G., Zhang, C., Sgarbossa, F., Strandhagen, J.O.: An agent-based simulation approach to model hospital logistics. Int. J. Simul. Model. **18**(4), 654–665 (2019)
9. Fragapane, G., Hvolby, H.-H., Sgarbossa, F., Strandhagen, J.O.: Autonomous mobile robots in hospital logistics. In: Lalic, B., Majstorovic, V., Marjanovic, U., von Cieminski, G., Romero, D. (eds.) APMS 2020. IAICT, vol. 591, pp. 672–679. Springer, Cham (2020). https://doi.org/10.1007/978-3-030-57993-7_76

10. Fung, W.K., et al.: Development of a hospital service robot for transporting task. In: Proceedings of the IEEE International Conference on Robotics, Intelligent Systems and Signal Processing, vol. 1, pp. 628–633 (2003). https://doi.org/10.1109/RISSP.2003.1285647

11. Galin, R., Meshcheryakov, R.: Automation and robotics in the context of industry 4.0: the shift to collaborative robots. In: IOP Conference Series: Materials Science and Engineering, vol. 537, p. 032073. IOP Publishing (2019)

12. Kam, H.R., Lee, S.H., Park, T., Kim, C.H.: RViz: a toolkit for real domain data visualization. Telecommun. Syst. **60**(2), 337–345 (2015)

13. Kumar, B., Sharma, L., Wu, S.L.: Job allocation schemes for mobile service robots in hospitals. In: 2018 IEEE International Conference on Bioinformatics and Biomedicine (BIBM), pp. 1323–1326. IEEE (2018)

14. Lavrenov, R., Magid, E., Matsuno, F., Svinin, M., Suthakorn, J.: Development and implementation of spline-based path planning algorithm in ROS/Gazebo environment. Trudy SPIIRAN **18**(1), 57–84 (2019)

15. Magid, E., Lavrenov, R., Svinin, M., Khasianov, A.: Combining Voronoi graph and spline-based approaches for a mobile robot path planning. In: Gusikhin, O., Madani, K. (eds.) ICINCO 2017. LNEE, vol. 495, pp. 475–496. Springer, Cham (2020). https://doi.org/10.1007/978-3-030-11292-9_24

16. Magid, E., Zakiev, A., Tsoy, T., Lavrenov, R., Rizvanov, A.: Automating pandemic mitigation. Adv. Robot. 1–18 (2021). https://doi.org/10.1080/01691864.2021.1905059

17. Open Robotics Foundation. Gmapping ROS package web page. http://wiki.ros.org/gmapping

18. Ozkil, A.G., Fan, Z., Dawids, S., Aanes, H., Kristensen, J.K., Christensen, K.H.: Service robots for hospitals: a case study of transportation tasks in a hospital. In: International Conference on Automation and Logistics, pp. 289–294. IEEE (2009)

19. Ramil, S., Lavrenov, R., Tsoy, T., Svinin, M., Magid, E.: Real-time video server implementation for a mobile robot. In: 2018 11th International Conference on Developments in eSystems Engineering (DeSE), pp. 180–185. IEEE (2018)

20. ROS Operating System. http://wiki.ros.org

21. Rösmann, C., Feiten, W., Wösch, T., Hoffmann, F., Bertram, T.: Efficient trajectory optimization using a sparse model. In: 2013 European Conference on Mobile Robots, pp. 138–143. IEEE (2013)

22. Rösmann, C.: Teb_local_planner ROS package web page. http://wiki.ros.org/teb_local_planner

23. Sagitov, A., Gavrilova, L., Tsoy, T., Li, H.: Design of simple one-arm surgical robot for minimally invasive surgery. In: 2019 12th International Conference on Developments in eSystems Engineering (DeSE), pp. 500–503. IEEE (2019)

24. Sun, Y., Coltin, B., Veloso, M.: Interruptible autonomy: towards dialog-based robot task management. In: 27th AAAI Conference on Artificial Intelligence (2013)

25. Thrun, S., Fox, D., Burgard, W., Dellaert, F.: Robust Monte Carlo localization for mobile robots. Artif. Intell. **128**(1–2), 99–141 (2001)

26. Zakharov, K., Saveliev, A., Sivchenko, O.: Energy-efficient path planning algorithm on three-dimensional large-scale terrain maps for mobile robots. In: Ronzhin, A., Rigoll, G., Meshcheryakov, R. (eds.) ICR 2020. LNCS (LNAI), vol. 12336, pp. 319–330. Springer, Cham (2020). https://doi.org/10.1007/978-3-030-60337-3_31

Dedicated Payload Stabilization System in a Service Robot for Catering

Petr Smirnov(✉) and Artem Kovalev

Laboratory of Autonomous Robotic Systems, St. Petersburg Federal Research Center of the Russian Academy of Sciences (SPC RAS), St. Petersburg Institute for Informatics and Automation of the Russian Academy of Sciences, 39, 14th Line, 199178 St. Petersburg, Russia

Abstract. The paper considers the implementation of robots in the service sector, as well as mechanisms for stabilizing the transported goods. The design of a mobile robotic platform is presented, which differs from analogs in the ability to stabilize the payload due to a combined solution based on the use of a PID controller, a suspension system and payload control. The design solutions for monitoring the payload are analyzed separately. The implemented mechanism is described, and the analysis is made mainly of its use in service robots limited by the layout of the premises. This device will solve common applied problems in the field of robotic service associated with the need to use such robots mainly on flat surfaces. The proposed solution allows to reduce the cost, simplify and optimize the work of the robot in the restaurant premises. Based on the proposed solution, a fully functional robot that can be developed, which does not require additional investments in the reconstruction of the premises of the restaurant, which provides assistance, or completely replaces the waiter when delivering food and drinks to the client's table, as well as attracting new customers due to its novelty and practicality.

Keywords: Waiter robot · Stabilization · PID-controller · Robot buffer · IMU-sensor

1 Introduction

Many robots are now replacing human labor in factories, which can improve productivity and increase the accuracy of the manufactured product, but this area is not the only area where robots can be used. One of the topical areas is the service sector. Currently, robot developers are trying to solve the following tasks: delivery of various goods and basic necessities, customer service in catering establishments, as well as cleaning the premises, preparation and disinfection of premises.

This article discusses the problem of customer service in catering establishments, which remains practically non-automated. Acceptance of an order and its delivery by a client is a monotonous work, which means that it can be easily algorithmized. With this planning, it is worth noting that the main problems of solving this problem of one or more premises are also constantly moving visitors to the institution, which can complicate the delivery of the order in its entirety. As a result, the device offers a robotic model that provides delivery and drinks to the client, which does not require redevelopment of premises.

© Springer Nature Switzerland AG 2021
A. Ronzhin et al. (Eds.): ICR 2021, LNAI 12998, pp. 194–204, 2021.
https://doi.org/10.1007/978-3-030-87725-5_17

2   Overview of Existing Solutions in the Field of Service Robots

There are many service robots on display today. Such devices help to deliver dishes to the client's table, and sometimes completely replace the waiter in a restaurant, which frees a person from constant monotonous work. This task is relevant and promising for the current developers of robots [1]. Thus, the authors of the article [2] presented a completely autonomous robot moving around a restaurant with a varied layout. The structure of the device consists of a wheelbase with a control system and an automatic lift with three levels for trays. Durinng delivery, the product is kept in a separate enclosure to maintain its temperature. At the client's table, the door of the drawbridge of the robot is lowered, and the desired tray with food rises to the level of the mechanism and rolls out. On the wheelbase there are motors that drive the four mechanical wheels of Elon. There is no suspension system in the design, which means that it is assumed that the robot motion is constrained to moving only on the flat surfaces. The power supply consists of two 24V lithium polymer (Li-Po) batteries to power the robot. In order for the robot to be able to serve restaurants with tables of different heights, a motorized lift table is installed between the base and the dumbwaiter [2]. The autonomous service robot Servi [3] from Bear Robotics (USA) is a device for delivering food around a restaurant, which can greatly facilitate the work of employees of restaurants and cafes. The battery of the robotic platform allows the device to operate for about 8–12 h. The movement of the robot waiter is powered by two motors. Positioning in the room is determined by two cameras, one of which is located at the base and looks up, and the second at the top and looks down.

The KEENON company is engaged in the production of intelligent robots for the automation of goods delivery and automatic disinfection of premises. One of such developments is the Delivery RobotT5. The robot relies on KEENON's independently developed SLAM synchronous localization and map construction system to run stably and efficiently in restaurants and other application scenarios. It relies on a series of sensors and multi-sensor fusion algorithms such as encoder, gyroscope (IMU), LiDAR ODOM, LiDAR, Image Module. The battery charge is enough for 15 h of operation [4]. The idea of delivering food in a restaurant was adopted by LG with the release of the CLOi ServeBot line of robots. This robot is capable of transporting up to four dishes at the same time due to 4 levels with trays. The robot cannot fully serve customers, but it facilitates the delivery of heavy and hot meals [5].

Haohai Robot restaurant, which opened in 2012, was one of the first restaurants to fully automate manual labor tasks usually performed by humans. The movement of robots is carried out along special marked paths required for their localization using optical sensors. The battery of each robot is designed for approximately 5 h of operation without recharging, the height of the robot is from 130 to 160 cm [6]. A similar idea of delivering food using robotic orienteering lines on the floor is used in a restaurant at Cixi Mall, Zheqiang City, China. The robot park consists of five robots, three of which stand at the entrance, inviting guests, and the rest serve as a waiter. The working time of the robot is also 5 h without interruption. The time required for recharging is at least two hours [7].

Pudu Robotics manufactures intelligent robots for automating the delivery of goods. BellaBot is one of the newest models from this company, dating back to 2020. This robot is equipped with multiple depth cameras Intel RealSense D435 with built-in IMU (Inertial Measurement Unit) sensors, which allows it to build a three-dimensional map of the scene and navigate the room using SLAM algorithms. Since one or several BellaBot robots can be used in one room, a decentralized architecture developed by the company and a flexible network communication scheme can be used to coordinate and interact with them. To ensure stability, the robot is equipped with a suspension with a linkage mechanism that allows it to adapt to the unevenness of the surface on which it moves [8]. Another example of this development is Bot Retail presented by Samsung at CES2019. This device, like the previous ones, is focused on restaurant-type establishments. The robot can help you choose a dish from the menu, showing its appearance, contents, taking into account your wishes, bringing the order and taking the dirty plates back to the kitchen [9]. Another example of this development is the Amy-Trackless Robot Waiter from CSJBO +. In this model, a laser sensor is used to determine the position of the robot in space, and a chassis with high balancing is used as a supporting structure [10].

The authors of the article [10] presented a robot serving customers in a restaurant in Da Nang, Vietnam. A proportional-integral-differentiating controller (PID controller) with a pulse-width modulation (PWM) generator, designed to control the movement of the device, is introduced into the software and hardware of this robot. As a result of the introduction of such hardware and specialized algorithmic support, it was possible to stabilize the movement of the robot, eliminating jerks and ensuring a smooth start and stop of the robot. A similar stabilization system was proposed by the authors of the article [11]. This stabilization solution was implemented on the basis of open source code for the operating system ROS with the application of restrictions in force in planning the movement. The proposed algorithm for fluid transportation, developed using the standard SMACH package for the ROS operating system, written in the Python programming language, provides a smooth movement of the device.

The article [12] proposes mathematical software for the humanoid robot TEO, which allows controlling the payload located on the tray while in motion. This solution calculates the actual zero moment point regardless of the slope and tilt vector of the robot. The authors of the article [13] proposed the idea of stabilizing a filled container using a 6-link manipulator while the robot waiter is moving. The presented method uses the direct transcription approach [13] to solve the problem of stabilizing the beverage tray. In the article [14], a similar solution was proposed for stabilizing the manipulator holding the object. The controller developed by the authors does not require torque sensors of the manipulator links. Experimental results confirmed the effectiveness of this control scheme, which ensures safe physical interaction in the case of intentional or unintentional contact with people, while maintaining the control object.

The authors of the article [15] proposed and experimentally tested a new method of creating trajectories for the free movement of a manipulator, in the capture of which a vessel with a liquid. The method is based on a linearized mechanical equivalent splash model. This simplified model of a spherical pendulum is used to obtain a set of parameters with which an exponential filter is designed and implemented in a cascade configuration with a common trajectory generator. According to the results, the method allows to significantly reduce the effect of splashing liquid during the movement of the manipulator with the vessel.

Based on the results of the above review of robotic tools used in the field of customer service in restaurants and public catering facilities, as well as object stabilization systems that are necessary to control the transported product, criteria for the developed robot were proposed. This device must deliver the order to the customer of the establishment in its entirety, avoiding collisions with static and dynamic objects during movement. In the solution, it is necessary to take into account the problem of unevenness in the floor when moving from room to room. The developed model must be equipped with a system for monitoring the speed of rotation of the engines. Also, in a robotic device, it is necessary to stabilize the transported tray with a payload, which will allow the platform to move in the institution, regardless of the quality of the floor covering, the presence of thresholds, slopes and minor obstacles in its path.

3 General Construction of a Robot Waiter

Consider the proposed schematic diagram of a service robot for performing the functions of a waiter (Fig. 1a). The movement of such a device is carried out by four motors (block 1 in Fig. 1a), rotating omnidirectional wheels, which allows the robot to move in any direction without the need to perform complex maneuvers. At level 2 in the presented diagram, there is a sensing unit, which includes wide-angle cameras, obstacle sensors [16] and a laser rangefinder (LiDAR), as well as pressure sensors, which are used to implement localization and navigation algorithms in the restaurant premises [17]. The laser rangefinder is offset to the edge of the device's circumference, allowing you to determine objects around the object (about 270°), the remaining blind zones are covered by 6 obstacle sensors. Wide-angle cameras of this device are necessary for visual localization, and to solve the disadvantages, laser rangefinders are used, in case it is impossible to determine an obstacle, for example, a chair leg. Pressure sensors in the robot are used for emergency shutdown of engines in a collision if the system could not detect obstacles or the above-described sensors failed. Also, inside this block there are a computing module and batteries. Trays with drinks and food are placed in an isolated compartment (Fig. 1, block 3) to ensure their safety, as well as protect the hardware. At level 4 of the device, there is a terminal for human-machine interaction (touch screen, cameras, array of microphones). The door that insulates the compartment in block 3 is controlled by two magnetic locks and can be unlocked by the client when the phone scans the QR code displayed on the screen of the interaction unit. The interaction scheme of the platform levels is shown in Fig. 1 b.

Due to the block organization of the robot, its structure satisfies the modularity criteria, and the robot is relatively easy to assemble and operate, as well as to replace and repair individual parts. The proposed sensing sensors are sufficient for the implementation of algorithms for determining the position of the robot on the map of the room, as well as for detecting and preventing possible collisions during its movement. The dimensions of the resulting model of this device are 540 mm in diameter and 1200 mm in height, which will allow you to ideally maneuver between tables in a restaurant or cafe.

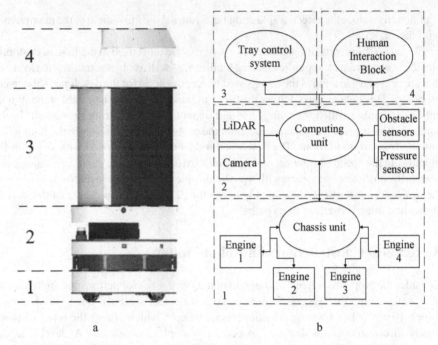

Fig. 1. Principal diagram of the service waiter robot: a) model; b) control diagram.

On the basis of the proposed model of a service robot and a review of existing stabilization solutions, a system for monitoring the stability of the platform and its payload was developed, combining the known approaches in this area. To solve this problem, the following solutions have been implemented.

A PID controller is introduced into the robot control system to control the speed of the DC motors that drive the all-directional wheels of the robot. This will maintain a constant speed of the motors, regardless of the presence of various loads and external disturbances. The use of PID control algorithms helps to achieve the desired effect while maintaining fast response and high stability. Thus, the application of the described solution in combination with the PWM method helps the robot to move faster, while maintaining the smoothness of movement and stability of the action under disturbances. Also, the problem of smooth start and end of the movement of the robot is solved, which makes it possible to reduce fluctuations in the useful load [18].

Based on the design features of the robot's omnidirectional wheels, the robot body is connected to the supporting elements by means of spring suspension. This structure assumes an independent way of connecting the wheels to each other, that is, the movement of one wheel of the axle is not associated with the movement of the other wheel on the same axle. The independent suspension was chosen in order to provide the strongest possible grip of the wheels with the floor surface, taking into account the peculiarities of their design. The suspension system used in this robotic device avoids unwanted system vibrations [19].

A stabilizing tray is introduced to ensure the stability of the payload in cases where the device is tilted relative to the surface. A construction based on a mechanical gyroscope is considered as one of the stabilizers' implementations. This mechanism is suitable for placement in a platform, has a small number of degrees of freedom, and therefore does not require high computing power. The device has small dimensions and the number of degrees of freedom.

Let us consider in more detail the control system of the tray with the payload, comparing with the available stabilizations.

4   Tray Control System with Payload

When comparing existing systems for stabilizing objects, in this case a tray with a payload, the key requirements for them are dimensions and the ability to work in a limited space of a mobile platform, as well as requirements for a control system. These characteristics are important due to the size limitations of the indoor platform. To meet these requirements, it is proposed to consider the stabilization mechanisms:

- Classic manipulator - any controlled mechanism capable of performing the functions of a human hand when interacting with objects. The executive mechanism is an open kinematic chain, the links of which are connected in series by joints. The advantages of using this mechanism are complete stabilization in space.
- Stewart platform – a kind of parallel manipulator that uses an octahedral strut arrangement [20]. In comparison with a classical manipulator, this design does not require high computing power, since in the case of solving inverse kinematics, we get the only solution.
- Gyroscopic platform - a device designed to stabilize individual objects or devices. The mechanism of the gyroscopic platform takes up a small volume and has a simple control system, in comparison with the above-described payload stabilization devices.

A comparison of the characteristics of the considered stabilization systems is given in the Table 1.

Based on the results of comparing solutions to stabilize the payload, the mechanism of the gyroscopic platform was selected. This mechanism is easy to implement, does not require a large volume occupied in the robot, which meets the criteria of an embedded system.

The proposed system (Fig. 2) consists of inertial measuring modules (IMU-sensor), a controller and servo drives that stabilize the nose. An IMU sensor is an inertial measuring device that allows you to determine a position in space. This system uses a linear-quadratic regulator to stabilize the motors. The proposed system will allow you to control the tray during movement or emergency braking. Emergency braking is understood as the behavior of the platform in the event of a sudden appearance of an object on its way [21].

Model Predictive Control stabilizes a system with a dynamic model $\mathbf{x} = \mathbf{f}(\mathbf{x}, \mathbf{u})$, along the target trajectory $\mathbf{x}^*(t)$, $\mathbf{u}^*(t)$ by minimizing the cost function $L(\mathbf{x}, \mathbf{u})$:

$$\min_{\mathbf{u}} \int L(\mathbf{x}, \mathbf{u}),$$

Table 1. Comparison of stabilization mechanisms.

Mechanism	Classic manipulator	Stewart platform	Gyroscopic platform
Number of degrees of freedom	6	6	2
Difficulty of embedding into platform in relation to dimensions	Large size, large workspace	Large size, small workspace	Small size, small workspace
Computational power requirement	High	Low	Low
Stabilization type	In space	On surface	On surface
Swivel independence	–	+	–
Ability to move stabilized object vertically	+	+	–

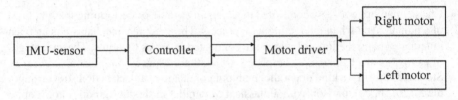

Fig. 2. Tray stabilization system.

$$\mathbf{x}(t_0) = \mathbf{x}_{init}, r(\mathbf{x},\mathbf{u}) = 0, h(\mathbf{x},\mathbf{u}) \leq 0$$

where $\mathbf{x}$ is dynamic model state vector, $\mathbf{u}$ is control vector, $\mathbf{x}_{init}$ is initial state of the system, $r(\mathbf{x},\mathbf{u})$ – terminal constraints, $h(\mathbf{x},\mathbf{u})$ – path constraints.

The linear-quadratic regulator finds the optimal control vector that stabilizes the dynamic system while minimizing the cost function. It is necessary to minimize the given cost function:

$$\min_u \sum_{k=0}^{N-1} \mathbf{x}_k^T Q \mathbf{x}_k + \mathbf{u}_k^T R \mathbf{u}_k,$$

where Q, R are positive definite matrices.

The discretized dynamic system is described as a linear model in the state space

$$\mathbf{x}_{k+1} = A\mathbf{x}_k + B\mathbf{u}_k,$$

where A is state matrix (system matrix), B is control matrix, $\mathbf{x}_k$ is the vector of the state of the system at time k, $\mathbf{u}_k$ is the control vector of the system at time k.

It is necessary to find the optimal control vector $\mathbf{u}_k = -K_k\mathbf{x}_k$ that will minimize the given cost function. The optimal control vector $\mathbf{u}_k*$ is found by solving the discrete algebraic Riccati equation (DARE):

$$\mathbf{u}_k^* = -K_k\mathbf{x}_k = (R + B^TS_kB)^{-1}B^TS_kA\mathbf{x}_k,$$

$$S_N = Q,$$

$$S_{k-1} = Q + A^TS_kA - (A^TS_kB)(R + B^TS_kB)^{-1}(B^TS_kA)$$

The equation is solved iteratively starting from the final condition $S_N = Q$ backwards in time. Formulation of the model predictive control problem with a quadratic cost function is as follows:

$$L(\mathbf{x}, \mathbf{u}) = \left\|\mathbf{x} - \mathbf{x}*\right\|_Q^2 + \left\|\mathbf{u} - \mathbf{u}*\right\|_R^2,$$

where T is time horizon, N is number of sampling steps, $\delta t = T/N$:

$$\min_{\mathbf{u}} \mathbf{x}_N^T Q\mathbf{x}_N + \sum_{k=0}^{N} \mathbf{x}_k^T Q\mathbf{x}_k + \mathbf{u}_k^T Q\mathbf{x}_k,$$

$$\mathbf{x}_{k+1} = f(\mathbf{x}_k, \mathbf{u}_k, \delta t), \mathbf{x}_0 = \mathbf{x}_{\text{init}},$$

$$\mathbf{u}_{\min} \leq \mathbf{u_k} \leq \mathbf{u}_{\max}.$$

The task is constructed in the form direct multiple shooting [22] and is solved by the sequential quadratic programming algorithm (SQP).

5 Experiment Result

Based on the proposed model, the gyroscopic platform system was tested. Figure 3 shows the operation of the tray stabilizing controller, tracking the set position in the event of emergency braking. Figure 3, a shows that the maximum deviation from the target position in the case of emergency braking was 0.1345 rad, and the minimum was −0.1067 rad. At a time interval of 120 s. after the disturbance, the system remains in a remains in a stable state (Fig. 3 b).

By introducing the proposed system into the service robot-waiter, it is possible to control the position of the payload during the movement of the robot. This design is similar in engineering to a mechanical gyroscope, allowing you to expand the ability to transport the payload without compromising integrity. Under the extension, transportation is assumed between rooms, or in the same room, which are located in different parallel planes with a passageway. Also, this design allows you to additionally check in the event of a malfunction of the suspension system. Compared to the Stewart platform, the resulting design is easier to assemble and sufficient to stabilize fluids during transport.

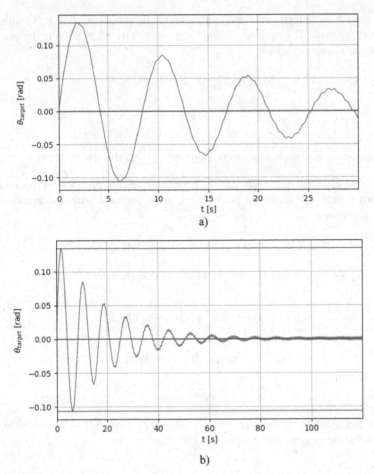

Fig. 3. Tracking the target position of the tray by the controller, after the disturbance: a) at an interval of 30 s; b) within 120 s.

6 Conclusion

In this work, the analysis of the available robotic solutions was carried out and the design of the robot waiter was presented, which allows to control and correct the movement of the mobile robot, taking into account the unevenness of the floor, as well as in the presence of dynamic obstacles that can provoke a sharp deceleration of the robot. Particular attention was paid to payload control systems in case of impossibility to stabilize the device. The selected solution based on gyroscopic stabilization, previously not used in practice in a specific task, is simple and easy to implement, not taking up a large amount of space. Thus, the proposed model is convenient for use in rooms that are not specially equipped for the operation of mobile robotic equipment, which is suitable for collaborative robotics and socio-cyberphysical systems [23, 24]. From a technical point of view, the proposed combined solution will allow control of the payload during delivery to the client of the establishment. The proposed design differs from similar solutions in that it allows simultaneous stabilization of not only the entire platform in motion, taking into account the unevenness of the floor, but also additional stabilization of the tray with the payload.

References

1. ISO 8373:2012 "Robots and robotic devices - Vocabulary", IDT
2. Cheong, A., Lau, M., Foo, E., Hedley, J., Bo, J.W.: Development of a robotic waiter system. IFAC-PapersOnLine **49**(21), 681–686 (2016). https://doi.org/10.1016/j.ifacol.2016.10.679
3. Osinova, A.A., Tatarinova, YA.V., Efa, S.G.: PR and innovation in the restaurant business, Siberian State Aerospace University named after academician M. F. Reshetnev. **7-2**. 278–280 (2012)
4. Ivanov, S., Webster, C., Berezina, K.: Robotics in tourism and hospitality. In: Handbook of e-Tourism, pp. 1–27 (2020)
5. Murphy, R.R., Gandudi, V.B.M., Adams, J.: Applications of robots for COVID-19 response, computer science, robotics, Cornell University (2020)
6. Zallio, M., Berry, D., Leifer, L.J.: Meaningful age-friendly design. case studies on enabling assistive technology. In: Ahram, T., Falcão, C. (eds.) AHFE 2019. AISC, vol. 972, pp. 779–790. Springer, Cham (2020). https://doi.org/10.1007/978-3-030-19135-1_76
7. Omair, M.A., Rakib, A.S.H., Khan, M.A., Mahmud, R.T.: An autonomous robot for waiter service in restaurants, Department of Electrical and Electronic Engineering. BRAC University, pp. 1–43 (2015)
8. Bulgakov, D.S.: Robotic cuisine in the hotel and restaurant complex Nizhniygorod science, no. 4 (2017)
9. Aymerich-Franch, L., Ferrer, I.: The implementation of social robots during the COVID-19 pandemic. ArXiv preprint. arXiv:2007.03941 (2020)
10. Jin, Y., Qian, Z., Gong, S., Yang, W.: Learning transferable driven and drone assisted sustainable and robust regional disease surveillance for smart healthcare. IEEE/ACM Trans. Comput. Biol. Bioinf. (2020). https://doi.org/10.1109/TCBB.2020.3017041
11. Thanh, V.N., Vinh, D.P., Nghi, N.T., Nam, L.H., Toan, D.L.H.: Restaurant serving robot with double line sensors following approach. In: 2019 IEEE International Conference on Mechatronics and Automation (ICMA) (2019). https://doi.org/10.1109/icma.2019.8816404
12. Wan, A.Y.S., Soong, Y.D., Foo, E., Wong, W.L.E., Lau, W.S.M.: Waiter robots conveying drinks. Technologies, **8**(3), 44 (2020). https://doi.org/10.3390/technologies8030044
13. Miguel Garcia-Haro, J., Martinez, S., Balaguer, C.: Balance computation of objects transported on a tray by a humanoid robot based on 3D dynamic slopes. In: 2018 IEEE-RAS 18th International Conference on Humanoid Robots (Humanoids) (2018). https://doi.org/10.1109/humanoids.2018.8624920
14. Nagy, Á., Csorvási, G., Vajk, I.: Path tracking algorithms for non-convex waiter motion problem. Periodica Polytechnica Electr. Eng. Comput. Sci. **62**(1), 16–23 (2018). https://doi.org/10.3311/ppee.11606
15. Zuiani, F., Vasile, M., Palmas, A., Avanzini, G.: Direct transcription of low-thrust trajectories with finite trajectory elements. Acta Astronaut. **72**, 108–120 (2012). https://doi.org/10.1016/j.actaastro.2011.09.011
16. Vigoriti, F., Ruggiero, F., Lippiello, V., Villani, L.: Control of redundant robot arms with null-space compliance and singularity-free orientation representation. Robot. Auton. Syst. **100**, 186–193 (2018). https://doi.org/10.1016/j.robot.2017.11.007

17. Krestovnikov, K., Saveliev, A., Cherskikh, E.: Development of a circuit design for a capacitive pressure sensor, applied in walking robot foot. In: 2020 IEEE 20th Mediterranean Electrotechnical Conference (MELECON), pp. 243–247. IEEE (2020). https://doi.org/10.1109/MELECON48756.2020.9140509
18. Krestovnikov, K., Cherskikh, E., Zimuldinov, E.: Combined capacitive pressure and proximity sensor for using in robotic systems. In: Ronzhin, A., Shishlakov, V. (eds.) Proceedings of 15th International Conference on Electromechanics and Robotics "Zavalishin's Readings." SIST, vol. 187, pp. 513–523. Springer, Singapore (2021). https://doi.org/10.1007/978-981-15-5580-0_42
19. Wescott, T.: PID without a PhD, Embedded Systems Programming (2000)
20. Margolius, I.: What is an automobile? Automobile **37**(11), 48–52 (2020)
21. Stewart, D.: A platform with six degrees of freedom. In: UK Institution of Mechanical Engineers Proceedings, vol. 180, no. 15, pp. 1965–1966
22. Ponomareva, S.V., Kutuzova, V.S., Pavlovich, A.A.: Calculation of uncertainties in operating strapdown inertial navigation systems on mobile objects. J. Mach. Manuf. Reliab. **49**(8), 723–730 (2020). https://doi.org/10.3103/S1052618820080099
23. Moritz, D., Hans, G.B., Holger, D., Pierre-Brice, W.: Fast direct multiple shooting algorithms for optimal robot control. In: Diehl, M., Mombaur, K. (eds.) Fast Motions in Biomechanics and Robotics, pp. 65–93. Springer, Heidelberg (2005). https://doi.org/10.1007/978-3-540-36119-0_4
24. Galin, R., Meshcheryakov, R.: Collaborative robots: development of robotic perception system, safety issues, and integration of Ai to imitate human behavior. In: Ronzhin, A., Shishlakov, V. (eds.) Proceedings of 15th International Conference on Electromechanics and Robotics "Zavalishin's Readings." SIST, vol. 187, pp. 175–185. Springer, Singapore (2021). https://doi.org/10.1007/978-981-15-5580-0_14
25. Cherskikh, E., Saveliev, A.: Survey on behavioral strategies of cyber-physical systems in case of loss of integrity. In: Ronzhin, A., Shishlakov, V. (eds.) Electromechanics and Robotics "Zavalishin's Readings" (ER(ZR)), pp. 463–474. Springer, Heidelberg (2021). https://doi.org/10.1007/978-981-16-2814-6_40

Collision Avoidance for Mobile Robots Using Proximity Sensors

Yucheng Tang[1], Ilshat Mamaev[1(✉)], Hosam Alagi[1], Bengt Abel[3],
and Björn Hein[1,2]

[1] IAR-IPR, Karlsruhe Institute of Technology, Karlsruhe, Germany
yucheng.tang@student.kit.edu
{ilshat.mamaev,hosam.alagi,bjoern.hein}@kit.edu
[2] Karlsruhe University of Applied Sciences, Karlsruhe, Germany
[3] STILL GmbH, Hamburg, Germany

Abstract. Due to the rise of e-commerce material handling industry
has been experiencing significant changes, especially in the COVID-19
pandemic. Notwithstanding the broad utilization of Automated Guided
Vehicles (AGVs) for many years, the demand for Autonomous Mobile
Robot (AMR) is rapidly increasing. One of the main challenges in
autonomous operation in an unstructured environment is gapless perception. In this paper, we present a concept for reactive collision avoidance using Capacitive Proximity Sensor (CPS), with the goal to augment
robot perception in close proximity situations. We propose a proximity-
based potential field method using capacitive measurement for collision
avoidance. A local minima problem is solved by applying tangential forces
around the virtual obstacle points. We evaluate the proof-of-concept both
in simulation and on a real mobile robot equipped with CPS. The results
have shown that capacitive sensing technology can compensate localization tolerance and odometry drift closing the perception gap in close
proximity scenarios.

Keywords: Reactive collision avoidance · Capacitive proximity
sensing · Narrow passage problem

1 Introduction

Autonomous mobile robots are becoming more eminent in various application
sectors, including logistics, service, healthcare, and agriculture. While AGV
nowadays already available as commercial off-the-shelf products like Kiva [8]
or Fifi [21], AMR are still mainly remain a research topic. Whereas AGV typically follow fixed routes along with visual markers, wires in the floor, etc.,
AMRs should be able to perceive their operating environment and navigate
autonomously using on-board intelligence [16]. The higher price of the AMR
on-board hardware is compensated by eliminating of the costly infrastructure
requirements, time-consuming commissioning, or process modifications. Especially in mixed environments where AMRs and humans work together, the

A. Ronzhin et al. (Eds.): ICR 2021, LNAI 12998, pp. 205–221, 2021.
https://doi.org/10.1007/978-3-030-87725-5_18

robot's perception of the environment is essential. This is because the robot must always react to the unpredictable actions of humans, such as incorrectly placed load carriers.

On the other hand, sensors for environmental perception also face challenges. In robotics, traditional optical sensors like cameras and laser scanners can offer high resolution and precise measurement capabilities for the robot. However, this precipitates high-performance requirements and still suffers from divergent light conditions, limited focal range, occlusions, etc. These disadvantages are particularly noticeable when the load is being picked up. Often the sensor is covered by the load carrier or the opening angle is not sufficient to see the load carrier. This leads to the fact that the load is often picked up *blind*.

There are two principal approaches for collision avoidance for autonomous mobile robots navigating in unstructured environments: deliberative and reactive [6]. The deliberative approach requires high computational power to plan the collision-free path in the given map and suffers from slow response times in unstructured environments. On the other hand, reactive approaches employ sensors to generate navigation behavior directly in the operational/task space.

In this paper, we present a concept for reactive collision avoidance using capacitive proximity sensors in a loosely structured environment. The goal is to augment robot perception in the close proximity of the robot to compensate localization tolerance and odometry drift. Our scenario focuses on a particular task of a collision-free drive-in underneath a trolley in a warehouse. As the robot has to lift the trolley for transport, usually optical sensors are located on the sides of the robot. Therefore, the scanner can only perceive the ambiguous pose of the trolley wheels, which leads to localization tolerance of several centimeters. Finally, we evaluate the proposed concept and hardware in a warehouse scenario in a simulation environment and on a real robot.

The main contributions of this work are:

- developing a proximity-based potential field method using capacitive measurement for collision avoidance,
- solving the local minima problem using tangential forces approach, and
- equipping a mobile robot equipped with Capacitive Proximity Sensor (CPS) as a proof-of-concept for augmented gapless perception.

2   State of the Art

We divide the relevant literature into two parts considering the methods for Reactive collection avoidance and its implementation and perception systems.

2.1   Reactive Collision Avoidance for Mobile Robots

Fox et al. [7] provide the dynamic window approach for collision-free driving, which generates a valid searching space and selects an optimal solution considering the constraints imposed by limited velocities and acceleration of the robots.

Wada et al. [24] use Markov model and Kalman filter to predict a dynamic obstacle and applied a rapidly-exploring random tree search method for trajectory planning in time augmented configuration space. Virtual Potential Field (PF) [11] proposed by Khatib et al. generate two kinds of artificial potential field to navigate the agent. The target position exhibits an attractive field while the obstacles in the system produce repulsive fields that guide the robot to the target point and bypassing the block simultaneously. Some other PF-based methods represent a widely used solution in the field of obstacle avoidance. Borenstein et al. [4] generate a polar histogram with obstacle density to navigate the agent towards the desired direction, Ulrich et al. [22] provide an obstacle expansion based on agent's diameter, and generate a masked polar histogram considered robot motion model. [23] iteratively run VFH+ to extend multiple nodes forward, thus introducing information closer to the global map, like RRT. However, these approaches consider agent holonomic (circular) or merge global and local planners.

Normally when encountering a non-circular robot, it will be treated as a circular robot with the longest diagonal as its diameter (VFH+ obstacle expansion). Nonetheless, when the robot is asked to pass through a narrow passage or encounter "piano movers' problem" [18], some novel approaches need to be implemented. Kondak et al. [12] formulate the problem of motion planning as a problem of the non-linear constrained optimization problem, Minguez et al. [14] combine the arc reachable manifold with robot configuration space that takes into account vehicle shape and kinematic constraints. However, the mentioned approaches for non-circular robots require high computational power, making them less reactive in loosely structured environments. Finally, Seki et al.[19] propose a potential field-based obstacle avoidance method using a non-holonomic rectangular robot and a LiDAR. This method is limited to 2D perception and suffers from the local minima problem. We propose a new proximity-based PF method and overcome the local minima problem by applying additional tangential forces.

2.2   Sensors for Mobile Robot

A wide range of sensors can be used in mobile robots. Sonar sensors have long been used in mobile robot obstacle avoidance applications, Yasin et al. [25] rotate an ultrasonic sensor mounted on the mobile robot for obstacle shape approximation and edge detection. In [9] localization method based on adaptive particle filter using solely sonar sensors is proposed. Almasri et al. [3] developed a new line tracking and obstacle avoidance technique with low-cost infrared sensors. Ohya et al. [15] proposed a template-vision-based obstacle detection method, where a single camera image is compared to a template picture recorded in the teaching phase. But they still used sonar sensors for dynamic obstacles due to computer arithmetic power problems at that time. Hiroaki Seki et al. [19] scan objects in the surrounding circular area to identify obstacles with the help of a LiDAR providing only 2D information. Lagisetty et al. [13] used a stereo camera intending to obtain 3D geometric information of the robot's surroundings and pose estimation of a robot. In general, 3D perception requires higher computational power and still suffers from ambiguous light conditions, material reflectance and transparency, close-range perception gap, etc. To overcome this limitations many sensor fusion methods have been proposed[2,5,20]. Rabl et al. [17] briefly introduce single-point capacitive proximity measurement for obstacle avoidance.

To address these challenges, we propose a concept for a non-holonomic mobile robot with integrated capacitive proximity sensors into all four lateral sides and capable of volumetric multi-obstacles detection in close proximity and achieving collision avoidance tasks using a proximity-based potential field approach.

3   Concept

In our scenario (Fig. 1), the task is that the robot can drive-in under the trolley or shelf without collision, and the problem is stated as follows.

1. A trolley is a metal basket of a shelf like in Kiva system however equipped with freely rotating wheels.
2. A nonholonomic four-wheeled mobile robot is considered in the scenario with a differential drive.
3. The shape of the robot is (or can be approximated by) a rectangle.
4. The width of the trolley should not be much larger than the robot, and the drive-in problem can be seen as a narrow passage problem or "piano movers" problem.
5. Global path planning is given. The robot is assumed to stop about one meter away from the center point of the target trolley based on the preliminary global path planning method. So R_G is set as $(1,0,0)$. Since the error is inevitable in the real environment, R_G is, in most cases, not the desired target point.
6. The process can be terminated when the robot has to go backward or predict an unavoidable collision.

3.1   Differential Drive

The mobile robot is operating in a two-dimensional task space. The pose information of the robot is defined by ξ, which consists of the translation in x and y as well as the rotation θ. In order to describe the motion of the robot, the elements of ξ must be differentiable over time to represent the velocity of the robot. In our scenario, the mobile robot is set as differential driven, so the kinematics input is provided as velocity vector ξ' without y-direction.

$$\dot{\xi} = [\dot{x}, \dot{\theta}].$$ (1)

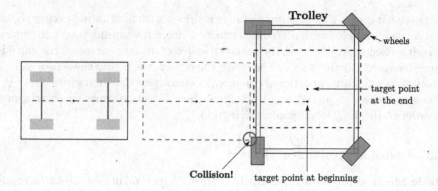

Fig. 1. Drive-in task with a rectangular differential drive robot and a trolley. The ambiguous pose of the trolley wheels and the target position error may lead to a collision.

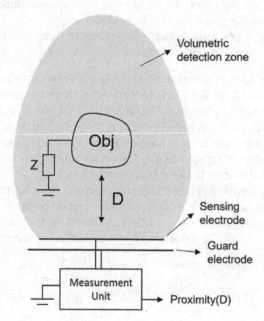

Fig. 2. Capacitive proximity sensor with active shielding (Guard electrode). The distance between the sensor (sensing electrode) and an Object (Obj) in the (volumetric detection zone) is approximated with a proximity signal (Proximity(D)), which shows an antiproportional exponential characteristic.

3.2 Capacitive Sensing

Our capacitive sensor can detect the proximity of an object and estimate its contact force in a case of contact. More details about the implementation are presented in a previous work [1]. In this work, we utilize only the proximity measurement. Figure 2 illustrate the electrode configuration, which is driven in single-ended mode. The *Sensing electrode* is driven with alternating exciter signal and actively shielded with a *Guard electrode* to form the sensing zone and reduce parasitic effects. An object in the *volumetric detection zone* increases the capacitance measured by the sensor. The closer the object, the higher the sensor signal, which shows an antiproportional exponential characteristic: $Proximity(D) \propto \frac{1}{D}$. The sensors can be placed in a way where their detection zones are overlapped in order to reach a lateral gapless detection.

3.3   Collision Avoidance Method

Basic Method for Non-holonomic Robot. A method of local obstacle avoidance for mobile robots with two driven wheels and rectangular bodies based on LiDAR data is proposed in [19]. The foundation of this method is PF that provides an attractive force towards the goal position and repulsive forces from obstacles that act on the robot. The attractive and repulsive forces are combined to a resultant force for generating movement command.

This approach deals with motion constraints of differential drive and takes the robot's shape into account as well.

- In terms of the motion constraints, the robot cannot move in the y-direction. Therefore the resultant force acts on two different action points. The position of these action points is assumed to be at the front end $r_f = (x_f, 0)^T$ and the rear end $r_r = (x_r, 0)^T$. When an obstacle point lays in front of the y axis in Fig. 3, a repulsive force is generated on the front action point and vice versa. The whole system is treated as the forces are applied to a "lever", whereby the fulcrum of the lever is the robot's center point.
- In a general potential field method, the repulsive force is determined by the distances between obstacle points and the center point of the robot. The shape of the robot's body should be considered in our case as well, so the repulsive force should be determined by the outline of the robot's body.

The repulsive forces are given by

$$F_{fj} = \frac{K}{|q_{fj} - p_j|^2} \frac{r_f - p_j}{|r_f - p_j|}, \text{ if } p_{jx} > 0, \tag{2}$$

$$F_{rj} = \frac{K}{|q_{rj} - p_j|^2} \frac{r_r - p_j}{|r_r - p_j|}, \text{ if } p_{jx} < 0, \tag{3}$$

where q_{fj}, q_{rj} are the intersections of the vehicle's body and the segments between obstacle points and the action points r_f, r_r respectively. K is the coefficient of repulsive force. As shown in Fig. 3, q_{fj} is on the contour of the robot for the side obstacle points, while q_{fj} is equivalent to r_f for the obstacle point which is in front of the robot.

Since the forces operate on two action points, the resultant force can not be determined by simply adding up all the forces mathematically. Assuming the resultant force acts on the front action point, the forces on the rear action point

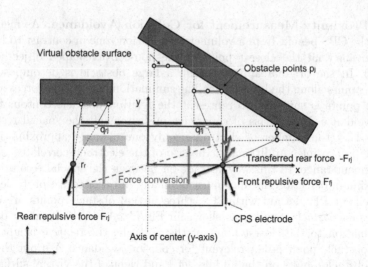

Fig. 3. Generation of repulsive forces from obstacle points. Sensor data is converted to distance approximation and a virtual obstacle surface is defined by three virtual obstacle points. The repulsive forces applied on the rear action point are transferred on the front action point in the opposite direction.

need to be transformed into the same action point according to the leverage theory (as the dashed green arrow in Fig. 3). That is also the reason only two action points are placed at $y = 0$ instead of, for example, 4 points on the corner. Then, the resultant force at the front action point is defined by

$$F = F_a + k_f \sum_{P_{jx}>0} F_{fj} - k_r \sum_{P_{jx}<0} F_{rj}, k_f + k_r = 1, \qquad (4)$$

where the coefficients k_f, k_r represent the action rate of the front and rear repulsive force, both of which in our case is always 0.5.

The attractive force $\mathbf{F}_a$ should pull the action point of the robot to the goal position with smooth motions. So as a reference, the amplitude of $\mathbf{F}_a$ is always 1 ($|\mathbf{F}_a| = 1$), and the direction of $\mathbf{F}_a$ is the tangential vector of a circle at the front action point r_f, the circle interacts with the front action point at the current position and the goal orientation vector at the front action point is a tangential vector of the circle. Without any obstacles, the vehicle moves along this circle and arrives at the goal position with considering the orientation.

Finally, the resultant force F affects the motion of the robot and can be divided into two orthogonal directions, namely x and y. The x-direction force is then directly converted to translational velocity, while the y-direction force works as torque on the center point of the robot which generates rotational velocity. As the formula shows,

$$F/|F| = (f_x, f_y)^T, \quad \begin{bmatrix} v \\ w \end{bmatrix} = C \begin{bmatrix} f_x \\ f_y \\ x_f \end{bmatrix}, \qquad (5)$$

where C is the velocity coefficient, which set a limitation on the rotational velocity.

Using Proximity Measurement for Collision Avoidance. As mentioned before, the CPS benefit from a volumetric detection zone in contrast to LiDAR, which means that the closest point of the non-convex-shaped object can be detected. In the original approach [19], a large obstacle is decomposed into obstacle points along the laser beam. The summation of repulsive forces at these obstacle points is sufficient to represent the relevant obstacle contour for collision avoidance. In the case of capacitive measurement, the spacial resolution is defined by the number of electrodes; only one distance approximation per electrode is possible. Additionally, the size of the electrode correlates with the measurement range. In this way, a trade-off between the spacial resolution and the maximum detection distance must be made. In order to get obstacle points to implement PF method with CPS, three virtual obstacle points are defined on a *virtual obstacle surface*, as shown in Fig. 5b. As the CPS allow distance approximation to the closest point of the obstacle, the relative height of the virtual obstacle point is not relevant for collision avoidance. We put the three virtual obstacle points on the middle, left, and right of the virtual surface centerline parallel to the ground. Mathematically, two points are enough to define the centerline of the virtual obstacle surface. However, introducing the 3rd point makes it possible to track the obstacle position by processing signals from adjacent sensors. Secondly, the measurement range of the LiDAR in the original approach is higher compared to CPS. Therefore the reaction time and the space for the collision avoidance action are limited. We propose to compensate this by introducing a multiplication coefficient for lateral repulsive forces while the amplitude of the attractive force is always 1.

$$\begin{bmatrix} F_{jx} \\ F_{jy} \end{bmatrix} = \begin{bmatrix} 1 & R \end{bmatrix} \begin{bmatrix} F_{jx} \\ F_{jy} \end{bmatrix}, \tag{6}$$

where R is the CPS repulsive coefficient, which entail a larger force in the y-direction. In addition, the CPS repulsive coefficient can be adjusted separately for each sensor. E.g., for sensors in the front of the mobile robot, the CPS repulsive coefficient is set to a higher value to avoid obstacles blocking the path. Whereas for the side sensors, the CPS repulsive coefficient is adjusted to minimize the oscillation in the case of two symmetrical obstacles while avoiding collisions with them.

Local Minima Problem. The general Potential field has a disadvantage of trapping into the local minimum, even if the solution above is no exception. [19] escapes from the local minimum by decreasing the coefficient of repulsive force K temporarily. Although changing coefficient K can help the robot get out of the local minimum, the robot will also drive towards the obstacle because of a smaller repulsive force. Since the measurement range of CPS is limited, the robot may go backward or oscillate. To solve the narrow passage problem, we propose using tangential fields around obstacle points. They appear when the robot detects obstacles on both sides simultaneously, as shown in Fig. 4. To drive the robot into the narrow passage or between symmetrical obstacles, a clockwise and counterclockwise tangential field around obstacles on the right side and on the left side, respectively, will be generated. The activation of local minima solution is based on all the values of the sensors in front of the y-axis. If the values of the sensors on two different sides exceed the threshold, it means that the passage is too narrow for the robot to drive in without collision. Further specific limitations will be mentioned in the experimental section.

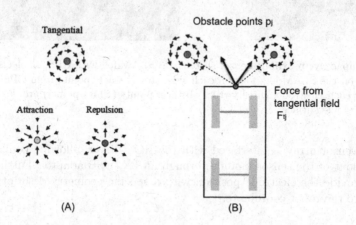

Fig. 4. (A) Three forms of potential fields [10] (B) Forces from tangential field will propel the robot pass through narrow passage.

4 Implementation

4.1 Hardware Setup

SLAMdog. SLAMdog is an AMR platform with four individual electromotors driving mecanum wheels. The dimension of SLAMdog is 48×75 cm. The system provides omnidirectional drive mode and additionally emulates differential drive mode. It is made of two layers of rectangular aluminum plate. Jetson TX2, battery and a LiDAR are mounted in the middle. There is a camera holder in the front of the robot for several camera mounting options, including Intel RealSense Depth Camera D435i and FRAMOS 435e cameras. A removable top plate was designed to install the CPS around the mobile robot (see Fig. 5).

Sensor Array for Obstacle Detection. The array consists of 16 electrodes and is driven by 2 sensor modules. Each electrode is square-shaped with a side length of 10 cm, providing a measurement range of about 10 cm. There are four electrodes on each side of the robot to ensure a 360° measurement range, as shown in Fig. 5a.

(a) 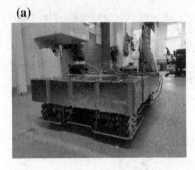 **(b)**

Fig. 5. Capacitive proximity sensor system. (a) SLAMdog with CPS: 16 electrodes are mounted on the SLAMdog; four on each side. (b) Obstacle points from CPS signal in Rviz: For each electrode, three virtual obstacle points (white points) are defined on a virtual obstacle surface.

The sensor array is interfaced with the ROS driver, allowing configuration and readout of the sensor module through an I2C-USB adapter. Further ROS-nodes provide the electrode position with a specific geometry description with respect to the robot coordinate.

4.2 Software Methods

Sensor Data Calibration. The CPS characterization is performed as a non-linear function for a well-coupled object (similar to a human or grounded metal) as shown in Fig. 6. For calibration of sensor data, a grounded profile beam serves as the measured object. The surface of the electrode and the profile were parallel during the entire test. The Object is placed precisely in front of the sensor plane along $x = [0, 200]$ mm. The maximum achieved sensing range in this setup is $d_{\max} = 80$ mm. The power regression result is

$$d_{\mathrm{tns}} = 199.633 \times \mathrm{data}_{\mathrm{tns}}^{-1.1591}. \tag{7}$$

Sensor Data Processing. The proposed method should be developed into a general package for ROS, so we improvise the whole method fitting move base package, an available navigation stack in ROS. The move base package can only receive two types of sensor signals, namely *LaserScan* and *PointCloud*. We provide the data from CPS as a form of PointCloud. Thus, the distance information from the above section should be converted to "Pointcloud". As explained in Sect. 3.3, each sensor electrode generated three virtual obstacle points according to the distance approximation, and a total of 48 obstacle points are used for generation of repulsive forces.

System Architecture: The nodes used to implement the collision free drive-in interact as follows:

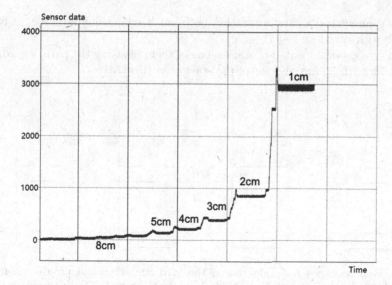

Fig. 6. The screenshot of the sensor data calibration. Coordinate axes are time and sensor data respectively, the average values of sensor data for the same distance will be used as data points of the power regression.

- **CPS node:** provides raw sensor data and their offsets to the CPS geometry tools node.
- **CPS geometry tools node:** pairs raw sensor data and sensor locations.
- **CPS data processing node:** processes raw sensor data and data from the CPS geometry tools node. It converts sensor data to points relative to robot coordinate.
- **Global path planning node:** is not the focus of this paper, provides a task-related trajectory based on map information, and in our experiments provides only a target location like (1,0,0).
- **Local path planning node:** subscribes to point clouds and target location, and implements modified potential field algorithm to send the velocity topic to the control node.
- **Robot controller node:** controls robot movement via a PID-controller, converts velocity commands to 4 motor current value. It provides odometry information as well.

5   Simulation

To evaluate the setup and method, several specific scenarios were designed. They depend on the location of the obstacles and whether the obstacles block the path.

- single obstacle, not blocking the path, e.g., profile on the side (Fig. 7a)
- single obstacle, blocking the path, e.g., profile in front of the vehicle (Fig. 7b)

- two symmetrical located obstacles, both not blocking the path, e.g., drive-in task with two desk legs (Fig. 7c)
- two symmetrical located obstacles, one of them blocking the path, e.g., drive-in task with an initial error of the start pose (Fig. 7d)

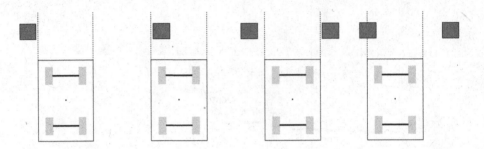

Fig. 7. Four scenarios for evaluation of the hardware setup and proposed software method. They are single obstacle unblocked, single obstacle blocked, two obstacles unblocked, Two obstacles blocked, respectively.

5.1 Evaluation with Laser Range Sensor

The mobile robot platform was modeled in a simulation environment for rapid and extensive testing of the software methods. This was achieved by the simulation software Gazebo, which is interfaced via the ROS framework.

We first test the original modified potential field approach with a laser range sensor. The proposed algorithm performs relatively well in all four tasks if the obstacle is a box. Since the measurement range is high, the robot intervenes early on the collision with tremendously smooth motion commands.

However, when the cross-sectional area of the obstacle is minor, such as table legs, the robot may oscillate. Since the resolution of the range sensor is 1°, small obstacles may fall into the measurement blind spot as the robot moves forward, as shown in Fig. 8 (left).

5.2 Evaluation with Sonar Sensor

At present, proximity-based sensors have not developed plugins for Gazebo yet; 16 sonar sensors are mounted on the robot to replace the proximity sensor's function. The data processing method is similar to one of CPS, namely each sensor generates 3 equidistant points on the plane. The only difference is that a CPS is plane and the three generated points are parallel to this surface, while a sonar sensor is a point and the points lie on the sector, as shown in Fig. 8 (right). In this way, initial parametrization of the algorithm can be done in a simulation using sonar sensors and then applied to the real-world system with CPS.

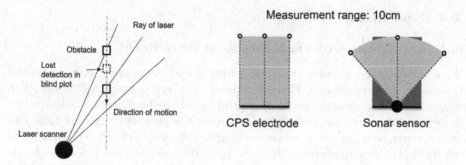

Fig. 8. Left: laser scanner. Loss of obstacle detection can cause sudden changes in speed and direction, resulting in oscillations. Right: CPS and sonar sensor. Sonar sensor is approximated as CPS in simulation, the red areas shows the difference in measurement range between the two sensors.

The robot succeeded in avoiding a single obstacle when it does not block the path. If the obstacle blocks the path, the closer the obstacle is to the center-line, the higher the repulsive force coefficient has to be set because a larger steering angle is needed to avoid the obstacle.

For the scenario as shown in Fig. 7c, the robot was able to finish the drive-in task without collision for the clearances down to 2 cm. When encountering two symmetrical located obstacles and one of them blocking the path, the robot may trap into the local minimum. With the solution mentioned in Sect. 3.3, the robot was able to escape from the local minimum and keep collision-free drive-in. However, the robot oscillates somewhat while escaping from a local minimum. We believe this is because of the sonar sensor's sector-shaped measurement range. The performance of the algorithm in the 4 evaluation scenarios simulated with sonar sensors was similar to the one with a laser scanner.

Table 1. Parameter for LiDAR and sonar sensor in simulation environment and for CPS on the real robot.

	LiDAR	Sonar sensor	CPS
Range of sensor	1 m	0.1 m	0.1 m
Detection points	360	48	48
Sampling time for control: Δt	0.1 s	0.1 s	0.1 s
Repulsive force coefficient: K	0.004	0.04	0.04
CPS repulsive force coefficient: R $(p_{fj} > r_f)$	1	10	30
CPS repulsive force coefficient: R $(p_{fj} < r_f)$	1	1	2
Velocity coefficient: C	0.05	0.05	0.05
Maximum angular velocity: w_{max}	0.2 [rad/s]	0.2 [rad/s]	0.2 [rad/s]

6 Experiment

6.1 Experiment with Omnidirectional Drive Robot

First, we designed a simple experiment with omnidirectional drive, in which the movement constraints of a differential drive robot are ignored. A PD controller was utilized to realize the servoing control based on the difference between the sensor signal on the left and right sides. After the parameter optimization, the robot could perform the obstacle avoidance and carry out drive-in tasks successfully. The robot constantly kept the same distance between two obstacles in the drive-in task, where the minimal clearance between obstacle profiles and the robot on each side was 2.5 cm.

6.2 Experiments with Differential Drive Robot

The SLAMdog succeeded in avoiding single obstacles such as profile, single table leg, human, etc. The repulsive force coefficient should be adjusted to be particularly large to avoid obstacles directly in the front, which cannot be used for multiobstacle scenarios.

When two obstacles are in front and not obstructing the path, the collision-free drive-in was executed using parameters shown in Table 1 until the distance between two obstacle profiles was 52 cm (Fig. 9). As the robot width is 48 cm, the minimum clearance achieved was 2 cm, which is similar to the performance in the omnidirectional mode (2.5 cm).

For the scenario as shown in Fig. 7d, namely one of the obstacles blocks the path, more place is needed since the mobile robot has to get around obstacles blocking the path by steering. In the experiments, the SLAMdog was able to drive through the obstacles with 56 cm distance. If the clearance was less than 8 cm, the robot was able to execute collision-free drive-in task with the help of the tangential field. However, due to the limited proximity measurement range and the kinematic constraints, robot can be forced to abandon the drive-in task. E.g., in case of an obstacle close to the center of the robot, the detection distance could be too short considering the minimum turn radius of the differential drive robot. The safety threshold was set to 0.5 cm.

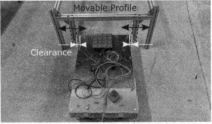

Fig. 9. Experimental setup with SLAMdog. The profiles (marked with red dashed boxes) can be adjusted according to the experiment requirements for the clearance. (Color figure online)

7 Results and Conclusion

This paper presents preliminary results of a collision-avoidance approach for a drive-in task using a capacitive proximity sensor. The sensor is mounted on an autonomous mobile robot and can measure the capacitive fluctuations of the electromagnetic field.

The proposed method is based upon *potential field* and allows obstacle detection based on proximity feedback. For considering the outline shape and motion constraints, we also leverage the method from [19] and improve it for the proximity measurement. *Tangential field method* addresses the local minimum solution for drive-in tasks.

To evaluate the capacitive proximity sensor, we use an omnidirectional robot and PD controller to verify that the CPS is up to the task of obstacle avoidance. To evaluate the proposed method in simulation, we approximate the behavior of the CPSs with sonar sensors. Similar outcomes are gained on the real robot. The 48 cm wide mobile robot was able to pass or drive-in through shelves or narrow passages with a gap more than 56 cm. While tolerance of 4 cm on both sides was achieved for arbitrary initial error of the starting pose causing in some cases oversteering, lower tolerance of 2 cm was acquired for a smaller initial error. This shares a similar result as the one of an omnidirectional robot.

In further studies, we plan to develop localization methods based on the proximity sensor and use the self-localization information to achieve a complete path planning pipeline. The capacitive measurement dependency on various materials like plastics, wood, human, etc. has to be investigated as well. Based on CPSs the robot would drive unobstructed into the shelf and obtain its relative position to maneuver accurately to the desired position. Furthermore, the tactile modality of the Capacitive Proximity and Tactile Sensor (CPTS) can augment the perception of AMRs, providing an additional estimation of the contact forces. In this way, a Center of Mass (CoM) monitoring can facilitate dynamically safe object transfer or light obstacles can be pushed by a robot for predefined interaction forces.

References

1. Alagi, H., Navarro, S.E., Mende, M., Hein, B.: A versatile and modular capacitive tactile proximity sensor. In: 2016 IEEE Haptics Symposium (HAPTICS), pp. 290–296 (2016). https://doi.org/10.1109/HAPTICS.2016.7463192
2. Alajlan, A.M., Almasri, M.M., Elleithy, K.M.: Multi-sensor based collision avoidance algorithm for mobile robot. In: 2015 Long Island Systems, Applications and Technology, pp. 1–6 (2015). https://doi.org/10.1109/LISAT.2015.7160181
3. Almasri, M.M., Alajlan, A.M., Elleithy, K.M.: Trajectory planning and collision avoidance algorithm for mobile robotics system. IEEE Sens. J. **16**(12), 5021–5028 (2016). https://doi.org/10.1109/JSEN.2016.2553126
4. Borenstein, J., Koren, Y.: The vector field histogram-fast obstacle avoidance for mobile robots. IEEE Trans. Robot. Autom. **7**(3), 278–288 (1991). https://doi.org/10.1109/70.88137

5. Cherubini, A., Chaumette, F.: Visual navigation of a mobile robot with laser-based collision avoidance. Int. J. Robot. Res. **32**, 189–205 (2013). https://doi.org/10.1177/0278364912460413. https://hal.inria.fr/hal-00750623
6. Evans, J., Patrón, P., Smith, B., Lane, D.M.: Design and evaluation of a reactive and deliberative collision avoidance and escape architecture for autonomous robots. Auton. Robots **24**(3), 247–266 (2008). https://doi.org/10.1007/s10514-007-9053-8
7. Fox, D., Burgard, W., Thrun, S.: The dynamic window approach to collision avoidance. IEEE Robot. Autom. Mag. **4**(1), 23–33 (1997). https://doi.org/10.1109/100.580977
8. Guizzo, E.: Three engineers, hundreds of robots, one warehouse. IEEE Spectr. **45**(7), 26–34 (2008). https://doi.org/10.1109/MSPEC.2008.4547508
9. Heilig, A., Mamaev, I., Hein, B., Malov, D.: Adaptive particle filter for localization problem in service robotics. In: MATEC Web of Conferences, vol. 161, p. 01004 (2018). https://doi.org/10.1051/matecconf/201816101004. https://www.matec-conferences.org/10.1051/matecconf/201816101004
10. Hellström, T.: Robot navigation with potential fields. UMINF (2011)
11. Khatib, O.: Real-time obstacle avoidance for manipulators and mobile robots. In: Proceedings, 1985 IEEE International Conference on Robotics and Automation, vol. 2, pp. 500–505 (1985). https://doi.org/10.1109/ROBOT.1985.1087247
12. Kondak, K., Hommel, G.: Computation of time optimal movements for autonomous parking of non-holonomic mobile platforms. In: Proceedings 2001 ICRA, IEEE International Conference on Robotics and Automation (Cat. No.01CH37164), vol. 3, pp. 2698–2703 (2001). https://doi.org/10.1109/ROBOT.2001.933030
13. Lagisetty, R., Philip, N.K., Padhi, R., Bhat, M.S.: Object detection and obstacle avoidance for mobile robot using stereo camera. In: 2013 IEEE International Conference on Control Applications (CCA), pp. 605–610 (2013). https://doi.org/10.1109/CCA.2013.6662816
14. Minguez, J., Montano, L.: Extending collision avoidance methods to consider the vehicle shape, kinematics, and dynamics of a mobile robot. IEEE Trans. Rob. **25**(2), 367–381 (2009). https://doi.org/10.1109/TRO.2009.2011526
15. Ohya, A., Kosaka, A., Kak, A.: Vision-based navigation by a mobile robot with obstacle avoidance using single-camera vision and ultrasonic sensing. IEEE Trans. Robot. Autom. **14**, 969–978 (1998)
16. Oyekanlu, E.A., et al.: A review of recent advances in automated guided vehicle technologies: integration challenges and research areas for 5g-based smart manufacturing applications. IEEE Access **8**, 202312–202353 (2020). https://doi.org/10.1109/ACCESS.2020.3035729
17. Rabl, A., Salner, P., Büchi, L., Wrona, J., Muehlbacher-Kárrer, S., Brandstötter, M.: Implementation of a capacitive proximity sensor system for a fully maneuverable modular mobile robot to evade humans. In: Proceedings of the Austrian Robotics Workshop (2018)
18. Schwartz, J.T., Sharir, M.: On the "piano movers" problem i. The case of a two-dimensional rigid polygonal body moving amidst polygonal barriers. Commun. Pure Appl. Math. **36**(3), 345–398 (1983). https://doi.org/10.1002/cpa.3160360305
19. Seki, H., Kamiya, Y., Hikizu, M.: Real-time obstacle avoidance using potential field for a nonholonomic vehicle. In: Silvestre-Blanes, J. (ed.) Factory Automation, chap. 26. IntechOpen, Rijeka (2010). https://doi.org/10.5772/9508
20. Tian, J., Gao, M., Lu, E.: Dynamic collision avoidance path planning for mobile robot based on multi-sensor data fusion by support vector machine. In: 2007 International Conference on Mechatronics and Automation, pp. 2779–2783 (2007). https://doi.org/10.1109/ICMA.2007.4303999

21. Trenkle, A., Stoll, T., Bär, R.: Fifi fürs lager. Logistik heute **2013**(6), 34–35 (2013)
22. Ulrich, I., Borenstein, J.: Vfh+: reliable obstacle avoidance for fast mobile robots. In: Proceedings, 1998 IEEE International Conference on Robotics and Automation (Cat. No.98CH36146), vol. 2, pp. 1572–1577 (1998). https://doi.org/10.1109/ROBOT.1998.677362
23. Ulrich, I., Borenstein, J.: Vfh/sup */: local obstacle avoidance with look-ahead verification. In: Proceedings 2000 ICRA, Millennium Conference, IEEE International Conference on Robotics and Automation, Symposia Proceedings (Cat. No.00CH37065), vol. 3, pp. 2505–2511 (2000). https://doi.org/10.1109/ROBOT.2000.846405
24. Wada, H., et al.: Dynamic collision avoidance method for co-worker robot using time augmented configuration-space. In: 2016 IEEE International Conference on Mechatronics and Automation, pp. 2564–2569 (2016). https://doi.org/10.1109/ICMA.2016.7558970
25. Yasin, J.N., Mohamed, S.A.S., Haghbayan, M.H., Heikkonen, J., Tenhunen, H., Plosila, J.: Low-cost ultrasonic based object detection and collision avoidance method for autonomous robots. Int. J. Inf. Technol. **13**(1), 97–107 (2021). https://doi.org/10.1007/s41870-020-00513-w

Analysis of Kinematic Diagrams and Design Solutions of Mobile Agricultural Robots

Iuliia Vasiunina$^{(\boxtimes)}$, Konstantin Krestovnikov , Aleksandr Bykov ,
and Aleksei Erashov

St. Petersburg Federal Research Center of the Russian Academy of Sciences (SPC RAS), 39,
14th Line, 199178 St. Petersburg, Russia
k.krestovnikov@iias.spb.su

Abstract. Automation and robotization in agriculture can reduce the amount of manual labor and increase yields and product quality. To perform tasks on agricultural land, the robot needs to move on open ground and cover significant distances. Thus, the main structural part of the agricultural robot is an autonomous mobile platform on which various functional equipment is installed. The rapid development of agricultural robotics makes it urgent to develop multifunctional platforms for applications in this area. To select the optimal kinematic scheme of the future robotic platform, it is necessary to analyze the existing solutions in this area and draw conclusions about the advantages and disadvantages of various options. This work is aimed at the search and selection of kinematic schemes for basic robotic platforms, the use of which is planned on agricultural land and in greenhouse complexes. The paper analyzes the design solutions and propellers used by the authors of research works and projects in the field of agricultural robotics. Based on the analysis, the most suitable kinematic schemes of mobile platforms were selected for this area, their properties and principles of operation were considered.

Keywords: Kinematic diagrams of mobile platforms · Types of movers for mobile platforms · Supporting systems of mobile platforms · Agricultural robotics

1 Introduction

The current level of development of robotics allows us to solve a wide range of industrial and civil problems. Agriculture is one of the topical directions for the implementation of robotic systems [1]. The main technological operations that must be performed for growing crops are related to soil cultivation, sowing and fertilization, plant care and harvesting. To solve this spectrum of tasks, which are significantly different from each other, an agricultural robot will need the use of specialized electromechanical devices for each type of work [2]. Combined with the need to move around the field or greenhouse complex, the creation of a universal solution becomes almost impossible. This problem can be solved by a modular approach, in which a mobile stand-alone platform becomes the base unit on which functional modules are installed.

© Springer Nature Switzerland AG 2021
A. Ronzhin et al. (Eds.): ICR 2021, LNAI 12998, pp. 222–231, 2021.
https://doi.org/10.1007/978-3-030-87725-5_19

Functional modules [3] include equipment for installation on a platform, the configuration of which depends on the tasks at hand. The modules are also designed to expand navigation capabilities, obstacle detection and connect additional batteries. Some functional modules can be self-powered.

The basic platform is an independent system consisting of propulsion, navigation, and computing subsystems, as well as mechanical and electrical connections for connecting functional modules. In the analysis [4], the authors argue that an increase in the design complexity of the prototype is required to create a universal mobile platform. The problem with creating a universal system is that the high mechanical complexity often leads to a difficult to control and mechanically unreliable platform. And in the study [5], the authors, when developing an agricultural platform, consider creating a prototype only with frames of constant geometry. This can also complicate the design, as a suspension must be used to avoid torsional moments and possible suspension of the wheels. For the correct choice of the kinematic diagram of a mobile robotic platform, it is necessary to consider possible options for design solutions and propellers, to assess their advantages and disadvantages when used in agricultural tasks. Further, the analysis presented is aimed at identifying the kinematic schemes that are most suitable for solving agricultural problems.

2 Design Solutions for Mobile Platforms

2.1 Carrying Systems

Carrier systems are the main components of the mobile platform, they involve the installation of all necessary subsystems and modules. Structurally, they can be divided into three types: frames, bearing bases and bearing bodies. Frame platforms are called platforms, the loads from the installation of modules and submodules of which fall on the beam structure. In platforms with load-bearing hulls, the loads are evenly distributed over the entire hull. And bearing bases can be called a combination of frame and hull bearing systems, they are also formed by beams, however, the beams are connected by the bottom, and not by cross members.

When designing a basic mobile agricultural platform, the subsequent installation of the functional modules must be considered. For this, the support system must have a sufficient mounting surface as well as suitable connections. The authors of [6] created a prototype of a mobile platform, the supporting system of which is a frame designed considering the installation of a seed selector on it. Similarly, in [7], the body of the mobile platform was designed in such a way that the platform is capable of plowing thanks to special wheels installed in the front of the body, sowing with a container and holes for planting seeds in the lower part of the body, and filling the planted seeds with earth using the attached towards the end of the platform of inclined metal sheets.

The existing constructive solutions for the bodies and frames of mobile platforms make it possible to increase the permeability and adaptability to changing environmental conditions. The improvement of cross-country ability by changing the geometry of the body is demonstrated in [8], the authors of which developed a prototype of a tracked mobile platform with an active connection implemented by a drive hinge. This connection allows you to change the geometry of the platform, and, therefore, the position of the center of mass to overcome obstacles, keeping the tracks in tension to continue moving. In a similar way, the frame geometry is changed in [9]. The mechanism for changing the geometry of the frame consists of two simultaneously operating motors and a hinge for connecting two parts of the frame. The mechanism can switch the platform between wheeled mode and walking mode. It can also adapt the platform to various obstacles by adjusting the folding angle.

To improve the maneuverability of mobility and adaptation to external conditions, the authors of the study [10] consider the advantages of using a passive connection or flexible frame. These frames reduce the load on the propellers and reduce torsional loads in the hull. An approach to the creation of flexible frames based on the principles and structures of wildlife is considered in [11]. Structurally, the frame includes two rigid subframes, on which the necessary functional modules can be installed. The stretchers are connected by four pneumatic artificial muscles and one artificial spine. A simpler and more realistic [12] connection of two subframes is applicable in agriculture is a hinge system consisting of two perpendicularly located hinges. This system provides up to 35° swivel with a vertical hinge and adapts the frame to rough terrain with a horizontal hinge. The horizontal hinge allows the frame to bend up to 16° and relieves the structure of additional torsional loads.

The configuration of the carrier system largely depends on the type of propellers used and their number. A significant variety of types of propellers and the principles of their installation does not allow identifying the most suitable options for solving agricultural problems and requires a comparative analysis.

3   Types of Mobile Platform Engines

3.1   Wheeled and Tracked Mobile Platforms

Wheeled mobile platforms used in agriculture are classified according to the number and type of wheels. In [13], mobile platforms are divided into four-wheeled and six-wheeled. Increasing the number of wheels increases flotation but adds bulk and complexity. Wheels are classified according to their appearance to regular wheels, universal omnidirectional wheels, and Elon wheels. Conventional and omnidirectional wheels can be driven, and non-driven, also conventional wheels can be swivel and non-swivel. The location of the wheels depends on the shape and size of the platform base, as well as on their type. In a study [14], the authors compared six types of wheels according to the following criteria: production complexity, stability on uneven surfaces, and the ability to work outdoors. We also found out the minimum diameter of the wheels, their carrying capacity and the number required for installation on the platform. The authors concluded that conventional wheels are the strongest of all types, and the omnidirectional wheels allow for the greatest platform maneuverability. At the same time, omnidirectional wheels have a complex design and are demanding on the quality of the travel surface.

To synthesize the kinematic scheme of a mobile platform, the authors of [15] carried out a mathematical analysis of the constraints imposed by the wheels on the movement of mobile platforms. Based on the analysis, it was concluded that there are five types of kinematic schemes for wheeled mobile platforms. The constraints imposed by the wheels were described using three vectors: the vector of the platform coordinates on the plane, the vectors of the angular coordinates of the swivel and non-swivel wheels, and the vector of the angle of the wheel about its horizontal axis. Based on these restrictions, it was concluded that there are five combinations of the degree of mobility (δ_m) and the degree of controllability (δ_s), and, consequently, possible combinations of different wheels.

When classifying mobile platforms according to the method of controlling the direction of movement [16], the following groups are distinguished: a group with rigidly fixed wheels (turning is carried out by changing the speed and / or direction of rotation of the wheels) [17]; steering group [18]; omnidirectional wheel group, both on Elon wheels [19] and on omnidirectional wheels [20].

The mobile platforms with the best cross-country ability include tracked platforms. The designs of mobile tracked platforms in [21] were divided into three groups depending on the number of tracks: two-tracked platforms [22]; platforms with four tracks having two main and two additional tracks [23]; platforms with six tracks [24], four of which are optional. The authors also divided tracked platforms into two types: fixed geometry and variable geometry. In fixed-type platforms [22], the position of the center of mass remains unchanged, so such platforms cannot rise to a height exceeding half the track diameter. Tracked mobile platforms with variable geometry have the advantage that, thanks to additional tracks, they change the position of the center of mass and can overcome steeper and higher inclines [23].

3.2 Walking Mobile Platforms

In work [25], walking mobile platforms are classified according to the number of pedipulators (supports): with two pedipulators; with four pedipulators; with six pedipulators; and by the type of gait: platforms with static and dynamic gait. Walking mobile platforms have a higher ground clearance than wheeled or tracked platforms, and therefore can better adapt to rough terrain. The authors of the study [26] concluded that walking platforms have better stability and many different gait options.

3.3 Combined Mobile Platforms

The developed locomotion systems that allow the platforms to move effectively on various surfaces, including various types of propellers, are called combined [27, 28]. By combining propellers, four categories of locomotion systems can be obtained: wheel pedipulators, track pedipulators, track wheels and track-wheel pedipulators. Thus, in [29], two types of propellers are installed on a mobile platform, and this mobile platform combines the advantages of wheeled platforms (fast movement on flat surfaces) and pedipulator platforms (high cross-country ability).

Mobile platforms with wheel-track systems combine the advantages of high-speed travel and the ability to travel on uneven ground. In [30], the authors developed a design, the propellers of which are an orthogonal combination of wheels and tracks and provide multidirectional mobility.

Prototypes of combined mobile platforms using all three types of movers are considered in [31, 32]. Their locomotion system includes wheels, tracks and pedipulators. This solution allows the platform to move on all types of surfaces and overcome obstacles.

Unlike most of the combined platforms, which have separate mechanisms and drives for each type of propulsion device, in [33] a transformation mechanism is implemented, with the possibility of directly switching the wheel morphology into a pedipulator. The process is the union of two semicircles of the wheel in a leg and vice versa.

Table 1 displays the satisfaction of the type of mover with the main frequently put forward requirements, where + meets the requirement, + \− does not sufficiently meet the requirement, - almost does not meet the requirement.

Table 1. Meeting design requirements.

	Driving at high speed	Passage on open ground	Overcoming obstacles	Simplicity of design
Wheeled	+	+\−	−	+
Tracked	+\−	+	+\−	+
Marching	−	+\−	+	+
Wheeled-tracked	+	+	+\−	+\−
Wheel-pedipulators	+	+\−	+	+\−
Caterpillar-pedipulator	+\−	+	+	+\−
Wheel-caterpillar-pedipulator	+	+	+	−

From this table, it follows that combined mobile platforms meet more requirements. However, in agricultural applications, there is no need to overcome significant obstacles, and the important criteria for selection are energy efficiency, simplicity, and reliability of the design. Further, the main kinematic schemes of mobile platforms will be considered, considering their applicability in agriculture.

4   Kinematic Diagrams of Mobile Agricultural Platforms

During the analysis aimed at identifying the kinematic schemes of mobile platforms most applicable in agriculture, the main bearing systems and propulsion systems were considered. The criteria for choosing a suitable kinematics are open ground passability, maneuverability, reliability, and simplicity of design.

Even though during the study, combined mobile platforms turned out to be the most adaptable to different conditions, they are rarely used in agricultural activities, since they have excessive design capabilities for working in fields and greenhouses. Therefore, their kinematic schemes will not be considered as possible solutions. As well as the kinematic diagrams of the walking mobile platforms adaptable to rough terrain. The need to support all the weight, the small surface contact area and the large number of drives significantly reduce the energy efficiency of walking platforms when solving agricultural tasks.

Caterpillar and wheel propulsion systems, the kinematic diagrams of which are shown in Fig. 1, are most often used in agriculture. Figure 1 has the following notations:

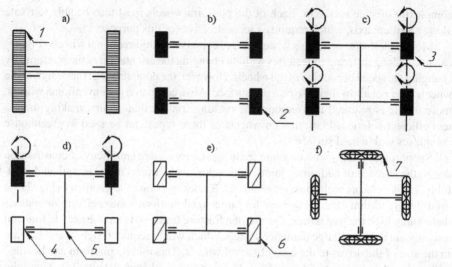

Fig. 1. Basic kinematic diagrams of wheeled and tracked agricultural mobile platforms: a) tracked mobile platform; b) four-wheel drive wheeled platform; c) platform on four swivel wheels; d) platform with two swivel wheels; e) platform on Elon's wheels; f) platform on omnidirectional wheels.

1 is a caterpillar, 2 is a drive non-swivel wheel, 3 is a drive swivel wheel, 4 is a non-drive wheel, 5 is a bearing system, 6 is an Elon wheel, 7 is an omnidirectional wheel.

Tracked mobile platforms (Fig. 1a) have a higher carrying capacity and maneuverability than wheeled ones. However, they have a large mass due to the complexity of the multi-link design of the tracked propeller and, therefore, consume more energy. Four-wheel drive (Fig. 1b) wheeled platforms with fixed wheels also have high cross-country ability on sticky soils and uneven surfaces. The wheels in them are kinematically connected in pairs and are driven by one engine and a transmission or two engines. Changing the direction of movement of tracked and all-wheel drive mobile platforms on fixed wheels can be carried out in a confined space by turning around its axis in place.

Four-wheel drive platforms on four swivel wheels (Fig. 1c) can be divided into two types depending on the angle of rotation of the wheel around the vertical axis. In platforms with a wheel turning angle of less than 50°, the transmission of torque to the wheels can be carried out using drives with hinges from a single traction motor. Changing the direction of movement in such platforms cannot be carried out in one place, however, the turning radius becomes smaller than that of mobile platforms with two swivel wheels (Fig. 1d). To turn the platform in place, without changing the orientation of the body, it is necessary to be able to turn the wheels along the vertical axis at an angle of 90°. The maneuverability of this solution is higher than that of tracked and wheeled platforms on fixed wheels. However, the design features of the hinges for transmitting the moment at an angle do not allow reaching this value of the angle of rotation of the wheels, therefore, the implementation of this kinematic scheme is possible only based on the motor-wheel principle. This feature makes it necessary to install traction motors with or without a gearbox with direct drive to each wheel, which increases the overall structural complexity of such a system. Each of the platform wheels must also be able to rotate along a vertical axis, which requires a separate drive for this purpose.

Mobile platforms on Elon's wheels (Fig. 1e) and on omnidirectional wheels (Fig. 1f) can move along different trajectories without changing the orientation of the platform, by changing the speed of rotation of the wheels. However, the complexity of the design of the wheels does not allow their use on a dirt surface. Also, compared to conventional wheels, more torque is required to overcome the rotating friction that occurs, making them a less efficient solution. Platforms on wheels of these types can be used in greenhouse complexes with a hard surface.

Supporting systems with constant frame geometry ensure simplicity of construction due to the absence of additional joints, which positively affects their strength and durability. Unlike frames with constant geometry, frames with variable geometry (Fig. 2) are used in agricultural machinery only for large-sized platforms that perform operations that require high tractive power. The use of a fracture frame is due to the need to transmit a significant torque to large diameter wheels, which would require a significant increase in the size of the drives in the case of swivel wheels. This mobile platform can be fitted with one traction motor and one drive M on the vertical joint 1 (Fig. 2a). This joint provides a frame flexing angle of up to 35°.

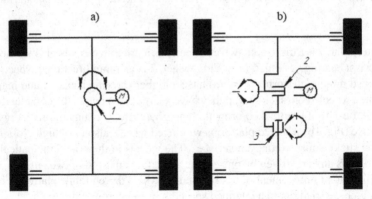

Fig. 2. Kinematic diagrams of hinged joints of frames with variable geometry: a) breaking frame; b) folding frame.

The frames shown in Fig. 2b are used to adapt to uneven surfaces. The main task that can be solved by the installation of a folding frame with a drive hinge or a hinge with an elastic element 2 and drive M (Fig. 2b), is to stabilize the frame for working across slopes up to 20°.

Frames with an installed non-drive hinge 3 (Fig. 2b) are used to reduce the likelihood of diagonal hanging of the platform wheels and reduce twisting loads when driving on uneven terrain. To prevent the rear subframe from tipping over, the non-drive hinge should be limited, and if driving on a level surface, the hinges should be locked in better stability. The use of the hinges (Fig. 2b) eliminates the need for wheel suspension while maintaining adaptability to the terrain, which can simplify the design.

5   Conclusion

The work analyzed the structures, propellers, and kinematic diagrams of mobile platforms in the direction of their application as basic autonomous agricultural robotic means. The analysis showed that wheeled and tracked propellers are best suited for moving on agricultural land. Elon's wheels and omnidirectional ones are not suitable for movement on a ground surface, but they can be used when operating in greenhouse complexes with a hard surface. The caterpillar drive, in contrast to the wheel drive, has a large support area on the surface, which can provide better cross-country ability. This is an actual option with a significant planned mass of a robotic platform, but less efficient and more complicated from the implementation side. The least suitable type of propulsion system for agricultural platforms is the pedipulator. This is due to the structural complexity of pedipulators and low energy efficiency due to the use of many servo-drives and the need for high torques.

Further research will focus on the development of a multifunctional agricultural robotic platform based on a kinematic scheme with four swivel wheels and a frame with fixed geometry. This design option allows you to change the direction of movement on the spot without turning the entire platform, which is important for greenhouse complexes with limited space and for fields with a high density of plantations.

References

1. Skvortsov, E.A.: Robots in agricultural reproduction process. Agrarian Bull. Urals **3**(133), 89–93 (2015)
2. Shanygin, S.V.: Robots as Means of Agriculture Mechanization. BMSTU J. Mech. Eng. **3**, 39–42 (2013)
3. Pavliuk, N.A., Smirnov, P.A., Kovalev, A.D.: Constructional and architectural solutions for service mobile platform with pluggable modules. Izvestiya Tula State Univ. **10**, 181–193 (2019)
4. Nie, C., Pacheco Corcho, X., Spenko, M.: Robots on the move: versatility and complexity in mobile robot locomotion. IEEE Robot. Autom. Mag. **20**(4), 72–82 (2013). https://doi.org/10.1109/mra.2013.2248310
5. Ipate, G., Moise, V., Biris, S.S., Voicu, G., Ilie, F., Constantin, G.A.: Design concepts of mobile robots for agriculture. In: 7th International Conference on Thermal Equipment, Renewable Energy and Rural Development, pp. 427–434. Drobeta Turnu Severin, Romania (2018)
6. Hassan, M.U., Ullah, M., Iqbal, J.: Towards autonomy in agriculture: design and prototyping of a robotic vehicle with seed selector. In: 2016 2nd International Conference on Robotics and Artificial Intelligence (ICRAI), pp. 37–44. IEEE (2016)
7. Gollakota, A., Srinivas, M.B.: Agribot—A multipurpose agricultural robot. In: Annual IEEE India Conference, pp. 1–4 (2011)
8. Paillat, J.L., Lucidarme, P., Hardouin, L.: Variable Geometry Tracked Vehicle (VGTV) prototype: conception, capability and problems. In: HUMOUS (2008)
9. Chou, J.J., Yang, L.S.: Innovative design of a claw-wheel transformable robot. In: International Conference on Robotics and Automation, pp. 1337–1342. IEEE (2013)
10. Deng, Q., Wang, S., Xu, W., Mo, J., Liang, Q.: Quasi passive bounding of a quadruped model with articulated spine. Mech. Mach. Theory **52**, 232–242 (2012)

11. Lei, J., Yu, H., Wang, T.: Dynamic bending of bionic flexible body driven by pneumatic artificial muscles (PAMs) for spinning gait of quadruped robot. Chin. J. Mech. Eng. **29**(1), 11–20 (2016)
12. Sharipov, V.M., et al.: Construction of tractors. A textbook for university students studying in the specialty "Automobile and Tractor Engineering". Moscow State University of Mechanical Engineering (MAMI), Moscow (2007)
13. Bechar, A., Vigneault, C.: Agricultural robots for field operations: concepts and components. Biosys. Eng. **149**, 94–111 (2016)
14. Shabalina, K., Sagitov, A., Magid, E.: Comparative analysis of mobile robot wheels design. In: 2018 11th International Conference on Developments in eSystems Engineering (DeSE), pp. 175–179. IEEE (2018)
15. Campion, G., Bastin, G., Dandrea-Novel, B.: Structural properties and classification of kinematic and dynamic models of wheeled mobile robots. IEEE Trans. Robot. Autom. **12**(1), 47–62 (1996)
16. Afonin, A.N., Aleynikov, A.Y.: Mobile robot BELSU-bot. Technique and technologies of the XXI century: monograph. Logos, Stavropol (2016)
17. Mrozik, D., Mikolajczyk, T., Moldovan, L., Pimenov, D.Y.: Unconventional drive system of a 3D printed wheeled mobile robot. Procedia Manuf. **46**, 509–516 (2020)
18. Cariou, C., Lenain, R., Thuilot, B., Berducat, M.: Automatic guidance of a four-wheel-steering mobile robot for accurate field operations. J. Field Robot. **26**(6–7), 504–518 (2009)
19. Tătar, M.O., Cirebea, C., Mândru, D.: Structures of the omnidirectional robots with Swedish wheels. Solid State Phenom. **98**, 132–137 (2013)
20. Tavakoli, M., Lourenço, J., Viegas, C., Neto, P., de Almeida, A.T.: The hybrid OmniClimber robot: wheel based climbing, arm based plane transition, and switchable magnet adhesion. Mechatronics **36**, 136–146 (2016)
21. Moskvin, I., Lavrenov, R., Magid, E., Svinin, M.: Modelling a crawler robot using wheels as pseudo-tracks: model complexity vs performance. In: 2020 IEEE 7th International Conference on Industrial Engineering and Applications (ICIEA), pp. 1–5. IEEE (2020)
22. Magid, E., Tsubouchi, T., Koyanagi, E., Yoshida, T.: Static balance for rescue robot navigation: losing balance on purpose within random step environment. In: 2010 IEEE/RSJ International Conference on Intelligent Robots and Systems, pp. 349–356. IEEE (2010)
23. Mavrin, I., Lavrenov, R., Svinin, M., Sorokin, S., Magid, E.: Remote control library and GUI development for Russian crawler robot Servosila Engineer. In: MATEC Web of Conferences, vol. 161, p. 03016. EDP Sciences (2018)
24. Nagatani, K., et al.: Redesign of rescue mobile robot Quince. In: 2011 IEEE International Symposium on Safety, Security, and Rescue Robotics, pp. 13–18. IEEE (2011)
25. Bruzzone, L., Quaglia, G.: Locomotion systems for ground mobile robots in unstructured environments. Mech. Sci. **3**(2), 49–62 (2012)
26. Luneckas, M., Luneckas, T., Udris, D., Ferreira, N.M.F.: Hexapod robot energy consumption dependence on body elevation and step height. Elektronika ir Elektrotechnika. **20**(7), 7–10 (2014)
27. Medvedev, M.Y., Kostjukov, V.A., Pshikhopov, V.X.: Method for optimizing of mobile robot trajectory in repeller sources field. Inform. Autom. **20**(3), 690–726 (2021). https://doi.org/10.15622/ia.2021.3.7
28. Kochetkov, M.P., Korolkov, D.N., Petrov, V.F., Petrov, O.V., Terentev, A.I., Simonov, S.B.: Application of cluster analysis with fuzzy logic elements for ground environment assessment of robotic group. SPIIRAS Proc. **19**(4), 746–773 (2020). https://doi.org/10.15622/sp.2020.19.4.2
29. Tătar, M.O., Gyarmati, M.: Locomotion unit for mobile robots. In: IOP Conference Series: Materials Science and Engineering, vol. 444, no. 5, p. 052024. IOP Publishing (2018)

30. Kumar, P., Saab, W., Ben-Tzvi, P.: Design of a multi-directional hybrid-locomotion modular robot with feedforward stability control. In: ASME 2017 International Design Engineering Technical Conferences and Computers and Information in Engineering Conference. American Society of Mechanical Engineers Digital Collection (2017)
31. Zhu, Y., Fei, Y., Xu, H.: Stability analysis of a wheel-track-leg hybrid mobile robot. J. Intell. Rob. Syst. **91**(3), 515–528 (2018). https://doi.org/10.1007/s10846-017-0724-1
32. Bruzzone, L., Baggetta, M., Nodehi, S.E., Bilancia, P., Fanghella, P.: Functional design of a hybrid leg-wheel-track ground mobile robot. Machines. **9**(10) (2021)
33. Chen, S.C., Huang, K.J., Chen, W.H., Shen, S.Y., Li, C.H., Lin, P.C.: Quattroped: a leg-wheel transformable robot. IEEE/ASME Trans. Mechatron. **19**(2), 730–742 (2013)

Author Index

Printed in the United States
by Baker & Taylor Publisher Services